# The Indian Economy and Its Performance Since Independence

# THE INDIAN ECONOMY AND ITS PERFORMANCE SINCE INDEPENDENCE

edited by

R. A. CHOUDHURY
SHAMA GAMKHAR
AUROBINDO GHOSE

DELHI
OXFORD UNIVERSITY PRESS
BOMBAY CALCUTTA MADRAS
1990

Oxford University Press, Walton Street, Oxford OX2 6DP
NEW YORK TORONTO
DELHI BOMBAY CALCUTTA MADRAS KARACHI
PETALING JAYA SINGAPORE HONG KONG TOKYO
NAIROBI DAR ES SALAAM
MELBOURNE AUCKLAND
and associates in
BERLIN IBADAN

© Oxford University Press 1990

HC
435
.I778
1990

Phototypeset by Taj Services Ltd., Noida, U.P.
Printed by Rekha Printers (P) Ltd, New Delhi 110020
and published by S.K. Mookerjee, Oxford University Press
YMCA Library Building, Jai Singh Road, New Delhi 110001

# Contents

*Foreword* viii
*Acknowledgements* ix
*List of Contributors* x

**Part I**

Introduction
by R. A. Choudhury, Shama Gamkhar and *Aurobindo Ghose*    1

**Part II: Background**

How is India Doing?
*by Amartya Sen*    7

Aspects of India's Development Strategy for the 1980s
*by Sukhamoy Chakravarty*    23

The Centre and the Periphery: Inter-State Disparities in Economic Development
*by Raj Krishna*    42

**Part III: Economic Performance Since Independence**

Development in the Indian Economy Since Independence
*by A. M. Khusro*    87

The Uneasy Coalition of Economic Interests
*by Dalip S. Swamy*    99

Indian Economy: Performance and Policy
by Kaushik Basu                                                    106

## Part IV: Strategy of Economic Growth

Key Components of the Strategy of Growth in India
by Ranjit Sau                                                      113

Some Reflections on the New Strategy
by Prem Shankar Jha                                                137

Contours of a Reorientation
by V. S. Minocha                                                   143

Some Premises of India's Development Strategy:
1950–90
by Kamal Nayan Kabra                                               151

Growth Strategy: Past, Present and Future
by Aurobindo Ghose                                                 169

Resource Mobilization, Resource Allocation and the
Economic Strategy
by Sanjaya Baru                                                    179

## Part V: Sectoral Performance—Agriculture

Agricultural Development in India Since Independence
by G. S. Bhalla                                                    194

India's Agricultural Performance: Growth Amidst
Neglect
by B. M. Bhatia                                                    206

Performance of Indian Agriculture and the Rural Sector
in the Post-Green Revolution Period
by H. Laxminarayan                                                 211

## Part VI: Sectoral Performance—Industry

Some Observations on the Rate and Pattern of
Industrial Growth
*by R. K. Roy*   234

Industrial Development: Issues and Policy Options
*by N. S. Siddharthan*   239

Privatization of the Development Process
*by Balraj Metha*   254

## Part VII: Concentration and Deprivation

Economic Class and Economic Policy in India
*by B. B. Bhattacharya*   259

Implications of Agricultural Development Policies for
Rural Poverty in India: A Note
*by K. Subbarao*   271

Poverty Eradication: A Review of Policies and
Programmes
*by S. D. Tendulkar*   276

Industrial Policy in India, 1947–85
*by Kamal A. Mitra Chenoy*   282

New Economic Policy: From Disenchantment to
Discontent
*by Balraj Metha*   287

On Economic Stagnation, Past Development Strategy
and New Economic Policy—A Summing-up
*by Arun Bose*   295

*Index*   307

# Foreword

Kirorimal College was host to a two-day seminar entitled 'Performance of the Indian Economy Since Independence' in 1985. It was a successful and rather unique seminar inasmuch as seminars that are both large and full of luminaries are seldom organized by a college; also, the topic was vast. The University Grants Commission very kindly provided the necessary funds.

The credit for all this goes to the Departments of Commerce and Economics of Kirorimal College. I would like to thank, particularly, Aurobindo Ghose and R. A. Choudhury for their tremendous effort in persuading various eminent economists to contribute. As is evident from the Introduction, a number of papers were specially written for this seminar.

The response from various quarters after the seminar encouraged us to approach other scholars to write on specified topics. The result is the present anthology, which covers a great many aspects of the Indian economy.

N. S. Pradhan

# Acknowledgements

The inspiration for the seminar, the source of the present volume, came from our late principal, Dr N. S. Pradhan. We owe him a debt altogether too extensive to be recorded. His encouragement was unfailing. We deeply regret his demise while this volume was in press.

The grants that made the seminar a practical reality came from the UGC under its Faculty Improvement Programme.

Colleagues in the Departments of Commerce and Economics, Kirorimal College, worked untiringly in its organization. Our special thanks go to Mr A. L. Sikri, our Librarian, for taking care of the logistics; and to Sri Madan Mohan for providing invaluable secretarial assistance.

Our primary debt is to the contributors to this volume, and to the participants who made the seminar a rich experiene. We wish to acknowledge our gratitude to authors and publishers for permission to reprint some of the papers: specific details are given below the relevant paper.

We express our indebtedness to Professors Amartya Sen, Arun Bose and Sukhamoy Chakravarty for actively encouraging the project. Our deep appreciation goes to Professors Sisirkumar Ghose, A. N. Oza and Kaushik Basu for intellectual stimulation, and to other friends, including Dr Badri Raina, Dr G. B. Upreti, Dr T. A. P. Singh, Mr Som Raj Gupta, Ms Shailaja Sivsubramanium and Mr G. J. Rama Rao for incisive interventions during the course of editing the volume.

To Ms Seema Mehra we wish to say thanks for help in preparing the diagrams.

Mr Kulbir Singh indeed accomplished a miracle in efficiently transforming the manuscript from hand-written scrawls to a state of decency.

To our friends and families we owe a deep personal debt for standing by us.

R. A. Choudhury<br>
Shama Gamkhar<br>
Aurobindo Ghose

# List of Contributors

Sanjaya Baru: Professor, Centre for Economic Studies, Hyderabad.

Kaushik Basu: Professor, Delhi School of Economics, University of Delhi, Delhi.

G. S. Bhalla: Professor, Centre for Studies in Regional Development, Jawaharlal Nehru University, New Delhi.

B. M. Bhatia: Professor, Centre for Policy Research, New Delhi.

B. B. Bhattacharya: Professor, Institute of Economic Growth, Delhi.

Arun Bose: Economist, Calcutta.

Sukhamoy Chakravarty: Professor, Delhi School of Economics, University of Delhi, Delhi.

Kamal A. Mitra Chenoy: Reader, Indira Gandhi National Open University, New Delhi.

Aurobindo Ghose: Lecturer, Kirorimal College, University of Delhi, Delhi.

Prem Shankar Jha: Journalist, New Delhi.

Kamal Nayan Kabra: Professor, Indian Institute of Public Administration, New Delhi.

A. M. Khusro: Professor, National Institute of Public Finance, New Delhi.

## List of Contributors

H. Laxminarayan: (the late) Director, Agro-Economic Research Centre, University of Delhi, Delhi.

Balraj Mehta: Correspondent, *Economic and Political Weekly*, Bombay.

V. S. Minocha: Professor, Department of Commerce, University of Delhi, Delhi.

Raj Krishna: (the late) Professor, Delhi School of Economics, University of Delhi, Delhi.

R. K. Roy: Resident Editor, *Economic Times*, New Delhi.

Ranjit K. Sau: Professor, Indian Institute of Management, Calcutta.

Amartya Sen: Professor, Harvard University, Boston.

N. S. Siddharthan: Professor, Institute of Economic Growth, Delhi.

K. Subbarao: Professor, Institute of Economic Growth, Delhi.

Dalip S. Swamy: Professor, Department of Business Economics, University of Delhi (South Campus), New Delhi.

S. D. Tendulkar: Professor, Delhi School of Economics, University of Delhi, Delhi.

# Introduction

R. A. CHOUDHURY, SHAMA GAMKHAR
AUROBINDO GHOSE

Twenty-four contributions by leading economists, academicians, journalists and policy-makers on the theme 'The Performance of the Indian Economy since Independence' are included in this volume. Twenty-one of these were first presented at a UGC-sponsored seminar hosted in 1985 by Kirorimal College, University of Delhi. These were subsequently revised for publication. Also included in this volume, as background readings, are three seminal contributions by renowned economists: Amartya Sen, Sukhamoy Chakravarty and Raj Krishna. The volume consists of seven parts: Part I contains this Introduction, Part II the background readings, and Parts III to VII the proceedings of various sessions of the seminar.

The need for a retrospective survey four decades after Independence, to take stock of the achievements and failures of the Indian economy, is evident. Viewed in the historical context of nearly two centuries of British rule, forty years may not appear to be long enough to erase all the marks of colonialism. Yet, it is not too short a period either. In this time span, the entire process of economic development could have been begun and completed by the Indian nation. What, then, has gone wrong, and why?

The contemporary relevance of this volume must be judged in the light of the crisis—economic, political and social—that has engulfed Indian society. Very many conscientious citizens—workers and peasants, students, academics, artists, scientists, administrators, policy-makers, social reformers and political activists—are keen to understand the nature of this crisis. An important part of understanding this crisis may emerge from learning how the Indian economy has fared and understanding its impact on the well-being of different sections of society—privileged groups as well as the masses.

We expect the volume to have a wide appeal, as the contributions are marked by an openness of approach and are not tied to dogma. There is here an interaction between very different and dissimilar approaches to the evaluation of economic performance. The approaches vary from the statistical-empirical method to the political-economy framework, to the more popular, liberal approach of the technology-institution paradigm. The political-economy approach itself swings between the classical approaches of Marx and Schumpeter to neo-classical methodology. What is refreshing is the mutual appreciation in the essays of the strengths and weaknesses of each other's approach. We feel that this volume succeeds in raising a number of new issues. Three key themes seem to emerge: (1) India's economic performance; (2) India's past development strategy; (3) The new economic policy being discussed since 1985.

On the country's economic performance, the views put forward range from the one that there has been no economic stagnation in India since Independence to the more common view that India has been suffering a low and stable or steady long-term rate of growth. This rate of growth, though positive, is one of the lowest among Third World countries. There are differences of opinion regarding the implications of this growth performance on the state of the economy. Amartya Sen, in 'How Is India Doing?', counterposes the strengths and weaknesses of Indian society to highlight its underlying duality—achievements on the growth front and in the development of science, technology and higher education, which coexist with persistent inequalities and deprivation. Yet another anomaly manifests itself in under-reporting within the formal sector and in the rapid expansion of the black economy. This calls for an enquiry into the credibility of the data base of Indian growth statistics.

On India's developmental strategy, pursued since Independence, all the contributors seem to agree that the growth strategy has failed. A new strategy is needed which envisages 'structural change'. However, opinions differ widely as to what constitutes this 'structural change': whether it would entail basic reforms within the existing socio-economic-political system or a change of the system itself. Several contributors have critically examined the strategy of heavy industrialization, liberalization, district-wise industrialization, modernization and technology imports. The institutional role played by the state in promoting monopoly capitalism comes in for sharp criticism. An analysis of the fiscal crisis of the state shows that the process of state capitalism had been inflationary and inequitous. It has led to the deceleration of industrial output and the growth in imbalances in agriculture—regionwise and cropwise.

The New Economic Policy adopted by the Rajiv Gandhi government comes in for close scrutiny. The growth impetus of this New Economic Policy is expected to come from nurturing production activities in areas which meet the consumption requirements of the elite. This would entail increased liberalization and privatization of industry, which reflect the class-bias basis of this policy. There is a welcome attempt in the essays to evaluate the New Economic Policy within the Schumpeterian framework. There seems general appreciation that there is need for a *truly* new economic policy for India, and that this should change the complex of productive forces and production relations in favour of workers, peasants and professionals.

The essays together may help explode several economic myths which have been used as the guiding forces of economic planning and policy-making in India. They seem to show that economic growth in underdeveloped countries by itself does not ensure a 'trickle-down effect' of the growth benefits to the poor and the unemployed. Several essays demonstrate that the 'strategy of growth' is in effect nothing but the strategy of 'state capitalism' or the development of capitalism under the aegis of the state, using the instruments of planning, public sector and public policy in accordance with the goals and interests of a capitalist class. Some contributors argue that export-led growth was an illusion and that more appropriate would have been a path of growth-led exports. The premise that bureaucracy is a neutral element in economic activity is challenged, and it is argued that the rentier-bureaucracy is an independent force or 'group' with its own objectives, programmes and targets.

Several of the essays seek to explain the paradox of a high rate of savings and unfulfilled basic needs, the fiscal crisis of the Indian state, the nexus between the technological and institutional aspects of economic growth, and the discriminatory and inequitious character of economic policy in India. They are also interesting in their varying interpretations of the same economic reality, thereby providing a comprehensive picture of our economic performance. For example, while a positive growth rate of the economy is highlighted in some of the essays, the character of this growth is found to be elitist in others. Income growth is consistently accompanied by the growth of poverty, unemployment and disparities. Similarly, macro-level food sufficiency has been found to be accompanied by micro-level food scarcity for a large majority of the populace. Again, while the much-touted Green Revolution raised the rate of growth of agricultural output, it is shown to have accentuated inter-personal and inter-regional disparities of income. All this has prompted Arun Bose to reach the disturbing conclusion that the 'main cause for concern about India's long-term economic performance is her unequal, uneven and in this sense "unreal" growth for a stable or growing majority rather than no growth'.

The papers presented at the seminar evoked much comment and discussion. Some of the remarks and comments have considerable contextual relevance. It is of no small interest that the following statement of ex-Prime Minister Rajiv Gandhi should have been referred to in the deliberations: 'We do not want controls. We want control. Controls lead to all the corruption, to all the delays, and that is what we want to cut out without losing control on the directions we are giving.' Another participant pointed out: 'Investment decisions in the public sector are largely dictated by what the political masters want and technologies are adopted because of other factors: What is the kickback abroad, what is the payment in terms of hospitality, etc'. A third participant remarked: 'It is not the policy makers but the peasant movement which will bring about land reforms. The peasant movement today is interested only in higher prices.'

Participants also tried to arrive at certain concrete lessons for the future: The technological and institutional aspects of growth need to be combined and dovetailed; the focus of future strategy should be shifted from growth to development, and for this it is necessary to attack the problems of poverty and unemployment directly rather than through the 'trickle-down effects' of growth; the neglect of agriculture must be corrected; and in agricultural development public investment and institutional reforms must be preferred to a direct incentives-oriented policy.

In the discussion on growth strategy, while all seemed to agree that the past strategy of growth had failed, particularly as regards poverty and unemployment, major differences arose as to the alternative strategy for structural change. This demarcated participants between those who envisaged a shift from one paradigm (capitalism) to another (socialism), and those who were in favour of removing structural bottlenecks within the existing socio-political framework. Appropriate institutions were considered as the other important aspect of structural change.

On the agricultural front, there was a difference of opinion regarding the scope of land reforms. Some participants agreed with Dandekar's view that 'the horses have already bolted', while others held that the existing data on asset distribution indicate sufficient scope for further land reforms. All seemed to agree that the only effective force to bring about land reforms is the peasant movement.

The discussion on industry was mainly geared to the relevance of the Schumpeterian framework to the Indian situation, and the concept of privatization. Certain distinctive features of the Schumpeterian framework, such as commitment to excellence, discipline, decision-making and risk-taking abilities (as observed in the East Asian Model) were identified. There was concern for the singular lack of initiative within the Indian public and private corporate sectors, as well as the phenomenon of non-economic factors dictating investment decisions in the public sector.

Two main instruments of economic policy—subsidies and public investment—were evaluated. Some participants cautioned against an injudicious use of subsidies at the cost of growth. The principal beneficiaries of this scheme have been the bureaucracy, rich farmers and industrialists. Further, it was pointed out that, as an instrument of redistribution, public investment has worked like subsidies for the betterment of the rich. It was also felt that the 'trickle-down' theory relies heavily on the private sector and capital-intensive method of production. This strategy can neither alleviate poverty nor lead to sustained growth. It was observed that this has only resulted in the emergence of anomalies such as macro-food security coexisting with micro-food scarcity and spatial redistribution of income from the food-poor states to the food-rich states.

One of the principal questions that faced the seminar was: Is the problem of inequality irreversible? The consensus on this was that to move towards this goal it was necessary to change the economic and social structure in rural areas through a mass mobilization and organization of agricultural workers and small farmers. It was felt that these would be the most effective agents of change with respect to technology, price support and subsidy.

In order to leap forward one has to look back. We hope that those who are concerned with the shape of things to come will find this volume useful.

# How is India Doing?*

AMARTYA SEN

'Thou by the Indian Ganges' side/Shouldst rubies find: I by the tide/of Humber would complain', wrote Andrew Marvell, the seventeenth-century poet, outlining to his coy mistress the things they could do if they had 'but world enough, and time'. While not many rubies have been found on the banks of the Ganges, India's reputation as a land of riches is as ancient as the history of its poverty. That mixed reputation has changed in recent centuries, and India is seen these days primarily as a land of poverty, famines, diseases, squalor, caste, untouchability, separatism, and chaos. This reputation is not altogether undeserved. But things do not stay stationary, and some changes have occurred in the last few decades. We have to ask: which way is India going? A sixth of humanity is involved.

I start with the economy. What did India look like at the time of independence in 1947? It was poor, obviously, but more strikingly, almost completely stagnant. In fact, many estimates suggest that a sizeable economic decline took place during the last decades of British rule. This is disputed by Alan Heston in his chapter on national income, in the recently published *Cambridge Economic History of India* (Raychaudhuri and

* This is a revised version of an article that appeared in *The New York Review of Books*, 21 (Christmas Number, 1982). Reprinted with the permission of the author and the publishers of *The New York Review of Books*. Some of the more general issues touched on in this article—including the contrasts between the successes and failures of China and India—have been further discussed in the author's 'Development: Which Way Now?', *Economic Journal*, 93 (December 1983), and 'Economic Distance and the Living Standard', in a forthcoming volume of essays in honour of S. J. Patel, to be published by Pergamon Press.

Habib 1982; Kumar and Desai 1983)—an impressive two-volume work that is indispensable for anyone seeking enlightenment on India's past. While Heston challenges the thesis of decline, his own estimates indicate a complete absence of growth of per capita income for the three decades preceding independence. Heston also accepts that in these years Indian food output per head was falling, despite the rather low growth of population (around 1 per cent a year).

The average expectation of life at birth in newly independent India was a mere 33 years. India also experienced a gigantic famine in 1943, shortly before independence; this killed around three million people. While the Great Bengal Famine was not directly related to the decline in the amount of food available per head (since it took place at a time when there was a comparatively good aggregate food supply), it brought out the disastrous vulnerability of several occupation groups in the Indian population to the vagaries of economic fluctuations (Sen 1981).

Judged against this background, India's economic performance since independence is bound to appear quite creditable. Its national product has grown steadily faster than population, and the process has speeded up from about 1 per cent per year before independence, to 3 to 3.5 per cent after independence—rather higher than that on average in the very recent years, and it is comfortably ahead of the population growth of about 2 per cent. Agriculture, no longer stationary, has grown enough for India to be self-sufficient in most years and often more than that. Some regions within the country (for instance, Punjab) have grown at rates high enough to compare with the fast-growing economies in the Far East. The popular world image of India as a model of Malthusian decline survives but the reality is different.

There have been no major famines since independence. While droughts and floods have threatened famine (for example, Bihar in 1968, Maharashtra in 1971–3, West Bengal in 1978), public action has prevented a traditional catastrophe from taking place. Life expectancy at birth has gone up from 33 years to 52 years. While the fall in the death rate led initially to a sharp increase in the rate of population growth, that growth has recently been declining because the birth rate has been falling. It still has a long way to fall, and there is little cause for smugness, especially since China and Sri Lanka have achieved so much more in reducing the birth rate than India has. But even the relatively moderate fall in the birth rate—from 44 to 36 per thousand during the last two decades—has now given India the third lowest birth rate among the 33 'low-income economies' covered by World Development Report 1982 (World Bank 1982: Table 18). Some regions in India, especially Kerala, have been more successful in cutting down the birth rate than have others.

The post-independence period has also seen some far-reaching changes in the legality of the caste system, and these have included making the practice of untouchability a criminal offence. India has been many years ahead of the West in introducing its own programmes of affirmative action and positive discrimination. The constitution of the Republic of India, which came into force in 1950, two-and-a-half years after independence, makes explicit provision for such actions. In the civil service a substantial number of jobs have been reserved for members of the 'Scheduled Castes'—officialese for traditional 'Untouchable' groups. As a temporary measure, a proportion of seats in the Lok Sabha (the lower house of the Indian Parliament) was reserved for 'Untouchables' (the others being 'general' seats open to all citizens). The same was done in the legislatures of the states. The number of 'Untouchables' in positions of power and influence has grown rapidly under these 'positively discriminatory' arrangements.

If all this sounds like a propaganda hand-out by a pro-India lobby, I should warn that I will presently argue that Indian society is a deeply troubled one, with extreme injustices heaped upon dreadful inequities. But we cannot begin to view India's problems and failures intelligently without acknowledging what has been achieved.

The expansion of science and technology in India—including nuclear power—has received some comment lately. Ved Mehta in his interesting and important book on the hold of the Nehru family on modern India has even argued that 'by some estimates' India 'ranks next to the United States and the Soviet Union in its number of highly trained nuclear scientists' (Mehta 1982: 158). India's higher education sector is vast. In the number of students enrolled in higher education as a percentage of the population aged 20 to 24, not only is India a considerable distance ahead of any other country of comparable income level, but there is in fact no country with even twice India's per capita income that comes anywhere close to its higher education ratio (World Bank 1982; World View 1982). In China, for example, the number of students in institutions of higher education is about 1 per cent of the corresponding age group, whereas in India this ratio is 8 per cent. In the number of doctors per unit of population, India is second only to China among all countries having an income per head no higher than twice India's.

I ought to discuss two other achievements of some importance before I take up the bad news. Ever since independence, it has been feared that, in view of its regional diversities, India would soon break up. It has also been doubted whether India is, in any sense, one country. The inevitability of disintegration was most plausibly argued. But this has not happened. The so-called most dangerous decades have come and gone. There have been regional tensions, but the social, cultural, and economic bonds have proved to be too strong to snap—or even to come close to snapping. I believe the historical basis of Indian unit is often underestimated by those who attribute to the innocent British the creation of a sense of 'Indianness', which in fact has deeper roots. The first volume of the *Cambridge Economic History of India* (Raychaudhuri and Habib 1982) brings out the extent of social and economic integration that obtained in pre-British India.

There are, of course, several peripheral groups (for instance, the numerically small but politically important tribes in extreme northeast India) and retaining their loyalty has often involved the use of force—even brutality. However, for most of the country separatism has proved to be a relatively weak force much overestimated by 'experts', foreign and domestic. While various internal rearrangements (such as revision of inter-state divisions) have occurred, the nation of two-thirds of a billion people with 14 major languages has survived remarkably intact.

The second achievement concerns the effects of the oil crises and the world recession. India is dependent on oil imports, though attempts have been made recently to find more oil within the country. Despite the hike in oil prices in 1973, which expanded India's import bill remarkably, its foreign exchange earnings also increased rapidly. While India's terms of trade declined sharply with the rise in oil prices, the volume of its exports increased much faster than the volume of its imports through the 1970s. India also earned large remittances from Indians working abroad, especially in the Middle East. India has had more difficulty in coping with the second round of oil price rises, in the late seventies, but all in all it has weathered the storm remarkably well. And in recent years—despite the world recession—the Indian economy has grown at an unusually rapid rate. Taken together these achievements are certainly impressive. What is the other side of the story?

'Speak of me as I am', said Othello (shortly before that imperialist agent gave his candid views on 'the base Indian' and 'a malignant and turban'd Turk'). To apply the same principle to India today offers much scope for criticism even without anyone's having to 'set down aught in malice'. One can, for example, point out that while the pace of India's growth has speeded up recently, its long-term average growth has been much lower than the world average; that Indian agriculture has got by with some help from good monsoons in recent years; that one reason India has weathered the oil crisis so well is that it is relatively near the Middle East. Even as it has suffered from the rise in oil prices, India has benefited from the consequent shift in world income from the West to the Middle East, which has been much more inclined to buy Indian goods, services, and skills.

These facts, however, do not really detract from India's achievements. Judged historically, the speeding up of India's economic expansion from, at best, just about 1 per cent at the time of independence, to 3 to 3.5 per cent, and rather higher since 1973, cannot be dismissed merely by noting that it is only recently that India's performance has become internationally respectable, partly because of the lowering of the world economic growth since 1973. Nor can the monsoons—on close analysis—be seen to be the major influence on the change in India's growth performance. And insofar as India has put the Middle East boom to good use, it has been able to do this because of its potential for domestic production, the availability of skilled and semi-skilled workers, and a willingness to seize economic opportunities as they arise. The real blots on India's performance lie elsewhere.

One of the major blots is the survival of regular malnutrition—as distinct from acute starvation and famines—in most parts of India. At least a third of the rural population seems to suffer from nutritional inadequacies. The deprivation is especially common for landless rural labourers, whose entitlement to food in the market economy of India rests on their ability to sell their labour and buy food. Depending on the varying changes for employment and relative prices, a great many of these families remain hungry a lot of the time. This class of rural wage labourers has been the traditional victim of South Asian famines (for instance, the Great Bengal Famine of 1943, the famine in neighbouring Bangladesh in 1974). While this class has not had to face a famine in post-independence India, it has had to live with regular malnutrition and endemic hunger.

Estimates of poverty in India are usually related to nutritional norms—such as the amount of calories people need. There have been a great many controversies among Indian economists and nutritionists on the choice of such norms (even on whether they are meaningful at all) as well as on the use of these norms for statistical analyses of India's performance in relieving poverty. While some estimates show an increase in poverty despite economic growth, others suggest a slight amelioration of the incidence of poverty. But there is no picture whatsoever of a decisive change for the better.

India's 'self-sufficiency' in food has to be assessed in the light of the limited purchasing power of the Indian masses. Their needs may be large, but their 'entitlements' in the market are small; that the economy produces enough to meet their market demand is not in itself a gigantic achievement. There has been no great 'shortage' in the market—no 'crisis' to deal with—but at least a third of the rural population has regularly—and quietly—gone to bed hungry and malnourished. The government has been able to ignore this endemic hunger because that hunger has neither led to a run on the market, and chaos, nor grown into an acute famine with people dying of starvation. Persistent orderly hunger does not upset the system.

Could India have done otherwise? It could be argued—indeed it is argued—that given the extremely low level of income from which India has started, it could not really do anything else until economic growth put the Indian people at a different level of economic prosperity altogether. Does this argument hold? The contrast with China is relevant here, but that raises a great many complex issues, some of which I shall take up later. Fewer problems are posed by a comparison with Sri Lanka, which belongs to the same region and has a political system not far different from India's.

For many decades Sri Lanka has followed the policy of providing extensive social services, including distribution of subsidized rice. The nature of that subsidy has varied over the year—sometimes cheaper rice was made available to all, at other times some rice was given free to anyone qualifying by a means test. While Sri Lanka's per capita income is of the same order of magnitude as that of India and Pakistan, and its total amount of available food (measured in calories) per unit of population is also quite comparable, cases of endemic hunger are much rarer in Sri Lanka than in the subcontinent. And the expectation of life at birth in Sri Lanka—estimated to be about 66 years—is far closer to the figures of rich countries than to those of India and Pakistan (52 and 50 years respectively). The rice policy is by no means the only factor responsible for the difference, but it has certainly contributed substantially to the result, and the general programme of government-financed social services—of which the rice policy and medical provisions are a part—has worked powerfully in that direction.

It is thus not quite the case that India's overall poverty rules out all policies other than the one it has followed. Food subsidies in Sri Lanka have cost no more than a small fraction of its GNP, and if they were similarly expensive in India, they would have amounted to something like just one year's growth of GNP at India's current rate of growth. But India's approach to social services has, in fact, been sadly unimaginative and breathtakingly conservative. The deal that the government of India struck recently with the International Monetary Fund, leading to the approval of the largest loan (exceeding $5 billion) that the IMF has ever given to any country, seems to involve a pattern of development that includes a further move in the direction of the no-nonsense South Korean model and that will have the effect of excluding ambitious programmes of social services. There is not much reason to doubt that this type of policy can bring dividends in high economic growth, but its impact on the quality of life will be slow. It is worth noting that South Korea, with five-and-a-half times the per capita income of Sri Lanka, still has no higher (in fact, a slightly lower) expectation of life than Sri Lanka. Nevertheless, the Indian leaders seem to have clearly decided on a strategy focused on growth, with an astonishingly conservative approach to social services.

This conservatism happens to fit quite well with the elitist character of Indian society and politics. The powerful groups have much to gain from high growth. If intensive public efforts were made to eliminate endemic malnutrition immediately, that would benefit groups that are less powerful. It is important to understand the elitist nature of India to make sense of India's policies. The elite groups in India are remarkably powerful, and while they are a small minority of a nation of 700 million people, they are still numerically large. The elite must not be confused with just the industrial leaders or the bourgeoisie. It includes millions of civil servants, business people, commercial farmers, educators, office workers, and small landowners. In fact, it includes many people who are themselves poor by international standards.

Nor is it the case that the Indian elite is unenlightened, or indifferent to the rest of the community. The moral and political consciousness of the Indian elite does not permit, for example, a major famine in India, and when a serious famine threatens, public intervention is swift and effective. Even reports on pockets of acute starvation by probing journalists—and there are many excellent ones in India—get prominent attention in newspapers and produce some response. On the other hand, removing the quiet presence of non-acute, endemic hunger does not have high priority in that elitist morality and politics.

The roots of elitism go way back in Indian history. The Hindu view of mankind—stratified and hierarchical—connects with it. To be born into one of the higher castes does not ensure elite status in the political economy; but in fact most of the elite comes from the upper and middle castes. The firm grip of the elite can be seen in practically every sphere of social activity in India. Recently, the historian Ranajit Guha (1982) has argued that it is difficult to disentangle the events of the history of

South Asia, since even the writing of history in the Indian subcontinent is so 'dominated by elitism'. As far as politics is concerned, it is remarkable that much of the leadership of all political parties in India—from the extreme right to the extreme left—comes from this elite background. It is not so much that the leaders join the elite when they establish themselves but that they typically come from that stratum already.

Some of the achievements of India that I discussed earlier reflect the success of elitism. The remarkable expansion of higher education is a case in point. This applies to liberal university education, and also to science and technology. The other side of the coin can be seen in the shocking neglect of elementary education. After thirty-five years of independence, only a miserable 36 per cent of adult Indians are literate. In this nation with a nuclear capacity, well-developed scientific know-how, and a higher education ratio perhaps eight times that of China, nearly two-thirds of the citizens simply cannot read or write.

Speculation on the influence of cultural history is usually rather treacherous, but there might well be some significance in the fact that in countries moulded by the less elitist Buddhist tradition, primary education is much more widespread and higher education much less so than in the land of Hinduism. This applies even to Buddhist countries in the same region, such as Burma and Sri Lanka; their adult literacy rates are 70 per cent and 85 per cent respectively (against India's 36 per cent) and their higher education enrollment as a proportion of the population aged 20 to 24 is 4 per cent and 1 per cent (as opposed to India's 8 per cent).

Underdevelopment of elementary education seems to go hand-in-hand with limitation of other social services. Kerala, the one state in India that has had a high level of literacy and schooling for a long time, also has a much better developed system of social services, including medical care. The expectation of life at birth in Kerala is, in fact, much closer to that of Sri Lanka than to that of the rest of India. But Kerala occupies an unusual position in Indian history. It has had rather different property laws and tenurial arrangements. Women have had a larger role in property inheritance. It has also been more open to outside influence. Christians came there by the fourth century and Jews shortly after the fall of Jerusalem, and both got on well with the Hindu kings and with the population; there were long-standing and close trading ties with many foreign countries including the Arab world; Kerala also elected the first communist government in India in the 1957 state elections. The dividing line between the elite and the non-elite has been under pressure for a long time in Kerala.

I mentioned earlier positive discrimination in favour of 'Untouchable' groups. Reserving civil service jobs and legislative positions has certainly had the effect of increasing substantially the number of 'Untouchables' in positions of power and influence. But there is little evidence that this has contributed substantially to improving the lot of the great majority of 'Untouchables' in the country. The high correlation of untouchability with economic disadvantage—in particular landlessness and poverty—makes it difficult to transform the general position of 'Untouchables' without very substantial economic change. Moreover, social conventions have been hard to break by purely legal means, such as the laws against the practice of untouchability.

In fact, in recent years the persecution of 'Untouchable' groups by members of some of the rural upper and middle castes seems to have intensified, and in some regions this oppression has even taken a sharply violent form. Members of 'Untouchable' communities seeking a better economic or social deal (e.g., less exploitative labour relations) have been subjected to harassment, beating, burning of homes, and even murder. While the offenders have been brought to justice in many cases (often only after newspaper reports and the resulting public outrage), the preventive measures have been quite inadequate, and incidents of such violence continue to occur in different parts of rural India. Because of the rural power structure—and the nature of the police force—it is difficult to wipe out this violence without a much firmer and broader use of central power.

It is also remarkable that those 'Untouchables' who are now in a position of influence, thanks to positive discrimination have—with a few exceptions—done very little to help others left behind. Recently, the Untouchable Battle Society (Dalit Sangarsh Samiti) has strongly criticized the inaction of 'Dalit legislators, members of Parliament, and ministers in the face of growing atrocities' against other Dalits. Positive discrimination has often done no more than recruit some of the ablest, or most advanced, 'Untouchable' members into the charmed circle of the Indian elite. One thinks of Marx's remark: 'The more a ruling class is able to assimilate the foremost minds of a ruled class, the more stable and dangerous becomes its rule.'

The elitist character of Indian society is brought out also by the treatment of women. Many women hold prominent positions in India—as parliamentarians, political leaders, academics, doctors, artists, and others—not to mention the most powerful Prime Minister the country has had. Although women in elite groups may still suffer from disadvantages, many doors are open to them. But the general position of women in Indian society is nothing short of scandalous. Their mortality rates are typically higher than men's (except for those above forty). The expectation of life at birth is lower for the Indian female than for the Indian male, and this pattern is quite contrary to that of the overwhelming majority of countries. Malnutrition too is more common among females. In studying the effects of the 1978 floods in West Bengal, I found that even among children under five, severe malnutrition was about 60 per cent more frequent for girls than for boys.

All this helps to explain the extraordinary fact that the so-called sex ratio—the percentage of females to males—in India has declined from around 97.2 per cent in 1901 to 93.5 per cent in the last census in 1981. This is, of course, an ominous and starting trend, since with modernization one would have expected a relative reduction of female mortality *vis-á-vis* male mortality. On the contrary, it appears that with the progress of modern medicine and health services in India, the opportunities have been much more effectively—and unequally—seized by men than by women. The traditional differences have been heightened by new opportunities, and as the absolute positions of both men and women have slowly improved in health and longevity, the relative position of women has fallen behind. This does not of course happen among the elite—not much anyway. The peculiarities and inequities of the respective mortality rates of men and women among the non-elite majority in India have not become a major policy issue in elitist India.

Insofar as elitism is seen as one of the main problems with India, a comparison with China is obviously relevant. With the establishment of communist China, anti-elitism immediately became one of the major emphases of its official policy, and during the Cultural Revolution this aspect of Chinese policy became particularly prominent. Certainly, anti-elitist achievements of China are very substantial. The traditional rural power structure was smashed effectively, the hold of the urban elite quite transformed. Schooling and medical services have expanded rapidly and are much more widely spread than in India. The general level of nutrition has vastly improved. Life expectancy—between 64 and 69 years according to various recent estimates—is much higher than India's miserable 52 years.

But anti-elitism has caused grave casualties too. The chaos and destruction in the old university system that took place during the Cultural Revolution have clearly extracted a heavy price, and while the system is currently being rebuilt, a great deal remains to be done. The tyranny imposed during the Cultural Revolution was also justified by the anti-elitist policy, and even the more moderate accounts suggest a merciless extremism—torture, 'punishments', killing—in the treatment of a considerable part of the population. India's record in this respect is obviously less disquieting. As Fox Butterfield, who was the *New York Times* correspondent in China, puts it in his disturbing book *China: Alive in the Bitter Sea*, except for the short period of the 'emergency', which ended in Mrs Gandhi's electoral defeat, India has maintained its political freedom; there have been no unchecked Public Security Ministry, no street committees, no network of forced-labour camps, no persecution of whole groups of people because they were intellectuals or had relatives who had once been landlords, no destruction of libraries and universities (1982: 447).

But in view of the price that India has to pay for its political system, it could be asked: are these liberties worth it? Would not better feeding, clothing, and health for the Indian population compensate for the loss of liberty which after all effectively concerns only a minority? (Sun Yefang 1981; Zhu Zhengzhi 1980). I believe this way of posing the choice is both banal and wrong. First, there is little evidence that matters of liberty do not concern most of the people, even in poor countries. Indeed, the response of Indian voters to Mrs Gandhi's 'emergency' rule demonstrated the wider concerns of one of the poorest electorates in the world. It is indeed remarkable that a community of voters who are ready to tolerate so much economic inequity and are so difficult to mobilize against elitist policies could be so quick to move in its rejection of tyranny.

Second, the choice posed is unreal. A regime in which basic liberties are severely suppressed, and in which the government cannot be voted out of office no matter what it does, is deeply unpredictable, and there is no guarantee that even large-scale starvation and famines would not occur under such a regime. Indeed, there is clear evidence now that in China during the three years from 1959 to 1961 a great many people died from lack of food.

The exact size of the extra mortality caused by the food problem remains controversial. One estimate, based on Chinese data sources, indicates that the extra mortality during a four-year period including the food crisis years was about 16.5 million. Another, also based on recently available Chinese data, suggests that 'the net loss in 1960-1 would have to be no less than 23 million', though other evidence suggests that 'the losses during the crises may not have been as acute' (Aird 1982: 277-8; Coale 1981: 89).[1]

No matter which of the various estimates we pick, there cannot be any serious doubt that there was truly appalling extra mortality during the food crisis years. The same statistical approach—focusing on extra mortality—was used to calculate the size of the Great Bengal Famine of 1943, and the extra mortality during the years from 1943 to 1946 was estimated to be around 3 million (much in excess of the official figure of 1.5 million). On that basis the Bengal famine of 1943 counts as the largest famine in South Asia in this century. The scale of Chinese mortality seems to have been much larger. So the Chinese catastrophe of 1959 to 1961 dwarfs even the pre-independence famines in India, and as I have already noted, there have been no major famines in the post-independence

---

[1] These analyses draw on Chinese work on mortality in the 1959-61 famine—in particular on Sun Yefang (1981) and Zhu Zhengzhi (1980).

period in India. Although the Chinese have an economic system that makes guaranteeing food to everyone much easier than in the Indian economy, it is China rather than India that has had sudden large-scale deaths from food shortages in recent times.

What is also remarkable is that the news of hunger and death in China could fail to become more widely known. It is only in the last few years—nearly twenty years after the event—that the extent of the calamity has been acknowledged, and this has happened after a major change in the Chinese leadership. In India even a fraction of that death toll would have immediately caused a storm in the newspapers and a turmoil in the Indian Parliament, and the ruling government would almost certainly have had to resign. Any government keen on staying in power would have had to avoid such starvation deaths from taking place at any cost. Thus the question of food and starvation is not unrelated to the issue of liberties, of newspapers, and, ultimately, of democracy. The Soviet famines in the thirties point towards the same lesson. So does the Kampuchean famine of more recent years.

What Wei Jingsheng called 'the fifth modernization'—the establishment of democratic rights—in his famous wall-poster message of December 1978 (after which he was sent to prison for fifteen years) is not only valuable in itself, as he emphasized, but it also has a crucial instrumental function in guaranteeing food and other necessities of life. The Chinese experience brings out the penalties of doing without 'the fifth modernization'. The Indian experience does not contradict the value of democratic rights—it confirms that value—but it also shows how easily terrible inequities can survive despite 'the fifth modernization'. The issue of democratic rights is part of a bigger social picture. In itself it does not make the picture, but if it is excluded, the picture has a crucial gap in it.

The strengths and weaknesses of the Indian system are clear enough. It permits endemic malnutrition and hunger that is not acute, so long as these happen quietly; it does not permit a famine both because it would be too acute and because it cannot happen quietly. It permits the injustice of keeping a large majority of the people illiterate while the elite enjoys the benefits of vast system of higher education. It tolerates the continuing disadvantages of those who formerly suffered from explicit discrimination, even though such discrimination is now made illegal, and even though 'positive discrimination' promotes a small number from the bottom stratum to positions of power and influence as new recruits of the elite. The elections, the newspapers, and the political liberties work powerfully against dramatic deprivations and new sufferings, but easily allow the quiet continuation of an astonishing set of persistent injustices.

This dichotomy seems to me to be the central point in judging how India is doing. It is doing quite well in many specific respects—for instance, in breaking the pre-independence stagnation and achieving a respectable growth of income per person, in guaranteeing many traditional liberties, in developing science and technology and higher education, in putting more dynamism into agriculture, in meeting the oil crises and the world recession. But this record has to be assessed in the light of the persistent inequities and the basic weakness of modern India that sustains them. It is a weakness that is not being conquered.

**REFERENCES**

Aird, John S., 'Population Studies and Population Policy in China', *Population and Development Review*, 8: 267–98, 1982.

Butterfield, Fox, *China: Alive in the Bitter Sea*, New York, Times Books, 1982.

Coale, Ansley J., 'Population Trends, Population Policy, and Population Studies in China', *Population and Development Review*, 7: 85–97, 1981.

Guha, Ranajit (ed), *Subaltern Studies I: Writings on South Asian History and Society*, Delhi, Oxford University Press, 1982.

Kumar, Dharma and Meghnad Desai (eds), *The Cambridge Economic History of India, Vol. 2: c. 1751 to c. 1970*, London, Cambridge University Press, 1983.

Mehta, Ved, *A Family Affair: India under Three Prime Ministers*, London, Oxford University Press, 1982.

Raychaudhuri, Tapan and Irfan Habib (eds), *The Cambridge Economic History of India, Vol. 1: c. 1200 to c. 1750*, London, Cambridge University Press, 1982.

Sen, Amartya, *Poverty and Famines: An Essay on Entitlement and Deprivation*, London, Oxford University Press, 1981.

Sun Yefang, *Jingji Guanli*, No. 2, 1981.

World Bank, *World Development Report*, 1982.

World View, *An Economic and Geopolitical Yearbook, 1982*, London, Pluto Press, 1982.

Zhu Zhengzhi, *Jingzhi Kezue*, No. 3, 1980.

# Aspects of India's Development Strategy for the 1980s*

SUKHAMOY CHAKRAVARTY

I

Indian development strategy as it evolved since the mid-fifties had largely been predicated on the basic understanding that the prime need before the country was to accelerate the rate of material capital formation. It was widely believed that the limiting factor in this regard was the shortage of savings. Mahalanobis added a major twist to the argument when he pointed out that the shortage of savings was mirrored in the inadequacy of the production of capital goods, an argument that would be strictly true only in a closed economy where wages were paid out at the end of the production period. His recommendation to step up the rate of expansion of capital goods as a solution to India's stagnation was a 'structuralist' one, not different in spirit from similar recommendations made by the Latin American economist Prebisch although argued from a somewhat different theoretical position.[1]

---

* This is an extended and revised version of the Fifth G. L. Mehta Memorial Lecture (instituted by ICICI, Bombay) delivered on 26 April 1984 at the IIT, Bombay. Reprinted with the permission of the author from the *Economic and Political Weekly*, 19–26 May 1984.

[1] I have discussed the analytic and policy significance of Mahalanobis' contributions in several places. For the former, particular mention may be made of Chapter V in my *Capital and Development Planning* (MIT Press, 1969). For the latter, see the survey I jointly made with J. Bhagwati, *American Economic Review*, Supplement, 1969.

Subsequently, the limitations of his argument were much emphasized but these consisted in pointing out the advantage of following an appropriate pattern of international division of labour, a factor which he did not explicitly consider although it was very much implicit in his argument. While his criticism has found many advocates, both at home and abroad, the crucial factor which seemed to have led to a diversion from the strategy in the mid-sixties was the growing proneness of the economy to inflation, itself based on the failure of agricultural supply to match the demand that was being placed on it due, in part, to efforts at accelerating industrialization, and, to a greater extent, on the slowdown of acreage expansion in agriculture and increase in population growth.

Once again, the savings shortage was re-established in the forefront of discussion although with a different physical emphasis. Considered statically, this meant that the supply of wage goods was relatively inelastic and constituted the crucial bottleneck to India's growth. Dynamically, the source of the crisis was found to lie in the disproportionate rates of growth of **industry and agriculture**. The situation changed briefly towards the end of the sixties and the early seventies (1969–71), and once again, during the years 1976–8, when India seemed to experience problems of domestic absorption, which were reflected in the growth of publicly held grain stocks and also in the accretion to the quantum of foreign exchange reserves. Investment in fixed capital construction was, however, sluggish, leading people to fear that the domestic market may also be a problem in achieving a reasonable rate of growth.[2]

In both cases, these worries were soon over-shadowed by violent fluctuations in exogenous variables, such as highly unfavourable weather conditions in 1972–3, 1979–80 and 1982–3, as well as by sharp adverse movements in the external

---

[2] Demand as a factor constraining growth in the context of India was discussed in the mid-seventies by K. N. Raj, P. Patnaik, D. Nayyar, among others. These contributions have all appeared in various issues of *Economic and Political Weekly*. My own initial contribution to this discussion came out also in *Economic and Political Weekly*, Special Number, 1979. Despite their common concern, explanations suggested by different authors have been far from uniform.

terms of trade. Interestingly enough, while these events led to sharp price increases, reduced rates of output growth, savings rates were not significantly affected, a phenomenon that has not been fully explained so far.

It is a noteworthy fact that over the entire period 1950–80, national accounts suggest a significant increase in the domestic savings rate as a proportion of gross domestic product even when the increase in the level of per capita income has been a very modest one judged by the same set of statistics.

It is equally true that the type of shortage of labour and entrepreneurial skills that India faced at the time the country became independent is nowhere visible to the same extent.

Of the traditional development economists' arguments which claim to explain why a poor country continues to remain poor, it is only the limited capacity to import which seems to remain as a persisting phenomenon. Yet the moot question remains whether a sharp rise in the net inflow of foreign capital is all that India needs to achieve the needed acceleration in growth rates, even if one were to leave out questions relating to equity. This is a question which has acquired all the more urgency in the decade of the eighties.

While not underestimating the need to augment India's capacity to import, an issue to which I return later, I would first like to examine whether there is not a role for 'demand' as a factor constraining growth in a country like India. Clearly the issue is not a normative one. What we are looking for is whether demand, understood as effective demand, can affect not merely the composition but also the growth rate of production, even in a country like India.

II

To begin with, it would appear to me necessary to state in a compact form the analytical basis of the widely held presumption that economic growth in a low income country is exclusively dependent on factors specific to the supply side.[3]

---

[3] J. Kornai has made a distinction between 'demand constrained' and 'resource constrained' systems. He finds that the capitalist economies are normally 'demand constrained' and socialist economies are typically

First, it is held that as a low income economy, in general, is one characterized by a low volume of capital stock, relative to labour, the rate of return on investment on the margin must be necessarily high thus helping to keep the inducement to investment at a high level. This would appear to be the assumption underlying much neoclassical theorizing on growth.

Secondly, with or without the help of the Keynesian theory of consumption, it is maintained that the ratio of consumption to income must be necessarily high, leaving very little scope for savings. Taken together with the first reason, this will typically imply a level of aggregate demand which will press heavily on aggregate potential output thereby producing a situation of actual or incipient excess demand.

While the above two factors deal with the level of demand, there are two other factors which are supposed to help maintain a high rate of growth of demand. One of these factors refers to the rate of population growth which being fairly high in India is supposed to be a major factor behind the widening of markets, a point much emphasized in the context of theories of secular stagnation, once very much in the forefront of discussions in mature capitalist economies.

The other factors refer to what may be called the structural change in the mode of production which follows from the growth of commercialization in the economy, which leads to increased monetization along with many concomitant changes.[4]

---

'resource constrained'. His analysis runs in terms of institutional features and action motivations in two regimes. I am more concerned with relating the argument to different stages of development. See J. Kornai, *Economics of Shortage*, Vols I and II (Amsterdam: North Holland, 1980)

[4] This factor constituted the foundation of the argument developed by Lenin in his work on the development of capitalism in Russia, which forcefully argued that the so-called 'populist' argument that capitalism could not develop in Russia was contradicted by the logic of analysis which Marx had developed. On the analytical plane, this amounted to a fairly detailed examination of the under-consumptionist theories which the French Swiss economist Sismondi had developed and which had met with much opposition from the classical school. Lenin's pamphlet, *A Critique of Economic Romanticism*, is worth reading for those who are interested in Sismondi.

The upshot of these arguments was that a labour-rich country once embarked on the path of capitalist industrialization could be expected to show high rates of growth, at least for a considerable period of time, provided supply side bottlenecks could be removed on the way.[5]

While, as we have seen, during the fifties there was a consensus on this point, we have to enquire a little more carefully today whether the consensus was not an overly hasty one.

### III

The argument on the inducement to invest is clearly a weak one. Analytically, it was grounded on a theory of capital which has been found on critical scrutiny to be lacking in coherence, let alone plausibility. While this is not the place to go into a review of recent literature on a relatively abstruse subject, it is necessary to mention that even if one could define away most of the objections to the concept of an aggregated capital-stock, the problem of inducement to invest will remain a formidable subject in its own right.

Given the presence of significant risk premia, and the high value attached to land and gold, it is by no means clear that a capital-poor country would be characterized by high rates of return on directly productive activities, especially in the absence of much complementary investment in social overhead capital.[6] The second argument is a much more substantial one and, in a

---

[5] Ironically enough, it appears that the argument fits much better the European experience of the fifties and the sixties. A very classical model was used by C. P. Kindleberger to explain European post-war growth experience. The Russian debate is very well presented in the work of the noted Polish historian A. Walicki. See especially his, *The Controversy over Capitalism* (Oxford University Press, 1974). R Luxemburg in her *Accumulation of Capital* was clearly influenced by this debate. Note especially her discussion of the views of Vorontsov.

[6] Keynes had raised a 'landtrap' argument which has been examined by Kaldor, Robinson, Raj, Samuelson and Rakshit, among others. While there is some variance of opinion, most authors do believe that there are some fundamental factors which give some credence to the argument, although Keynes may have considerably exaggerated its importance.

sense, forms the logical crux of the supply-side argument. Many capital-poor, land-scarce economies are characterized by what may be called a state of 'primitive stagnation', to borrow an expression used by the late Joan Robinson.[7] In such an economy, a great deal of net output, given the seed-yield ratio, accrues as rent which is very largely consumed. There is little capacity to save on the part of small peasant proprietors/share-croppers and others because of the small size of operational holdings. So far as the modern sector is concerned, it is much too small to change the overall dimensions of the savings-income ratio.

Such a situation can with some justification be regarded as a saving-constrained situation as any sudden increase in investment can lead to the price of consumer goods rising relatively to money wages, thereby triggering off an inflationary spiral. Granted this however, it is not clear that the story, quite a plausible one in itself, is best told in the form of causation running from savings to investment. It may be more appropriate to stress the reverse causal link running from investment to saving, in which case, the problem of demand appears, although not in the form of a simple tale of *under-consumption*. On the impact of population growth on the inducement to invest I cannot do better, within the present space, than to quote the following paragraph from Kalecki who put the argument with clarity and succinctness. He wrote, 'It should be noticed that some authors have taken into consideration other channels through which growth in population may stimulate economic development. They have maintained that an increase in population encourages investment, because the entrepreneurs can then anticipate with some certainty the broadening of markets for their products. What is important, however, in this context is not an increase in population but an *increase in purchasing power*. An increase in the number of paupers does not broaden the market. For instance, increased population does not necessarily imply a higher demand for houses; for without an increase in purchasing power the result may well be the crowding of more

---

[7] See Joan Robinson, *The Accumulation of Capital* (Macmilan and Co., 1973), pp. 256–8.

people into an existing dwelling space' (emphasis added).[8] I have quoted the above paragraph from Kalecki because it states and illustrates what appears to me the most crucial point in regard to the effect of a steadily growing population on maintaining a regime of higher level of effective demand, i.e. the question of a steadily increasing level of purchasing power. However, the proposition is, on the face of it, a paradoxical one, because if increased population leads to increased output, then this should lead automatically to an increase in purchasing power. Kalecki then would seem to be suggesting a state of affairs where additional availability of labour does not yield extra output or leads to a more skewed distribution of income.

The first situation can arise under conditions of self-employment if the marginal productivity of labour in traditional agriculture is zero or negative, a possibility which was at the centre of much theoretical discussion in the sixties. However, such an extreme assumption is tantamount to assuming that land is an absolutely limiting factor and no alternative use of labour is permitted. In this case, however, the supply bottleneck is supreme and the situation is resource constrained rather than demand constrained. A somewhat milder set of assumptions, however, restores a role for demand. Assume that labour has a positive marginal product in industry but not in agriculture and also assume that labour is transferable between sectors. Further assume that the wage level is already at a subsistence minimum defined in terms of 'food'. Given a minimum rate of profit,[9] then the classical adjustment rules through changes in prices lose their operative significance. In Kornai's language, output in the industrial sector becomes demand constrained unless the supply of infrastructure acts as an independent constraint.

Industrial growth can be accelerated in this situation provided

---

[8] M. Kalecki, *Theory of Economic Dynamics*, 2nd edition (New York: Monthly Review Press, 1965), p. 181.

[9] Is there such a thing as a minimum rate of profit which is above zero? Ricardo thought so. If we allow for holding of money, this may be a justifiable assumption. Whatever may be the theoretical reasons behind holding money, there is little doubt that real life investors do expect a rate of return higher than real rate of 'interest'.

agriculturist's real income net of own consumption of 'food' can increase at a higher rate.

It is possible that such an increase in agriculture is not possible without a substantial increase in the absorption of industrial inputs by agriculture. This situation will then resemble the more classical arguments for a balanced growth of industry and agriculture. But if we allow for increasing returns to scale in industry, an element of cumulation is built in, which gives a greater role for demand in triggering off a growth spiral. The same thing can happen if exports show an unusual buoyancy and industry can be reorganized so as to take advantage of such a situation. A similar situation occurred in Japan during the eighteen nineties and more especially during the fifties and sixties.

The argument sketched out above is similar to Kaldor's recent argument on the importance of 'foreign trade multiplier'.[10] However, my argument differs from Kaldor's in attaching relatively little importance to the point as to whether Say's law is violated or not as there would appear to be relatively little consensus as to what Say precisely meant It differs from Nurkse's in so far as I believe that vertical linkages are more important than horizontal inter-commodity shifts in demand. It is also true that in some respects my argument is closer to the Smithian view of the demand process as compared with the more recent demand-centred position such as that of Keynes. But it has at least three Keynes-like features: (*a*) failure of all markets to clear because of the inflexibility of real wages; (*b*) adjustments are brought about by changes in quantity rather than through prices; (*c*) an external market can lead to stepping up the growth rates.[11]

---

[10] See N. Káldor, 'What is Wrong with Economic Theory?', *Quarterly Journal of Economics*, Vol. LXXXIX, August 1975, pp. 347–57.

[11] In my contribution in *Economic and Political Weekly*, Special Number, 1979, I had placed explicit emphasis on the last two features, arising from the macro economic impact of administered price decisions regarding agriculture and also from the Kalecki type interpretation of 'external markets' represented by budgetary deficits. I, however, think that 'real wage resistance' is an important feature which cannot be ignored, even though the existence of an 'informal sector' allows for a greater flexibility

It differs from the Keynesian argument because it is not money wages that are rigid. Also, inter-industrial relationships are critical to the whole process.

However, the empirical plausibility of this model would appear to depend on the assumption that labour has a zero or negligible productivity on the margin in agriculture with the existing set of techniques. It is well known that this assumption has been questioned a great deal in more recent discussions with 'empirically fitted' production functions regularly showing up results which contradict the postulate of a zero marginal productivity of labour in agriculture. However, it would appear that so long as the marginal productivity is substantially below the wage rate at which the industrial sector employs labour and so long as the minimum supply price of capital is relatively high, the rate of growth of demand for industrial products coming from agriculture will prove a very important causal factor in securing a dynamic balance in a growing economy.

As mentioned already, we may like to say that what this argument does is to restate the traditional case for 'balanced growth', rather than a separate role for demand as a constraint on the entire growth process. Let us recall that within the context of the traditional balanced growth model, the overall rate of growth is determined by the capacity to save whereas only the composition of growth is determined by income elasticities of demand for different products.

What is being maintained in contrast is that both the rate and the composition are simultaneously determined, and that too as a part of a process where no pre-existing constraint on saving is being postulated. It is, however, not being asserted that an increase in monetary demand is all that is needed, a simplification that does not apply to our situation, if exceptional harvests are excluded.

One may wonder at this stage whether the argument given here will not apply to the so-called 'classical model' of growth much popularized by Lewis. How did Lewis avoid the possibility that demand could be a constraint on growth? First, by mostly concentrating on the assumption that the capitalist

of its operation in the Indian context. I would also like to emphasize here the 'mark-up' pricing rule used by the industrial sector.

sector is self-contained in the sense that it produces all the necessary commodities. There is no product exchange between the capitalist sector and the 'subsistence' sector. Labour alone is imported into the industrial sector. In this case, which he calls Model I, he could concentrate only on the question of labour supply and ignore the question of inter-sectoral trade.[12]

Thus, he eliminated the possibility that profits in the industrial sector may be squeezed dry because of adverse movements in terms of trade. Furthermore, and also critical to the argument, profits equal savings which in his model are automatically reinvested. Thereby he avoids the problem of an independent inducement to investment. With low wages, in terms of food, unchanged terms of trade and an upwardly moving marginal productivity of labour function based on accumulation of petty capital, Lewis could with some reason argue that the whole development process consists in the fact that a low saving economy is transformed to a high saving economy. Thus, for him demand factors are not the inhibiting ones on the growth process. Neither under-consumption nor under-accumulation bothers him. What is essential for Lewis is that the capital output ratio is not allowed to rise so long as real wages stay the same, which he thought that competitive conditions will ensure.

How does the Indian experience corroborate the central insights which Lewis deduced from what has been called classical growth process? Not very well beyond a point, as far as I can judge. India has become a relatively high saving economy without getting perceptibly closer to what may be called the turning point when marginal returns to labour tend to get equal across the sectors. It is also clear that the terms of trade movement against industry can express only a part of the story, the part that pertained to the period between mid-sixties and mid-seventies.

In fact, it remains a puzzle that higher savings do not seem to have resulted in higher rates of growth. While arithmetic and casual observation may partially support that the capital-output

---

[12] See W. A. Lewis, 'Reflection on Unlimited Labour' in *International Economics and Development, Essays in Honour of R. Prebisch*, edited by L. E. de Macro (Academic Press, 1972).

ratio has risen on the margin, it is not clear to me what are the factors which have contributed to this process on an economy-wide basis. Above all, we have to remember that viewing the growth rate as a product of the marginal capital–output ratio and the savings ratio is at best an equilibrium relationship and often little more than an accounting framework. In either case, it does not tell a causal story. We have to probe deeper.

IV

Is it possible to say that the rise in capital–output ratio has something to do with the operation of demand factors in our development process? Normally, this would be answered in the negative. Common wisdom has been that this is a sign of the increased inefficiency of resource utilization. But this is in my opinion only a part of the story and for some sectors may be a large part of the story. But there are some economy-wide processes which cannot be ignored and they are at least in part connected with demand factors. While statistical exercises bearing on this point have yet to be fully carried out, we have factual evidence on the following points:

*a*. Deceleration in the rate of growth of public investment from the mid-sixties onwards implied that capacity could not be fully utilized in certain capital goods sectors, e.g. the fact that steel investment could not be stepped up sufficiently meant in turn that heavy engineering sectors could not utilize their capacity fully. Increased investment in fertilizers, chemicals, etc. which came up on a relatively larger scale in the seventies generated more demand abroad than at home. On the whole, the cut-back in public investment in the sixties and subsequent shift in the investment pattern implied that in sectors where we had built capacity ahead of demand, because of scale considerations, we did not derive the benefits we expected.

*b*. Shift in emphasis away from a public irrigation-based strategy of development in agriculture to the strategy of the 'Green Revolution' along with support price operations have led to income distributional changes which are not yet fully understood. While I believe that by now the earlier 'immiserization' thesis put forward in the early seventies cannot be maintained in the areas affected by the 'Green Revolution', not many would like to endorse the conclusion recently reached by Blyn that it has 'reduced income inequality'.[13] However, it will possibly be agreed to by most that while the immiserization theory would appear not proven and in some specific areas there is evidence to the contrary, what has probably happened is that incremental incomes have accrued to the upper deciles to a larger extent because of the initially skewed distribution of asset-holdings. In its turn this has implied that incremental demands have been directed towards non-traditional consumer goods and also towards greater savings. Recent NCAER survey data showing a higher marginal propensity to save in the rural sector in comparison with urban wage-earners would constitute an indirect evidence for the second half of the proposition. While urban sector production has become more capital-intensive, suggesting much slower labour absorption rates, combined with the impact of the 'Green Revolution', this has not made it possible for us to benefit from the adoption of mass production methods in the case of items such as consumer durables which have shown higher rates of growth than necessities.

I think that the effect on the capital–output ratio has been more unfavourable than it needed to be, as the increase in production has been largely fragmented because of the operation of our industrial policy. Whether it was necessary for India to go in for the production of these goods is a moot question, but there is no justification for inefficient production of these commodities.

c. The cost of energy-related investment has gone up very substantially, at a time when the direct and indirect energy requirements of Indian agriculture have risen substantially, especially in the areas affected by the 'Green Revolution', which constrain additionally the demand stimulating potential of investment through vertical and horizontal linkages.

Home demand is, however, not the only source of demand. There is also the necessity to take into account the role of exports. Indian export performance has been much criticized and one major deficiency of India's development strategy has been found to lie in its adverse discriminating treatment towards exports. Some would maintain that by maintaining an overvalued real exchange rate, India has not been able to derive the benefits of income and employment growth from trade. Once again, if true, this will have an effect on the marginal

[13] See G. Blyn, 'The Green Revolution Revisited', *Economic Development and Cultural Change*, July 1983.

capital–output ratio. The experience of newly industrializing countries of East Asia operating in densely populated areas has been found to be worthy of emulation by many economists. While I do not underestimate the need for stepping up our export performance and also do not deny that our import substitution in some sectors has been excessively costly, I fear that at this stage India is unlikely to emerge as a leading actor on the export front. I have three main reasons for this conclusion. First, the relative size of the non-tradeable sectors is a vastly bigger one in the Indian case, which is posing major problems of management even for meeting home demand where one can naturally be more relaxed. Secondly, there is a limit to which efficiency wages can be reduced so as to generate adequate export competitiveness. Thirdly, the technological changes currently taking place in the world economy have introduced considerable uncertainty regarding the newly emerging international division of labour. For example, we have as yet no clear indication of how the large-scale application of microprocessors will change relative comparative advantages amongst the countries in regard to traditionally labour–intensive manufacturers. Furthermore, while the elasticity of world trade with respect to world product was well above unity during the fifties and sixties, it is not clear whether this episode will again be repeated at least within the next half-decade or more. This will mean that countries which are heavily trade-dependent will have to put up strong competition, which India will need to match. The scenario is somewhat reminiscent of what Keynes wrote in his famous essay 'National Self-Sufficiency' in *Yale Review* in 1935. While the first point will possibly not be disputed, even though it can be maintained that we should be able to do much better than we have done in the past, the second point may be disputed. In a recent paper, G. S. Fields has studied the relationship between export-led growth and labour markets.[14] His conclusions based on a comparative study of seven countries in East and South-East Asia would appear to me to support my relatively pessimistic forecast unless we succeed in lowering the wage rates prevailing in industrial sectors to

---

[14] See G. S. Fields, *Export-led Growth and Labour Markets*, Warwick Discussion Papers, 1982.

'market clearing' levels. While I do not know what is meant by the market clearing level in a situation marked by profound dualism, it is unlikely to equal the current wage rate in the Indian organized sector. Most probably it will be less and sometimes much less. As such wage reduction is not possible, this will constitute an additional reason for my conclusion. Economists have in these circumstances argued for the adoption of dual exchange rates. But this has generally met with considerable resistance from those who believe that only an unified exchange rate is administratively feasible. The upshot is that the present world conjuncture is not especially encouraging for our exports, especially for manufacturing exports. Agricultural exports constitute a different type of problem. They may well have potential in the area of non-staple exports which can be exploited given a suitable policy environment.

If my overall judgment on the export scene is broadly correct, then with our fast deteriorating land–man ratio, we have to look for a strategy of growth which places maximum emphasis on land–saving innovations. Unfortunately, as these innovations are also turning out to be more capital-intensive than envisaged before, especially if ecological degradation is to be avoided, we are caught in a dilemma from which we cannot escape by demand stimulation alone through following a simple redistributive policy or from adopting a policy of cheap money for investment because of the inflation proneness that the economy has displayed over the last decade or so.

We need, in our situation, not merely an increase in 'thriftiness' on the part of our upper income groups, both rural and urban, which can be offset only by larger volumes of *real public investment* which will increase the productivity of labour in the wage goods sectors and in the capital goods sectors which are linked with them. The combined impact of these policies will be to generate a higher rate of growth along with a better distribution of incomes. Demand raising influences operating through higher real investment, especially public investment in sectors mentioned above along with growth of employment opportunities in agriculture and rural public works will help us in realizing the potential output that may be created through reduction in capital–output ratio in existing sectors which can be seen to constrain growth as of today. This implies much greater selectivity in project choice as well as a clear identification of key sectors, from our present point of view, of the 1980s.

The crux of the process seems to lie in non-inflationary methods of transference of investible resources into the hands of the State and their efficient deployment. Anybody who has cared to look at the fiscal sociology of India would be obliged to conclude that our tax system in practice has undergone a very profound transformation from what it was designed to be in principle. It is a non-solution to ask for a sharp increase in tax rates when we know for sure that they would be evaded in collection, nor do I think that the problem lies merely in the inefficiency of the tax collecting machine. Our present crisis of the 'tax state', to borrow an expression from Schumpeter, lies in the fact that new social groups with considerable amount of economic power have emerged which look at the economic system as if it were only a grants economy. Without bringing about a new political consensus on the costs and benefits of development financing, no major alteration can be brought about.

Possibly the only practicable answer in the short run to the resource problem would lie in greater mobilization through public enterprises and through providing attractive enough financial instruments where people especially in rural areas would be inclined to put their money. While the first device can work only through increasing the efficiency of public sector along with cutting down unproductive expenditure, the second depends on maintaining a non-inflationary environment. Perhaps a substantial improvement in either direction is too much to hope for. In that case, a substantial widening of the direct tax net which involves people belonging to the so-called unorganized sector is inescapable if the present syndrome of modest growth with inflation were to be avoided.

v

The Indian economy entered the decade of the eighties in rather adverse circumstances. While some progress has been undoubtedly achieved with regard to import substitution in the oil sector, it is not clear, despite this year's bumper crop, whether any trend improvement in the rate of growth of foodgrains *vis-à-vis* agriculture has been achieved. On the other hand, we have a difficult situation with regard to pulses and edible oils. Our export pick-up, even when world recovery accelerates, if at all, is yet to be demonstrated. We also know that public investment may be further constrained by the declining inflow of net external capital. In the circumstances, the following components of a policy package would appear to me to be deserving of special attention:

    *a.* rapid transformation of the rice economy, especially in the eastern region, where adequate ground water potential exists which can without much difficulty be tapped during winter and summer seasons provided supporting infrastructural facilities are created, permitting conjunctive use with surface water;
    *b.* a major co-ordinated effort at boosting oilseeds production, especially non-traditional varieties such as sunflower, etc.;
    *c.* wholehearted attention to maintenance and repair of existing major irrigation works as well as power stations.

These are some of the relatively low cost supply side strategies. But if these are accompanied by a suitable implementation of rural development programmes with an eye on the requirements of small and marginal farmers and agricultural labour, these can have a valuable impact on the demand for industrial products, both capital goods as well as industrial consumer goods and intermediates, helping to move them into more efficient zones. The industrial policy must be framed so as to bring down 'costs' by inducing firms to reap economies of scale, to reduce 'idle time' on machines and by bringing down capital cost through quicker implementation of projects.

I would not place any undue reliance on the import of technology as the solvent of all our problems. I recognize that our capital stock is outdated in certain sectors. But its replacement has to be necessarily a time-phased affair with timing depending on our own specific needs and resource availabilities. It is necessary to stress that without a substantial step up in the domestic production of capital goods, technological absorption and adaptation problems cannot be successfully tackled. The fact that among the developing countries, India was among the first to develop the 'capital goods sector' should not be a handicap. Rather it is one of the few major achievements which we have to our credit. We need to modernize and modernize it fast, especially in certain sectors where advances in materials science and/or advances in microprocessors have led to substantial reduction in costs. Several such sectors can be identified.

We need further to distinguish also between 'stable' and 'unstable technologies'. Where technology is stable and also vital to the performance of the key sectors in the Indian economy, we need to acquire it if we do not have it. Where technological development is very fast and our chance of getting 'locked in' with an inefficient technology are substantial, we have to be much more careful in devising our import policy. As a matter of fact, criteria for cost-benefit analysis for technology acquisition are significantly different from those for ordinary commodity producing sectors. We need operational guidelines in this respect which are much less time-consuming than the existing ones. Perhaps we need to implement the concept of technology missions in regard to our key sectors.

According to some experts, the world is going through a third or possibly even a fourth 'Industrial Revolution' with information emerging as the key unifying concept. To profit fully from this newly emerging situation, it is very necessary that we give greater importance to building our scientific and managerial capability.

I believe that today material capital is losing out in relative terms with regard to human capital. Once upon a time, it was assumed that natural resources were the key to development. Coal and iron were supposed to be the sinews of economic growth. I am not suggesting that they are not any longer important. But organization, motivation and creativity would appear to me to be just as important, if not more. While we have acquired considerable skill and expertise in running complex industrial processes, our innovativeness as a nation is yet to be shown. This would appear to be one of the challenges of the eighties. The other major related area of concern for me is whether we can bring in new technology without increasing the extent of socio-economic *dualism* that prevails today. This to my mind poses one of the most serious problems involving our social cohesiveness. International demonstration effects which have had very unfavourable effects on the growth pattern of some Latin American countries, now recognized by the policy-makers of those countries, are beginning to gain in strength in India today. We should not succumb to this as if it represented an inexorable force of nature. Our cultural resources are relevant for designing our development pattern. This may sound an odd thing for an economist to say. But experience of the last one hundred years clearly demonstrates that technology is not merely a product of growing knowledge of the forces that govern nature, but also of our human concerns and human organization, where culture matters.

A society oriented towards the needs of the upper 10–15 per cent of its population can do very well, even with our proven resource endowment, provided we know how to manage things somewhat better. But a society which has wider objectives in mind has to do very much more.

It must find, along with new technology, newer ways of involving people in the development process. This is a much more demanding job and requires for its success involvement of masses of people. While some of it may be organized through the market system, our job as economists and social scientists is to find other organizational possibilities as well. However, some of these possibilities which exist notably in the creation of rural infrastructure, cannot be successfully carried out with centralized methods of planning. By their very nature, they require as nodes of implementation much smaller units. Our efforts at 'block level planning' have been inhibited by the absence of a community-oriented outlook which in any event is being subjected to cruel onslaughts by the fast-growing commercialization of rural commons. While our experience in this regard is not historically without precedent, we are not necessarily condemned to repeat everything that went before. Once again we have a major task of social innovation.

We need, in this context, to attach much greater importance to education, in the widest sense of the term. We also need to achieve newer modes of integrative behaviour without which tasks in the eighties which relate to poverty eradication cannot be successfully tackled.

Looking back, it seems to me that while our achievement during the last thirty odd years of planning have by no means been insignificant in the area of agricultural production, industrial diversification and technology acquisition, we have not been able to make a major impact on the lives of vast masses of our people. However, consciousness has very much increased. This can be a source of very positive developments, even when we are likely to face more difficult external circumstances. For this purpose, our planning needs to take into account the vastly changed circumstances compared with what prevailed when the first Planning Commission was constituted.

# The Centre and the Periphery: Inter-State Disparities in Economic Development*

RAJ KRISHNA

## 1. INTRODUCTION

There is growing evidence to show that inter-regional (inter-state and intra-state) disparities in various dimensions of development have remained undiminished in spite of considerable overall development over the last three decades. The states are getting grouped into 'bhadralok' and 'shudra' states in respect of their levels and rates of development. In the United Nations terminology, a serious 'North-South' problem is emerging within the country, though, in view of the map of areas identified as 'backward', it would be better to call it the 'Centre-periphery' problem rather than the North-South problem. For most of the least developed areas lie in the heartland; while most of the outlying areas seem to be less deprived.

The problem requires the focused attention of all planners involved in the allocations of resources. For, unless resource allocation is made deliberately and increasingly 'region-conscious' and inter-regionally progressive, the vast mass of poverty and unemployment, concentrated in a few states, will continue to grow

In this paper I set out selected facts about inter-state disparity

---

* Reprinted with the permission of the author's wife from the volume, *Facts of India's Development*, G. L. Mehta Memorial Lectures, ICICI, Bombay, 1986.

levels and trends, and propose a few essential ingredients of a policy for more balanced development.

Ultimately, of course, it is inter-personal (i.e. inter-household) inequality in the distribution of income and assets which needs to be reduced. The reduction of inter-regional inequality is merely a means to this ultimate end. But it is an important means for two reasons. First, millions of poor households are concentrated in a few regions; therefore the development of these regions can bring about a rapid reduction in the size of the poverty population. Second, since the bulk of public investment flows into basic industry and infrastructure development, a tilting of this investment, particularly in infrastructure facilities, in favour of the less developed regions, can trigger other investments which in turn will generate new employment and income-streams for the poor.

## II. DISPARITY INDICATORS

Indicators of inter-state disparities can be conveniently grouped into six categories: (1) indicators of income, poverty and unemployment; (2) agricultural indicators; (3) industrial indicators; (4) infrastructure indicators; (5) social service indicators; and (6) resource allocation indicators.

A few selected indicators are tabulated in Tables 1 to 8. The data support the following overall picture.

## III. INCOME, POVERTY AND UNEMPLOYMENT

About 72 per cent of the total poverty and unemployment in the major states is concentrated in seven states: U. P., Bihar, West Bengal, M.P., Maharashtra, Tamil Nadu, and Andhra Pradesh. If Orissa and Karnataka are added to this list, 83 per cent of the poor population of 15 states would be accounted for (Table 1).

The same seven states also contain two-thirds of the total pool of unemployment in the country. (The all-India total was 16.35 million person-years in 1977-8 in the age group 15 to 59 years, see Table 1.)

The unemployment rates, too, are very high in these seven states. In five of these (Andhra Pradesh, Tamil Nadu, Maharashtra, West Bengal and Bihar), the rate exceeds 8 per cent. The

## TABLE 1
### Poverty, Income and Unemployment (Major States)

| State | Percentage of Population Below the Poverty Line[a] 1972–3 | Percentage Share in All-India Poverty Population[b] 1972–3 | State Domestic Product Per Capita (Rs) 1970–1[c] | 1977–8[e] | 1973–4 to 1975–6[d] | Percentage Share in All-India Unemployment 1977–8[e] | Percentage Unemployment Rate 1977–8 (Per cent) |
|---|---|---|---|---|---|---|---|
| 1 | 2 | 3 | 4 | 5 | 6 | 7 | 8 |
| ANDHRA PRADESH | 54.9 | 8.5 | 584 | 607 | 928 | 11.9 | 10.8 |
| ASSAM | 46.9 | 2.6 | 538 | 552 | 791 | 0.5 | 1.8 |
| BIHAR | 54.6 | 11.5 | 402 | 434 | 645 | 8.8 | 8.1 |
| GUJARAT | 41.1 | 4.0 | 842 | 786 | 1134 | 3.9 | 6.4 |
| HARYANA | 23.1 | 0.9 | 845 | 973 | 1399 | 1.2 | 6.9 |
| KARNATAKA | 50.7 | 6.3 | 682 | 730 | 1045 | 6.4 | 9.6 |
| KERALA | 56.9 | 4.4 | 584 | 584[f] | 948 | 11.6 | 26.0 |

| | | | | | | | |
|---|---|---|---|---|---|---|---|
| MADHYA PRADESH | 58.6 | 0.9 | 488 | 494 | 776 | 3.1 | 3.1 |
| MAHARASHTRA | 47.7 | 8.6 | 807 | 991 | 1349 | 10.2 | 8.2 |
| ORISSA | 68.6 | 5.4 | 493 | 501 | 793 | 3.7 | 8.2 |
| PUNJAB | 21.5 | 1.0 | 1030 | 1298 | 1586 | 1.3 | 5.0 |
| RAJASTHAN | 46.0 | 4.3 | 623 | 542 | 853 | 1.9 | 3.4 |
| TAMIL NADU | 59.6 | 8.7 | 595 | 657 | 942 | 16.6 | 16.1 |
| UTTAR PRADESH | 52.6 | 16.7 | 486 | 503 | 715 | 7.0 | 4.3 |
| WEST BENGAL | 56.9 | 9.2 | 737 | 769 | 1033 | 9.4 | 10.4 |

[a] Calculated on the basis of rural and urban poverty ratios given by the Prime Minister in the Lok Sabha on 12 March 1980. See *Indian Express*, 13 March 1980. The rural poverty line is Rs 41 and the urban Rs 47 of consumption per head in 1972–3 prices. Projected population figures for March 1973 are used. [b] Calculated on the basis of column (2). [c] Source: *Monthly Abstract of Statistics*, June 1979. All figures in 1970–1 prices. [d] Report of Seventh Finance Commission, Annexe VII. 3. In current prices. [e] *Draft Sixth Five Year Plan 1978–83, Revised*, p. 150. Age group 15–59 years. [f] 1975–6.

rate is, of course, also high in Kerala, Karnataka and Orissa (Table 1).

Data collected recently in the 32nd round of the National Sample Survey (1977–8) also show definitely, for the first time, that the poorest households suffer from the highest rates of unemployment. In households spending less than Rs 11 per capita per month on consumption, the unemployment rate was as high as 29 per cent in the urban areas and 22 per cent in the rural areas. In households spending Rs 11 to 21, and Rs 21 to 34 per capita per month, the unemployment rates were as high as 14–16 per cent and 10–12 per cent respectively. In higher expenditure brackets the unemployment rates fall steadily; and in households spending Rs 100 or more per month the rate was only 2 per cent in the rural areas and 4 per cent in the urban areas (PC 1979: 150).

These figures belie the theory held in some quarters that only

TABLE 2

*Coefficients of Inter-State Variation of Rural Poverty Ratios**

| Year | Coefficient of Variation |
|---|---|
| 1 | 2 |
| 1957–8 | 25.19 |
| 1959–60 | 25.14 |
| 1960–1 | 28.34 |
| 1961–2 | 22.93 |
| 1963–4 | 23.28 |
| 1964–5 | 26.36 |
| 1965–6 | 25.60 |
| 1966–7 | 20.94 |
| 1967–8 | 23.21 |
| 1968–9 | 23.81 |
| 1970–1 | 25.05 |
| 1973–4 | 24.34 |
| Average | 24.52 |

* Calculated from basic data in Ahluwalia 1978: 17.

## TABLE 3
### Inter-State Agricultural Indicators

| State | Farm Output/ Rural Population 1975–6 (Rs)[a] | Growth Rate of Grain Production 1961–2/ 1978–9 (per cent per annum)[a] | Fertilizer Nutrients per Cropped Hectare 1978–9 (kgs)[a] | Net Irrigated Area/Net Sown Area 1975–6 (per cent)[b] | Major and Medium Irrigation Potential 1982–3/ Ultimate Potential (per cent)[b] | Minor Irrigation Potential 1982–3/ Ultimate Potential (per cent)[a] |
|---|---|---|---|---|---|---|
| 1 | 2 | 3 | 4 | 5 | 6 | 7 |
| ANDHRA PRADESH | 506 | 1.7 | 46.3 | 31 | 65 | 52 |
| ASSAM | 453 | 2.2 | 2.5 | 22[c] | 15 | 26 |
| BIHAR | 341 | 1.8 | 17.2 | 33 | 44 | 60 |
| GUJARAT | 607 | 4.2 | 31.4 | 15 | 43 | 89 |
| HARYANA | 1032 | 5.1 | 37.4 | 48 | 62 | 88 |
| KARNATAKA | 592 | 3.0 | 32.3 | 13 | 60 | 60 |
| KERALA | 479 | 1.1 | 33.4 | 10 | 59 | 34 |
| MADHYA PRADESH | 459 | 0.9 | 9.0 | 10 | 32 | 50 |
| MAHARASHTRA | 555 | 2.5 | 19.4 | 10 | 43 | 55 |
| ORISSA | 515 | 1.4 | 9.3 | 17 | 44 | 43 |
| PUNJAB | 1161 | 6.4 | 94.8 | 75 | 78 | 86 |
| RAJASTHAN | 600 | 2.5 | 7.7 | 17 | 71 | 78 |
| TAMIL NADU | 442 | 1.9 | 68.1 | 43 | 82 | 86 |
| UTTAR PRADESH | 427 | 2.5 | 45.5 | 46 | 55 | 81 |
| WEST BENGAL | 511 | 2.5 | 30.6 | 24 | 78 | 53 |
| ALL INDIA | 519 | 2.6 | 29.8 | 24 | 53 | 65 |

[a] CMIE 1979: Vol. 2.  [b] PC 1979.  [c] 1973–4.

TABLE 4

Natural Resource Indicators

| State | Forest Area/Reporting Area Ratio 1975-6 (per cent)[a] | Proportion of Net Sown Area with Assured Water Supply[a] (per cent) | Percentage Share in All India Mineral Reserves[b] |||||
|---|---|---|---|---|---|---|---|
|  |  |  | Coal | Iron | Manganese | Chromite | Bauxite |
| 1 | 2 | 3 | 4 | 5 | 6 | 7 | 8 |
| ANDHRA PRADESH | 23 | 28 | 3 | – | – | – | 30 |
| BIHAR | 16 | 92 | 42 | 24 | – | – | 2 |
| GUJARAT | 8 | 21 | – | – | – | – | 2 |
| HARYANA | 2 | 19 | – | – | – | – | – |
| KARNATAKA | 15 | 18 | – | – | 25 | – | – |
| KERALA | 28 | 100 | – | – | – | – | – |
| MADHYA PRADESH | 32 | 60 | 21 | 18 | 15 | – | 6 |
| MAHARASHTRA | 17 | 26 | 3 | – | – | – | 5 |
| ORISSA | 41 | 100 | 6 | 21 | 39 | 86 | 50 |
| PUNJAB | 4 | 72 | – | – | – | – | – |
| RAJASTHAN | 6 | 15 | – | – | – | – | – |

| | | | | | |
|---|---|---|---|---|---|
| TAMIL NADU | 15 | 54 | — | — | — | — |
| UTTAR PRADESH | 17 | 48 | — | 4 | — | — |
| WEST BENGAL | 13 | 100 | 23 | — | — | — |
| ASSAM | 25 | 100 | — | — | — | — |
| HIMACHAL PRADESH | 22 | 28 | — | — | — | — |
| JAMMU-KASHMIR | 61 | 95 | — | — | — | — |
| TRIPURA | 60 | 100 | — | — | — | — |
| MEGHALAYA | 37 | 100 | — | — | — | — |
| NAGALAND | 17 | 100 | — | — | — | — |
| MANIPUR | 27 | 100 | — | — | — | — |
| UNION TERRITORIES | — | 96 | — | — | — | — |
| INDIA | 22 | 48 | 100 | 100 | 100 | 100 |

[a] CMIE 1979.
[b] Computed from figures in CMIE 1979, only ratios of large reserves computed.

the workers of better-off households can afford to remain unemployed. It is clear that in India the poorest suffer the most, and the least poor suffer the least, from involuntary unemployment. The correlation between the incidence of poverty and the incidence of unemployment across households is plainly positive.

On the other hand, the correlation (across states) between per capita income and the incidence of poverty is clearly negative, as we would expect. In other words, states with a relatively high per capita income have a low poverty ratio (the percentage of people below the poverty line) and vice versa. Thus, for

TABLE 5

*Industrial Indicators*

| State | Value Added by Manufacture Per Capita 1976-7[a] (Rs) | Percentage of Workers Engaged in Manufacture 1971[b] | Share in Central Government Gross Blocks March 1978 (per cent) |
|---|---|---|---|
| 1 | 2 | 3 | 4 |
| ANDHRA PRADESH | 119 | 9 | 4 |
| ASSAM | 118 | 9 | 3 |
| BIHAR | 78 | 5 | 25 |
| GUJARAT | 322 | 12 | 6 |
| HARYANA | 203 | 10 | 1 |
| KARNATAKA | 207 | 10 | 4 |
| KERALA | 140 | 16 | 3 |
| MADHYA PRADESH | 111 | 7 | 16 |
| MAHARASHTRA | 413 | 13 | 8 |
| ORISSA | 98 | 6 | 6 |
| PUNJAB | 236 | 11 | 2 |
| RAJASTHAN | 94 | 7 | 2 |
| TAMIL NADU | 227 | 11 | 5 |
| UTTAR PRADESH | 91 | 7 | 4 |
| WEST BENGAL | 237 | 14 | 9 |

[a] CMIE 1979.
[b] GOUP 1979.

instance, income per capita in the Punjab (averaged for the three years 1973–4/1975–6) (Rs 1586) is nearly 2½ times the income per capita in Bihar (Rs 645). But the poverty ratio in Bihar (55 per cent) is 2½ times the poverty ratio in Punjab (22 per cent) (Table 1). If states are ranked according to their per capita income and their poverty ratio, the correlation coefficient between two rankings turns out to be (−0.5). This correlation is significant, but not very high, because there are many states where the average income is relatively high but the poverty ratio is also high, e.g. West Bengal and Maharashtra. In these two states, the existence of modern industrial complexes in and around a metropolis has raised the average income per head to a high level, but the hinterlands are steeped in abject poverty.

In any case, average income indicates only the general level of income but not its distribution. The poverty ratio on the other hand reflects the distribution as well as the level of income. Therefore the correlation between poverty ratio and per capita income need not be very high.

The above discussion covers only the inter-state dispersion of poverty, income and unemployment in the latest year for which data are available. But it is obviously more important to establish whether disparities in these fundamental indices of economic condition have been increasing or decreasing. Although many researchers have tried to study trends in inter-state income disparity (for example, Williamson 1965, Mahajan 1972, Majumdar 1978 and Mathur n.d.), the paper by Ashok Mathur has covered the longest period with all available data on per capita state income. The main finding of his work is that during the decade 1950–1 to 1960–1, there was a small decrease in the coefficient of variation (CV) of State Domestic Product (SDP) per capita across states—from 25 per cent in 1950–1 to 24 per cent in 1960–1. In the middle year of the decade, 1955–6, the CV had fallen to 21 per cent, but it rose back to 24 per cent by 1960–1. These results for the first planning decade are based on constant (1960–1) price estimates of SDP by the NCAER.[1] For the next 15 years, 1960–1 to 1975–6, constant price estimates of the SDP made by State Statistical Bureaus show that the CV rose from 20 per cent in

---

[1] National Council of Applied Economic Research.

TABLE 6

Infrastructure Indicators

| State | Proportion of Villages without Adequate Water Supply 1977–8 | Power Consumption Per Capita 1977–8 (KWH) | Percentage of Villages Electrified December 1978[a] | Road Length per Hundred Square Kilometres 1975–6[c] (Kilometres) | Composite Infrastructure Index 1977–8 |
|---|---|---|---|---|---|
| 1 | 2 | 3 | 4 | 5 | 6 |
| ANDHRA PRADESH | 58 | 82 | 55 | 37 | 95 |
| ASSAM | 69 | 36 | 11 | 69 | 85 |
| BIHAR | 24 | 89 | 28 | 54 | 104 |
| GUJARAT | 18 | 207 | 49 | 25 | 123 |
| HARYANA | 50 | 173 | 100 | 58 | 148 |
| KARNATAKA | 3 | 135 | 58 | 53 | 104 |
| KERALA | 36 | 100 | 97 | 225 | 148 |
| MADHYA PRADESH | 10 | 95 | 26 | 21 | 64 |
| MAHARASHTRA | 11 | 210 | 63 | 37 | 113 |
| ORISSA | 23 | 116 | 30 | 31 | 80 |
| PUNJAB | 11 | 227 | 100 | 82 | 207 |
| RAJASTHAN | 52 | 87 | 32 | 16 | 74 |
| TAMIL NADU | 7 | 159 | 99 | 85 | 145 |

| | | | | |
|---|---|---|---|---|
| UTTAR PRADESH | 27 | 82 | 32 | 61 | 118 |
| WEST BENGAL | 2 | 119 | 31 | 157 | 148 |
| HIMACHAL PRADESH | 61 | 55 | 48 | 32 | 76 |
| JAMMU KASHMIR | 80 | 65 | 62 | 6 | 75 |
| NAGALAND | 38 | 31 | 27 | 41 | 75 |
| TRIPURA | 41 | 10 | 10 | 56 | 53 |
| MANIPUR | 32 | 5 | 12 | 39 | 52 |
| MEGHALAYA | 33 | 33 | 9 | 16 | 49 |
| SIKKIM | – | – | 22 | 33 | – |
| AVERAGE/TOTAL[b] | 26 | 121 | 39 | 42 | 100 |

[a] CMIE 1979
[b] Including Union Territories
[c] PC 1978.

TABLE 7

Social Service Indicators

| State | State Government Expenditure on Health Per Capita 1977-8[c] | State Government Expenditure on Education Per Capita 1977-8[c] | Literacy Rate 1976[a] (per cent) | Composite Quality of Life Index (PQLI) 1975-6[b] (Kerala-100) |
|---|---|---|---|---|
| 1 | 2 | 3 | 4 | 5 |
| ANDHRA PRADESH | 17 | 33 | 36 | 21 |
| ASSAM | 12 | 27 | 43 | 23 |
| BIHAR | 8 | 18 | 31 | 23 |
| GUJARAT | 18 | 39 | 54 | 24 |
| HARYANA | 19 | 35 | 47 | 52 |
| KARNATAKA | 16 | 40 | 50 | 38 |
| KERALA | 23 | 64 | 86 | 100 |
| MADHYA PRADESH | 14 | 26 | 36 | 15 |

| | | | | |
|---|---|---|---|---|
| MAHARASHTRA | 19 | 39 | 65 | 58 |
| ORISSA | 13 | 30 | 38 | 35 |
| PUNJAB | 26 | 50 | 56 | 62 |
| RAJASTHAN | 23 | 35 | 32 | 31 |
| TAMIL NADU | 16 | 35 | 56 | 36 |
| UTTAR PRADESH | 9 | 25 | 36 | 5 |
| WEST BENGAL | 16 | 30 | 53 | 46 |
| JAMMU KASHMIR | 44 | 50 | 30 | – |
| INDIA[d] | 16 | 33 | 46 | – |

[a] PC 1979. Age 15–35.
[b] CMIE 1979. Includes infant mortality rate, and life expectancy at birth.
[c] ICSSR 1979.
[d] Including other states.

1960–1 to 22 per cent in 1975–6. Thus it seems that in the 50s inter-state income disparity showed a small decline but in the 60s and early 70s this disparity has been increasing.

The fact of increasing income disparity during the 70s is confirmed by the most recent data given in columns 4 and 5 of Table 1. The CV of state SDP per capita (at 1970–1 prices) has risen again from 26 per cent in 1970–1 to 33 per cent in 1977–8.

There is only one study of trends in the poverty ratio in different states, calculated on a uniform basis, for a long period (Ahluwalia 1979). This study computed rural poverty ratios in 14 major states for 12 survey years during the period 1957–8 to 1973–4, and concluded that the ratio for 14 states taken together did not have a significant trend over this period. The ratio averaged 50.2 per cent over the period.

Examining the trend in the rural poverty ratio in each state separately the study showed that the ratio increased significantly in only two states, Assam and West Bengal, and declined significantly in only one state, Andhra Pradesh. In all other states, the ratio did not record any significant upward or down-ward trend.

But the study did not compute the inter-state coefficient of variation (CV) of the rural poverty ratio in each year. The CV series computed with the data given in the study is given in Table 2. The inter-state CV of the rural poverty ratio averaged 24.5 per cent over the period, and recorded no significant trend.[2]

These results show that the rural poverty ratio, as well as its dispersion, remained undiminished over the 15-year period. But it is some consolation that it did not increase.

Unfortunately, a view of the trend in the inter-state variation in unemployment is not possible because the person day unemployment rates in different states in 1972–3 and 1977–8 are not comparable. The former relate to the whole labour force; the latter only to the labour force in the age group 15 to 59 years. But assuming that the inclusion/exclusion of children may not affect the inter-state dispersion significantly, we may compare the inter-state CV of unemployment rates in 1972–3

---

[2] The estimated trend coefficient is not significant, and the r° coefficient is only 0.1.

and 1977–8. The CV appears to have increased very slightly from 67.9 per cent to 68.3 per cent.

Thus we confront a situation in which the ratio of maximum to minimum per capita state income and poverty ratio is 3:1, and the ratio of maximum to minimum unemployment rate is 14:1. We also find that in the 60s and 70s the dispersion (CV) of per capita state income was increasing and the dispersion of poverty and unemployment remained undiminished.

## IV. AGRICULTURAL INDICATORS

A well-known recent study of agricultural growth at the district level (Bhalla and Alagh 1979) has revealed that growth has been extremely disparate across regions. Of 289 districts covered by the study, as many as 71, or about one-fourth, recorded negative growth during the period 1962–5 to 1970–3. In another group of 62 districts, growth was positive but low: less than 1.5 per cent a year. Thus in nearly half (46 per cent) of the districts, agriculture was stagnant or declining, only 50 districts (less than one-fifth of the total number) achieved a high growth rate exceeding 4.5 per cent and a large number of districts (106) averaged only a moderate growth rate of the order of 1.5 to 4.5 per cent per annum.

In eight states (Andhra Pradesh, Bihar, Kerala, Madhya Pradesh, Maharashtra, Orissa, West Bengal and Himachal Pradesh), there was not a single high growth district. In four of these states (Andhra Pradesh, Bihar, Maharashtra and Orissa), the largest proportion of the districts included in the study belonged to the negative growth category. In Punjab, Haryana, Rajasthan and U.P., on the other hand, the largest proportion of districts belonged to the high or moderate growth groups.

This evidence shows that the geographical pattern of agricultural growth has been highly uneven, with production booming in some regions and sinking elsewhere.

State-level data on other indicators (Table 3) corroborates this picture. Thus the highest farm output per head (Rs 1161 in Punjab in 1975–6) was more than three times the lowest in Bihar (Rs 341). The growth rate of food production over the 18 year period 1961–2 to 1978–9 in Punjab (6.4 per cent per annum) turns out to be seven times the rate in Madhya Pradesh (0.9 per cent).

When we look at the relative status of the states with regard to the absorption of two major inputs, irrigation water and fertilizer, similar disparities are apparent.

In 1978-9, 95 kilograms of fertilizer nutrients were applied per cropped hectare in Punjab. Rajasthan, on the other hand, had the lowest level of fertilizer use—only 8 kilograms per hectare. Orissa and Madhya Pradesh too used less than 10 kilograms and Bihar only 17 kilograms per hectare.

In Tamil Nadu, the major and medium irrigation potential created by the end of the Sixth Plan period is expected to be as high as 82 per cent of the estimated maximum. But it would be only 32 per cent in Madhya Pradesh. In four other states too (Bihar, Gujarat, Maharashtra and Orissa) the potential created will be only 43 to 44 per cent of the maximum.

Of the known minor irrigation potential, whereas Gujarat, Haryana, Punjab, Tamil Nadu and Uttar Pradesh would have utilized 80 to 90 per cent, Kerala, Orissa and Madhya Pradesh would have utilized only half or less.

An important implication of these facts is that some of the poorest states, such as Bihar, Orissa and Madhya Pradesh, still have a vast amount of unutilized water potential.

The same is true of their mineral and forest resource potential. Madhya Pradesh and Bihar alone are known to be generating 48 per cent of the total value of mineral production in India. Together, they carry 63 per cent of the total known coal resources and 42 per cent of the iron ore resources of India. Orissa alone has 21 per cent of India's iron ore, 39 per cent of the manganese, 86 per cent of chromite and 50 per cent of bauxite reserves. West Bengal again has nearly a quarter of total coal deposits. And yet all these states have very high poverty ratios. Madhya Pradesh, Andhra Pradesh, Kerala, Orissa and the Himalayan states are endowed with rich forest belts. But all these states are among the poorest in India.

These data contradict the facile theory that the poor regions are poor because of their poor natural resource endowment. It seems that many of the poor regions are blessed with a rich natural resource base. What keeps them poor is not the paucity of natural resources but the insufficiency of investment.

Accidents of politics and *laissez-faire* economics concentrated early investments in particular regions—port states, areas producing exportable crops, centres of military importance, etc. Other regions were neglected except for revenue collection. The initial disparity in investment thus produced by early history tends to be self-perpetuating. Areas with a high initial rate of capital formation continue to have a growing infrastructure base, and a pool of skills and surpluses for reinvestment. They not only have ample resources of their own but also a steady inflow of labour and capital from low investment regions. In the low investment regions, on the other hand, the vicious circle of insufficient infrastructure, income and market growth, and the export of skills and surpluses, sets in.

Policy makers can break this vicious circle in the backward regions only with a deliberate and massive investment push of the same magnitude as the luckier regions received in the past. The investment package should, however, be tailored to overcome the peculiar constraints and utilize the special endowments of each region. They should also be so designed that they do not reproduce the pathology of gross inequalities *within* the region.

## V. INDUSTRIAL INDICATORS

Only two indicators would suffice to prove the persistence of disparities in the field of manufacturing: value added by manufacture per capita (VAMP) and the proportion of workers in manufacturing (PWM). In 1976–7 the highest VAMP was recorded in Maharashtra (Rs 413) and Gujarat (Rs 322). At the other end were Bihar and U.P., with low VAMP levels of the order of one-fourth to one-fifth of the Gujarat and Maharashtra levels. The middle group with VAMP exceeding Rs 200 included Haryana, Punjab, Karnataka, Tamil Nadu and West Bengal (CMIE 1979).

The situation with respect to the proportion of workers in manufacturing (PWM) is similar. In 1971 PWM was 12 per cent or more only in Gujarat, Maharashtra and West Bengal. In the industrially backward states (Bihar U.P., Madhya Pradesh and Rajasthan), it was only 5 to 7 per cent (GOUP 1979).

It is important to note that some of these states remained

backward in industry inspite of the fact that a substantial proportion of the gross capital stock of Central Government (non-departmental) enterprises is located within their boundaries. As much as 25 per cent of the aggregate Central investment (as at the end of March 1978) was located in Bihar alone; and 16 per cent in Madhya Pradesh alone (Table 5). And yet both PWM and VAMP remain extremely low in these states. These facts suggest that more massive investment in a few capital-intensive industries is not sufficient to generate widespread and sustained industrial development in otherwise backward regions. The investment policy for these regions must be structured to have strong intra-regional multiplier effects.

### VI. INFRASTRUCTURE

When the status of different states in respect of infrastructure levels (particularly the availability of water, power and transport) is examined, it appears that among major states Punjab and Maharashtra have the highest consumption of power per capita (227 and 210 KWH); and U.P. and Andhra have the lowest (82 KWH). In hill states the consumption is even lower (31 to 36 KWH) (Table 6).

So far as rural electrification is concerned, Punjab and Haryana in the north, and Kerala and Tamil Nadu in the south, have completed the electrification of their entire countryside. But again, in the whole middle belt, comprising Rajasthan, U.P., Bihar, Madhya Pradesh, West Bengal and Orissa, less than one-third of the villages have been electrified so far.

In respect of road length (kilometres per square kilometre of area in 1975–6), the most advanced are Kerala and West Bengal with 225 and 157 kilometres respectively. Rajasthan, Orissa and Madhya Pradesh have only 16 to 31 kilometres. Jammu and Kashmir has only 6 kilometres. The low level of road development in Madhya Pradesh and Orissa explains to some extent the gross under-utilization of their rich soil, forest and mineral resources (Table 6).

As regards (drinking) water supply, Planning Commission figures show that at the end of 1977–8 more than half of the villages were without an adequate supply in six major states

(Andhra, Assam, Haryana, H.P., and Jammu and Kashmir), about one-third in five states and about a quarter in U.P. and Bihar (Table 6).

The Centre for Monitoring Indian Economy, Bombay, has constructed an interesting composite index of the level of infrastructure development for 1977–8. The index is a weighted sum of eight indicators measuring the availability of power and road and railway transport, and the development of irrigation, communications, health, education and banking facilities. This index stood at the highest level in Punjab (207) and at the lowest level (74) in Rajasthan. Among the hill states, too, the level is low (75 to 76) in Himachal Pradesh, Jammu and Kashmir and Nagaland, and even lower (49 to 53) in Tripura, Meghalaya and Manipur.[3]

## VII. SOCIAL SERVICES

The Centre for Monitoring the Indian Economy has also estimated the Quality of Life Index (PQLI) for all states for 1975–6. This index has been calculated with the methodology developed by the Overseas Development Council to compute the PQLI indices for all countries. The index includes infant mortality rate and life expectancy at birth as indicators of the health status of the population, and the literacy rate as the indicator of the educational status. These three indicators are combined with appropriate weights.

The PQLI has turned out to be the highest for Kerala (100) and the lowest for Uttar Pradesh (5). The index exceeded 50 for only three states (Haryana, Maharashtra and Punjab). For five states besides Uttar Pradesh, it was lower than 25 (Andhra Pradesh, Bihar, Gujarat, Madhya Pradesh and Assam). For the rest of the states, it ranged between 25 and 50.

The fact that Gujarat had a low PQLI illustrates a general point. Economic backwardness is generally associated with a low level of social service development, but it is possible for particular regions to be economically better off and socially backward, and vice versa. Gujarat has a high industrial

---

[3] The weights are: power (20), irrigation (20), roads (15), railways (20), postal services (5), education (10), health (4) and banking (6).

development status but remains backward in social service development. Kerala, on the other hand, suffers from a high incidence of poverty and unemployment; but it has managed to acquire a high social service rating because of the high priority given to the development of health and education services not only by successive post-independence governments but even by the ruling princes in earlier times.

Other specific indicators of social service development, summarized in Table 7, show that the literacy rate still ranges from 31 per cent in Bihar to 86 per cent in Kerala; the state expenditure on health from Rs 8 per capita in Bihar to Rs 26 in Punjab; and the expenditure on education from Rs 18 per capita in Bihar to Rs 64 in Kerala.

### VIII. SOME POLICY IMPLCATIONS

The factual review so far quantifies the persistence of, and in some cases even an increase in, inter-state disparities in the movement of various indices of development. It also throws up some propositions which have important policy implications.

First, since poverty and unemployment are geographically concentrated in some areas, there must be a mechanism to channel relatively more investment resources to these areas. Even agricultural growth, which can reduce rural poverty and unemployment, has been concentrated in a few areas; therefore measures must be taken urgently to step up agricultural growth in poorer areas.

Second, many poor areas have very rich, and still undersurveyed and underutilized, natural resource endowments. These areas need massive doses of investment to relax the particular constraints which have blocked a fuller use of their natural resources.

Third, concentrated investment in a few capital-intensive enterprises cannot, by itself, reduce widespread poverty in less developed regions. A more balanced investment package is needed for these regions.

Fourth, whatever else the investment package may contain, it must invariably include the provision of the water-energy-transport infrastructure. and the upgradation of literacy and skill levels. For these are the indispensable pre-requisites of development anywhere.

Fifth, much poverty can and does exist in the hinterlands of states like West Bengal and Maharashtra even though their average income may be high due to the existence of one or more urban-industrial enclaves.

This last consideration points to the need for studying and dealing with disparities at levels below the state—the district and the block.

There have been two recent exercises in which some below-the-state indicators have been analysed. First, the National Sample Survey (NSS) collected unemployment data in 1972–3 for sixty-five regions. Second, a Committee of the Planning Commission headed by Professor S. Chakravarty analysed in 1973 data on fourteen indicators for almost all the districts of India.

The NSS data for regions has been published in the Sixth Five Year Plan (Revised). As expected, it shows significant variations in unemployment rates even across the sub-regions of individual states. For example, in Bihar the rate was 8 per cent in the south and 14 per cent in the north. In Jammu and Kashmir it was 17 per cent in the valley and only 1 per cent in the highlands. In Maharashtra it varied from 6 per cent in the coastal areas to 15 per cent in the eastern regions. In Orissa the rate was the highest (17 per cent) in the coastal region, in Karnataka, in the inland northern region (11 per cent) and in West Bengal in the western plains (14 per cent). Such disaggregated data indicate the zones where anti-poverty measures are most urgently needed.

The Chakravarty Committee, using three statistical techniques (including principal component analysis), identified 169 backward districts, lying mostly in a Central heartland belt across U.P., M.P. and adjoining states, a Western Rajasthan-Gujarat belt and a Himalayan belt. (This is why the Indian backwardness problem is better described as a Centre-periphery problem, rather than a North-South problem.) The Committee also traced the major assets and handicaps in each belt and the investment strategy appropriate for it. It is significant that though the investment package indicated stresses on agriculture or small industry or large industry for different regions, infrastructure development and skill upgradation were found to be the critical needs everywhere.

IX. INFRASTRUCTURE POLICY

The double character of infrastructure services (water-supply, energy and transport) deserves emphasis in this connection. They are essential both as items of consumption and as inputs for production and capital formation. Access to them should, therefore, be regarded, *inter alia*, as the basic right of every area/community particularly since in poor countries the state has to provide or heavily subsidize, most of these services.

Benefit-cost analysis can be used to choose between alternative modes of providing these services; but it should not be used to decide whether any particular area/community should or should not have them. All areas/communities must be considered as entitled to them.

This notion of infrastructure entitlement underline the launching of the Minimum Needs Programme (MNP) and the Revised Minimum Needs Programme in the Fifth and Sixth Plans. In the Revised Sixth Plan document the objectives set down are to provide a safe water supply system to all villages, to provide access roads to all villages with a population of 1000 or more, and to provide electricity connections to 50 per cent of all villages by 1988. In addition all adults in the age group 15–35 and all children in the age group 6–14 are to be brought into the appropriate educational stream by 1988.[4] More than half of the remaining coverage under all these items is to be accomplished by 1983 with an outlay of Rs 477 crores (PC 1979). It is a matter of the utmost importance that in any further revisions of the Plan these minimum infrastructure targets and outlays are not cut down.

It is pertinent to recall here the infrastructure policy of two Asian countries (Taiwan and South Korea) whose achievement of rapid development along with substantial distributive progress has received much attention in recent years. Taiwan accelerated its annual growth rate of per capita income from 2.7

---

[4] There are also similar targets for primary health care, housing for the landless, nutrition and the upgradation of urban slums.

per cent in the 50s to 5.8 per cent in the 60s; and the Gini coefficient of inequality remained steady up to 1968 and *declined* by 11 per cent over the following 4 years (Ranis 1977). South Korea achieved a growth rate exceeding 8 per cent per annum in the 70s and its poverty ratio was barely 7.6 per cent in 1976 (Rao 1978). One of the key elements of the policy which produced these results was heavy investment in decentralized infrastructure. In Taiwan 60 per cent of the total road mileage was servicing the rural areas, and the proportion paved had risen from 7 to 50 per cent by the end of the 60s. A country-wide rural electrification grid had been established and rural and urban power rates were equalized. The education-cum-science expenditure rose from 8 per cent of the total budget in 1953 to 15 per cent in 1968. The number of research workers was as high as 80 per 100,000 of the farm population. The result was regionally balanced growth, with industry in rural areas producing 60 per cent of total consumer goods output, and generating 50 per cent of total industrial employment (Ranis 1977). Similarly in South Korea almost all villages are connected by roads; 91 per cent of all households have electricity; and more than half of all villages have community telephones. The literacy rate has been raised from 12 to 90 per cent. And the proportion of workers with secondary and higher education has been doubled from 16 to 32 per cent (Rao 1978).

The clear lesson of these success stories is that an active infrastructure and education policy favouring the less developed areas is essential, *inter alia*, to minimize the rural–urban and inter-regional imbalances that tend to arise in the course of development.

### X. A MULTI-LEVEL PLANNING SYSTEM

Besides an active infrastructure policy the policymix needed for reducing inter-regional imbalances must comprise: (a) the creation of efficient planning and implementation systems at state, district and lower levels, with considerable decentralized powers; and (b) the devolution of much larger financial resources from the Centre to the states and from the states to districts/blocks, according to new and more progressive formulae.

A consensus has existed in India for a long time, especially since the Fourth Plan period, about the need for regional/district block level planning or a balanced multi-level planning system on the ground that over-centralized planning is necessarily inefficient in a large, subcontinental economy. The decentralization of more funds and powers to local bodies (elected/administrative and or voluntary agencies) has also been on the national agenda ever since the beginning of planning. But the fact remains that so far no effective planning machinery has been created even at the state level, not to mention lower levels (except in Gujarat, Maharashtra, U.P. and Karnataka). And no significant devolution of funds and powers to local authorities has come about except in Gujarat and Maharashtra. Central and state politicians and bureaucrats relay the rhetoric of decentralization but resist and undermine any real decentralization. The latest indications are that the outlook for any decentralization may be even bleaker in the future than in the past. But the rational case for and the structure of multi-level planning must continue to be articulated.

A fairly strong planning machinery has been operating at the Central level. But similar outfits need to be developed at the state, district and block levels and in some cases at the level of large geographical units, with common features, cutting across normal administrative boundaries, such as river basins, forest belts and hill ranges. The structure and methodology of planning at all levels, though they may be different in detail, must have many common features.[5]

The first issue is the optimum division of functions. Avoiding the extreme centralist or decentralist views, it seems that in a reformed, rational system (*a*) the planning of some sectors should be transferred almost entirely from the Centre to the state and lower levels, (*b*) the planning of schemes in some other sectors must be shared by all levels according to the size or geographical incidence of the schemes, and (*c*) industrial planning must be done concurrently at all levels.

Planning for the following sectors can and must be decentralized to the state and lower levels: agriculture, land development, animal husbandry, fishery, forestry, housing, water supply,

---

[5] When necessary, we use the word 'region' or 'area' to denote any of these levels.

health, sanitation, school education and adult education, and local marketing.

Sectors where a division of responsibility according to the size or the geographical incidence of the scheme would be appropriate would include: irrigation, mining, energy, higher education, and transport.

In these sectors, large-scale projects of inter-state or national importance should be the responsibility of the Centre and others of the state. Thus railways, major ports, national highways, a few Central educational and research institutions, large power generation and transmission projects of inter-state importance, large-scale mining and large-scale irrigation projects can belong to the Central sector and all the rest to the state sector.

In some of these fields, there is a case for greater rather than less centralization. Thus the planning and management of major irrigation schemes (with culturable command area, CCA, exceeding 10,000 hectares), major power generation schemes (with capacity exceeding 200 MW) and some more universities can be centralized with advantage.

Some division of responsibility along these lines already exists in these sectors. But it has to be streamlined and rationalized according to clear principles. Otherwise ugly controversies of the kind which flourished in 1978 and 1979, about the transfer of the so-called Centrally-sponsored schemes to the states, will recur.

In classifying sectors or schemes in the manner suggested the principle involved is that planning (*i*) for all agricultural and allied sectors and (*ii*) for infrastructure and social service sectors, must be decentralized to the maximum possible extent (except for projects of national importance), because activities in these sectors are either location-bound or natural resource bound (as in the case of agriculture and allied sectors), or they are universal necessities (as in the case of infrastructure and social service sectors). In all these sectors, detailed local knowledge is critical for successful planning.

The case of manufacturing is different. A great deal of manufacturing is footloose. Proximity to material and/or markets does influence the location of manufacturing activities.

But many branches of manufacturing are not tied to any one of these factors. Industrial history shows that there are important manufacturing countries and regions which are distant from their materials and markets and yet remain dynamic and competitive (Japan is a prime example). Therefore, unlike agricultural infrastructure and social service planning, industrial planning has to be located at every level. There is no clear case for locating it at any particular level. Manufacturing possibilities have to be explored and appraised all the time at every level and the location of each activity has to be decided on the basis of the comparative advantage of different locations.

The hard core of planning at any level is always the task of determining the total investment to be made in the area over a given period, and its allocation between sectors, sub-regions and projects (schemes or activities).

In order to perform this task, the planning body at any level must be a strong specialized and relatively autonomous agency with a sufficient number of wholetime technologists, economists and administrators. The agency must have (*a*) the power to allocate the total investment within its jurisdiction subject to the formal approval of the political authority, (*b*) the power to appraise and clear important projects before they are considered by the political authority, (*c*) the power to send its own observations on all economic policy papers considered by the political authority, (*d*) the power to formulate or help departments to formulate important projects, (*e*) the power to collect necessary data from all government agencies and from the field, and (*f*) the power to evaluate the operation of schemes in the field independently, publish its findings and ask for corrective action. The Central Planning Commission is reasonably effective because all these powers have been traditionally available to it. If state governments consider establishing or strengthening their planning machinery, they should give the machinery similar authority.

Investment decisions are different from routine financial decisions and if they are to be rationally made, the apparatus to help formulate, appraise and evaluate projects, plans and policies should be a strong and specialized outfit. Otherwise there is no point in having it at all.

A plan necessarily consists of a set of schemes or projects. Therefore, the quality of a plan is the result of the quality of individual schemes included in the plan. Since the need for appraisal and evaluation is already widely accepted, it is necessary to stress the urgent necessity of strengthening the project formulation agencies in every department and at every level of planning. In every sector (department) project formulation must be entrusted to composite teams of technologists, economists and administrators working on a wholetime basis. While on project formulation, duty officers must be relieved of all routine executive duties because routine work and project formulation work are incompatible. A great deal of fresh data collection, thinking, designing and analysis is required to make good projects. This work must, therefore, be recognized as specialized, wholetime work.

Often schemes fail not because implementation is bad, but because the schemes themselves are bad. Many of them can hardly be called schemes at all. When large-scale industrial, irrigation or power projects are formulated, considerable sums are invested in project formulation. Expert bureaus and consultancy organizations are engaged in the task. But in agricultural, small-scale industrial and infrastructure fields, scheme formulation is often casual and amateurish. The hastily concocted schemes are structured to fail and they invariably fail.

Therefore, to make public investment produce the desired social benefits, substantial investments must be made in the immediate future in the creation of competent scheme formulation capacity. The same kind of detailed work should go into the preparation of small and medium schemes as is now devoted to the formulation of large-scale projects.

It is at the district and block levels that strong project formulation bureaus need to be established most urgently. Otherwise, the vast sums (of the order of Rs 2600 crore) allocated in the Sixth Plan document for area development are likely to be wasted. In scores of blocks some academic agencies, social work agencies and private consultancy organizations have done excellent professional planning work. It is high time that on the basis of the knowledge generated and experience gained by these agencies the area planning work is fully professionalized. As a result of recent work, a strong consensus has emerged about the essential ingredients of good area planning. It is accepted that area planning has to be comprehensive or integrated in the sense that it should cover the growth of crop production, animal husbandry, forestry and fishing, local industry, infrastructure and social services.

The area plan should be based on a scientific inventory of all the natural resources of the area. It should not be assumed that the natural resources of the area are fully known or can be known by simple observation. The truth is that in the country as a whole only 63 per cent of the area coverable by systematic hydrogeological surveys had been actually surveyed up to 1975. And only 46 per cent of the total geographical area of the country had been covered by systematic mineral resource surveys. The available estimates of mineral reserves are often based on incomplete mapping. Similarly, the extent of detail available about soils and forest resources varies from area to area; for some areas it is adequate but for others it falls far short of planning requirements. Before a good area plan can be made, it is necessary that all available data on natural resources be pooled and gaps in the data be filled by fresh surveys.

Investment in natural resource surveys has very high social return, for it identifies new income-raising possibilities and enables a number of productive schemes to be formulated with a high probability of success. The Chandrapur resource inventory should be cited in this connection. The inventory brought out the following facts which amateurs could never know:

> As many as 72,000 additional underground water outlets can be set up in the area without affecting the recharge; the irrigated area can be increased 17 times; and the forestry resources of the area can support four new paper mills, tussar cultivation and wood-working units.

Such data can be easily translated into sound schemes for investment and employment.

In addition to the natural resource inventory, a benchmark socio-economic survey is necessary for area planning. The survey should collect basic data about the productive assets of the area, output and input flows, consumption levels and the extent of poverty, the pattern of employment, unemployment and skills available, the trade of the area and people's access to infrastructure and social services.

Armed with natural resource data and socio-economic data,

planning teams can easily put together a development plan for the area, including specific schemes for the development of every sector.

A manpower budget must be a part of the plan. In fact, it is the manpower budget for full employment which makes comprehensive planning necessary and possible. When the objective is to provide employment to every single unemployed or underemployed person in the area, so that every family is enabled to have a minimum annual income of Rs 3500 (at 1977–8 prices), planning has to be multi-sectoral. For except in areas where productivity is already high and population density low, it is not possible to plan local full employment without accelerating activity in a number of sectors. The objective of the manpower budget is simply to ensure that the proposed activities in all sectors would together absorb the present labour surplus as well as the additions to the workforce over the next five to ten years at an income level close to the poverty line.

Needless to say, the individual schemes included in an area plan should be technically sound. Their costs and benefits should be carefully calculated. In the case of irrigation, transport and industrial schemes optimum locations must be chosen and detailed blueprints prepared.

The cost of every scheme as well as the whole area plan should, of course, be calculated in detail. All bankable schemes relating to soil improvement, irrigation, fishing, forestry, animal husbandry and small-scale industries should be submitted for sanction to financial institutions. And non-bankable schemes relating to transport, water supply, electrification, health and education, etc., should be presented to the concerned departments or corporations. So far as these latter sectors are concerned, planners in some areas may only be able to work out needs on the basis of the minimum physical standards specified in the Five Year Plan and leave it to the departments and corporations to formulate detailed schemes.

The schemes already being implemented in the area by the departments of the state governments should, of course, be subtracted from the total area plan in arriving at the additional finance required.

A large allocation for area development, as distinguished from allocations for sectoral developments, can fulfil its purpose only if there is no rigidity about the types of activities that may be financed out of it. The area development agency should have delegated authority to formulate and implement schemes in any sector as required for the balanced development of the area. Only such decentralized planning can supplement and reduce the deficiencies of rigid sectoral planning. By its very nature, sectoral planning cannot provide for the specific priority needs of poor areas and poor families. Area planning alone can do so.

It is necessary to emphasize that while comprehensive area planning is undertaken, on-going schemes and any immediately identifiable new schemes should continue to be implemented. There is no justification for postponing all action until a comprehensive area plan is made. Every available individual scheme, with some merit, should be implemented without delay. But a year or two must be devoted, side by side, to the preparation of the comprehensive plan. For such a plan would give a perspective on the full potential of the area, the requirement of full employment and the investment needed over a period of five to ten years.

On the question of the implementation of area development programmes, a few important issues and suggestions can be highlighted for consideration.

First, since autonomous corporations and agencies have consistently peformed better than departments, area development work should be increasingly entrusted to autonomous bodies. Everyone recognizes that the dairy corporation, the fertilizer corporation, the agricultural finance and refinance corporations, some of the small farmers' agencies, drought-prone area agencies and command area authorities and some of the banks have proved to be reasonably effective delivery systems. The lesson of this experience is that on the official side non-departmental agencies should be the main instruments for area development work. They should be given a clear objective, substantial autonomy, sufficient finance and a fully professional management and technical expertise.

Second, more and more work should be entrusted to non-official agencies. Many of these agencies have good leaders and professionals working in the field. Government departments should help them, legally, administratively, technically and financially, to make and implement area plans. The voluntary agencies can perhaps take up the responsibility of making and implementing area plans in at least 300 blocks. The agencies which already have high-grade planning and action capabilities will have to help and train other agencies and their workers.

Regarding coordination at the district level, it is an established principle that a high-power rural development planning and coordination body must exist at that level. It should be chaired by the Collector; and it should have representatives of all the government agencies, financial institutions, and semi-official and non-official agencies doing development work in the district. This body, on the Maharashtra pattern or the U.P. pattern, or the SFDA pattern, should have the decentralized responsibility and power to get area plans made and to have them implemented by all departments and institutions in a coordinated way. It should allocate the unallocated area development fund placed at its disposal. These unallocated area funds should be additional to the amounts budgeted for the sectoral departments.

In due course, when panchayats are re-elected and revitalized (in states where they are now weak or defunct) the responsibility for area planning and development can be progressively trasferred to them.

XI. RESOURCE ALLOCATION

The next issue to be considered is that of the equity of inter-state financial allocations.

In considering this question, it is necessary to examine together the equity of Finance Commission transfers, Planning Commission transfers and 'other' transfers, because at the state level the resources made available by the Centre under different arrangements are substantially substitutable.

Successive Finance Commissions have noted that transfers earmarked for specific purposes have not always been utilized for those purposes; and there has been no regular and systematic monitoring of the actual use of earmarked funds nor, of course, any penalty charged for their diversion. Even the Planning Commission, which settles with the state governments their total plan outlay as well as the sectoral allocation in advance, discovers every year that actual spending by most state governments has deviated widely from the planned allocation. But again the Commission is unable to do anything about it. 'Other' transfers are made *ad hoc*, to enable state governments to cover excessive overdrafts of meet extra expenditures on calamity relief and other contingencies. The relief outlay is earmarked, but overdraft and other assistance obviously is unallocated budgetary support. Thus it is clear that the state governments can and do actually use a large part of the total Central funds going to them under various headings according to their own development and non-development priorities.

There is also another important linkage between Plan and non-plan outlays. Finance Commission transfers influence, to a significant extent, the size of the surpluses/deficits in the states' revenue accounts from year to year, particularly in poorer states. These revenue surpluses/deficits in turn determine the 'own resources' of the state available for development and hence their total plan outlay levels settled with the Planning Commission.

For all these reasons, it is more meaningful to consider equity in the distribution of the total Central transfer rather that in particular segments of the transfer.

Over the 29-year period ending in 1978–9, the Finance Commission transferred to the states a total sum of Rs 23284 crores and the Planning Commission Rs 22072 crores. In addition, the Finance Ministry made *ad hoc* transfers of the order of Rs 12085 crores. Thus the aggregate resource transfer over the 29-year period adds up to Rs 57441 crores.

There have been two important studies of the equity of these transfers as between states. Gulati and George (1978) have shown that during the period 1956–77, five relatively high-income states (Punjab, Haryana, Gujarat, Maharashtra and West Bengal) received a per capita amount nearly equal to the average for 15 states (Rs 774); six middle-income states (Kerala, Tamil Nadu, Assam, A.P., Orissa and Karnataka) received 13 per cent more than the average; but the four low-income states (U.P., Bihar, Rajasthan and Madhya Pradesh) received 8 per cent less than the average. The distributive bases of the three kinds of transfers have been different. But this result indicates that the overall transfer has been regressive. If the total transfer had been progressive, high income states should have received less and low-income states more than the average and the middle-income states should have received amounts close to the average. But in fact the middle and high income states received more than the average. This is particularly disturbing because the four low-income states account for 41 per cent of the total poverty-stricken population of the major states (Table 1).

The National Institute of Public Finance and Policy reached a similar conclusion about the regressiveness of total transfers during the Annual Plan and Fourth Plan periods in one of their exercises. They noted that:

> during both the periods, the three poorer states of Uttar Pradesh, Madhya Pradesh and Bihar, received per capita federal transfers which were significantly lower than the all-states' average. During the Annual Plans, in fact, the poorest state of Bihar received the lowest per capita federal transfer (NIPFP 1978, p. 70).

However, they have also drawn a different inference with another methodology. The Institute found that:

> None of the elasticities (of per capita total transfer with respect to per capita total for the Third, Fourth and Annual Plan periods estimated separately) is significantly different from 0, even at the 10 per cent level of confidence. The contention that higher per capita transfers have been given to the poorer states or otherwise cannot be said to have been established (NIPFP, 1978, pp. 67–8).

The discrepancy in the results obtained about the equity of transfers with the two methods (grouping and regression) can be statistically explained. For an overall judgement it is sufficient to note that a non-significant elasticity (of transfer with respect to income) implies, at best, that the transfer was neutral—neither progressive nor regressive. But an examination of the basic data shows that though some of the poor states (Assam, Orissa, Rajasthan and Kerala) did receive larger than average transfers in some periods, three of the poorest states (U.P., M.P. and Bihar) received amounts much below the overall average per capita and some higher-income states received above-average transfers.

Examining Plan transfers alone, we find that during the whole planning period 1951–2 to 1978–9, Central Plan assistance given to 14 major states amounted to Rs 279 per capita. But four states (West Bengal, Tamil Nadu, Uttar

Pradesh and Bihar), which carry 42 per cent of the total poverty population of the country, received only Rs 246 to 251 per capita which is 11 per cent less than the all-state average. The two states with the highest per capita income (Punjab and Haryana) received the highest per capita Central Plan assistance, Rs 497 and Rs 529 respectively (GOUP, 1979).

If total per capita plan outlay over the whole 28-year period is considered, it averaged Rs 734 for all the 14 states. But, again, the outlay has been the highest in Punjab and Haryana (Rs 1660 to 1670) and the lowest in Bihar (Rs 479), West Bengal (Rs 586), Uttar Pradesh (Rs 636) and Tamil Nadu (Rs 660) (GOUP, 1979).

In other words, in four states with 45 per cent of the total population of 14 states, the level of state Plan investment per head has been the lowest. And in three states (Punjab, Haryana and Gujarat), accounting for only 10 per cent of the total population, per capita state Plan investment has been the highest. The ratio between the average state Plan investment, as well as average Central Plan assistance, in the three better-off states and the four low-income states has been about 2.5:1.

If this inequity of the level of state Plan investments between the sparsely populated and luckier states on the one hand, and the densely populated poorer states on the other, continues, the gap between regional incomes and poverty ratios will continue to increase. It is imperative, therefore, that all the formulae according to which Centrally collected resources are transferred to the states are made steadily more progressive.

In the formulae used by the Finance Commissions as well as the Planning Commission so far, the main factors are: (1) population, (2) tax collection, (3) some index of backwardness, and (4) outlays required for large irrigation and power projects or for the upgradation of particular services. The emphasis on the population factor to which 60 to 90 per cent weight has been given in different formulae is unexceptionable. But allocations in proportion to tax effort and the expenditure on big projects generally tend to be regressive because tax collections and project formulation capabilities are systematically higher in states with higher per capita income. It is, therefore, desirable that these criteria be omitted altogether from all allocation formulae. Allocations need to be made only in proportion to population and an appropriate index of backwardness. But, the index of backwardness has to be more satisfactory. It has been noted above that per capita income is a poor index of backwardness because it does not reflect the distribution of income between different income classes, Indices of backwardness, made up of several weighted indicators, are also unsatisfactory because the indicators as well as the weights chosen remain arbitrary. It has, therefore, been suggested that the simplest and the most desirable index of the backwardness of a state is simply its poverty ratio.[6] Central resources transferred to the states under all headings can be allocated in proportion to the total size of the poor population in each state (poverty ratio multiplied by the total population). This procedure would simplify and unify the allocation formulae and render the total allocations more progressive than ever before.

Another reform of the resource allocation process which must be considered is that the allocation formula be applied to the total Plan outlay of each state, and not merely to Central assistance. Central assistance should in fact be derived as a residual after deducting the projected 'own resources' of a state from the target outlay. This reform is essential because the proportion of Central assistance to total Plan outlays has been falling from about 63 per cent in the first four Plans to only 36 per cent in the projections of the current Sixth Plan. Thus even if the distribution of Central assistance is made highly progressive, the distribution of total Plan outlay will remain regressive, because nearly two-thirds of it comes from the states 'own resources' which are, of course, much larger in states with a higher per capita income than in the poorer states.

Total investment in a state includes not only state Plan outlay but also Central Plan investment and private investment. The geographical distribution of direct Central Plan investment in key mining and manufacturing sectors and in large irrigation-power systems has depended on the location of national or inter-state level resource pools (water, mineral, oil and gas reserves). This part of Central investment must continue to be distributed strictly according to techno-economic criteria,

---

[6] In the Minute of Dissent in the Report of the Seventh Finance Commission.

though more investment must be made in resource exploration and project formulation in less developed regions. In fact, all key industry investment needs to be kept outside all transfer formulae. However, Central outlays (under the remaining Centrally sponsored schemes) on infrastructure and social services can and should be distributed more progressively across states.

As regards the distribution of private investment, the government can only influence it through incentives. But the flow of medium and long-term credit from financial institutions is more directly influenceable by the government. Unfortunately inequity has characterized inter-state bank and cooperative credit flows as well. Gulati and George have shown in another paper (CDS 70), that over the seven years, 1969–70 to 1975–6, Group A (Gujarat, Haryana, Maharashtra, Punjab and West Bengal) states received 70 per cent more institutional[7] finance per capita than the all-state average, Group B (Tamil Nadu, Kerala, Orissa, Assam, Karnataka and Andhra Pradesh) states received 3 per cent more, Group C (U.P., Rajasthan, Madhya Pradesh and Bihar) states 49 per cent less and Group D (Himachal Pradesh, Jammu and Kashmir, Tripura, Manipur, Nagaland and Meghalaya) hill states 40 per cent less. The corresponding figures for Reserve Bank advances to cooperatives are 90.4 per cent, 57 per cent and 89 per cent. This inequity can and must be reduced through the influence of the Reserve Bank. The pattern of credit flows for natural resource-bound investments and the working capital needs of historically established activities may not be alterable; but flows for financing universal or footloose activities can be made more equitable. We have so far discussed the distribution of funds devolved by the Centre. But the quantum of total devolution is a more basic issue. The devolution of large sums to the states by the Seventh Finance Comission (Rs 23000 crores for the five years 1979–80 to 1983–4) and Rs 13400 crores proposed by the Planning Commission in the Draft Sixth Plan (1977–8 to 1982–3) has been criticized as excessive. But these transfers

---

[7] Including commercial bank credit and investments, term lending to industry and loans, given by the Agricultural Refinance and Development Corporation and the Rural Electrification Corporation.

would be no more than 28 per cent of the total projected tax revenue and capital receipts of the Central Government. There is no case for decentralizing revenue collection: about 68 per cent of total tax collection can stay in the hands of the Centre as in recent years. But if regional disparities are to be reduced, a greater spending must accompany a greater decentralization of functions. The devolution ratio which is now 28 per cent may be steadily raised to 30 or even 40 per cent over time.

Secondly, the devolved funds must not be allocated by the Central Planning Commission (CPC). The CPC can reserve what is needed for the Central Plan and for large irrigation power and transport projects. But the inter-sectoral allocation of funds devolved for state Plans must be left to the states. The current practice (and in reality the farce) of the CPC trying to allocate every lakh of Plan rupees for every sector, in every state, every year, must be given up; for, except in the case of large projects, the CPC has no special knowledge to contribute and the states feel free to reallocate nominally allocated funds. The states must get the bulk of the devolved funds unallocated, and allocate them according to their own needs and priorities.

And they, in turn, must treat their district Plan authorities the same way. Keeping back a part of state Plan funds for state level projects they must devolve the rest, unallocated, to the strengthened district planning authorities. Other states can emulate, and improve upon such a dualistic system which Maharashtra already has. Even in the allocation of funds among districts, the states can use the poverty population criterion (or a close proxy of it) which I have suggested for the inter-state allocation of Centrally devolved funds.

### XII. CURRENT SCHEMES OF BACKWARD AREA DEVELOPMENT

The present policy for the development of backward areas comprises a set of special schemes under which plan funds are provided over and above the funds allocated for general sectoral programmes. The special schemes can be classified into:

*a.* Schemes focusing on areas with special features (the desert development programme, the drought-prone area programme, the command area development programme, the hill area development projects and sub-plans, the North Eastern Council set-up, and the tribal area sub-plans and tribal development agency projects).

  b. Schemes focusing on target groups (small farmer development agencies and the special component plan for scheduled castes).

  c. Schemes providing incentives and concessions for particular activities in backward areas (concessional finance from financial institutions, tax relief, investment subsidy, transport subsidy, and priority in a few material allocations and hire-purchase of machinery, for industries located in 247 backward districts/areas, and relaxed viability and loan repayment norms for extension of electricity by the Rural Electrification Corporation in backward areas).

Large sums have been provided for all these schemes in the Fifth Plan and the Draft Sixth Plan. For hill and tribal area development alone the allocation has been raised from Rs 450 crores in the Fifth Plan to Rs 960 crores in the Sixth. For backward classes development it has been raised from Rs 295 to Rs 580 crores (PC 1979, p. 115). Provision for other schemes is additional. The Central provision alone is: SFDA[8] Rs 360 crores, DPAP[9] Rs 235 crores, IRD[10] part in CAD[11] Rs 78 crores, IRD Rs 98 crores, and Desert Development Rs 821 crores (PC 1979, P. 307).

A few comments on this spectrum of programmes are in order here. The twin principles of additionality and reservation underlying them have to be endorsed without hesitation. Special programmes/allocations, earmarked for backward areas/target groups, are clearly needed in addition to general sectoral programmes. For our whole development experience shows that the geographical distribution of general sectoral programmes tends to leave large parts of the country unaffected. And the multiplier effects of general sectoral programmes are too weak to benefit the backward classes.

Experience also shows that without reservation weaker sections would never get their due share in any developmental

---

[8] Small Farmer Development Agency.
[9] Drought Prone Area Programme.
[10] Integrated Rural Development.
[11] Command Area Development.

deliveries by the state (of inputs or assets or credit, or social services). To cite only three instances, without special schemes 5.4 million children of backward classes would not be receiving scholarships for education today (PC 1979, p. 201); and 6 million small and marginal farmers would not have been beneficiaries of institutional credit under the SFDA scheme; and 2 lakhs of poorest households would not have received assets and other assistance in Rajasthan within two years. Therefore, the continuing need for special schemes with earmarked benefits for target areas and target groups must be recognized without any qualification.

Second, we need clarity about the relation between sector programmes, area programmes and class programmes. Developmental (investment/production/social service) activity is always sectoral; and our whole administrative apparatus is organized mainly into single sector agencies. For correcting regional imbalances, however, shift to the area-orientations is indispensable. This orientation implies that within an area efficient single-sector agencies must continue to operate, but on the basis of a coordinated multi-sectoral plan designed to ensure that within a decade or so the chosen mix of activities does eliminate poverty and unemployment in the area.

Under all the schemes cited above, the list of sectoral activities to be developed turns out to be more or less the same: the development of intensified and diversified cropping, horticulture, animal husbandry, fishing, forestry, small industry, infrastructure (water· supply, energy and transport) and social services (health and education) (MFA 1978). The particular mix of these would, of course, differ across regions according to local needs and resources at different stages of development. But there is need for a unification of Central funds for all special schemes into a single national area development fund (until area planning is fully decentralized). This would make a large pool of finance (about Rs 2360 crores) available out of allocations already made.

A great drawback of all backward area schemes is that there is hardly any feedback about the actual physical progress of these schemes in the field. There is a widespread feeling that most of the sub-plans are paper plans without techno-economic teeth and without corresponding real action on the ground. Leakage of vast funds into the bureaucracy itself and/or the local oligarchy is also suspected. These feelings will remain until area planning is made a professionalized and specialized activity in the hands of strong project formulation bureaus in every district/block; and regular, detailed and independent monitoring/evaluation of progress is organized.

Although the amounts of funds earmarked for area development schemes nominally appear to be large, we have seen that total development outlays (per capita) available to less developed areas (including special allocations) remain small in comparison with those in the more developed regions. Therefore, the whole set of current arrangements for the allocation of funds needs to be reconsidered.

The effect of industrial and transport subsidies also remains unevaluated. But the scrappy evidence available suggests that subsidies have an inducement effect only if and where the basic infrastructure is accessible.

### XIII. SOME PROMISING SCHEMES

In the preceding section we have noted the schemes specifically meant for the development of backward areas/classes. But there are other schemes which have proved their capacity to raise hundreds of thousands of people above the poverty line, directly, in three to five years, in particular regions. It is important that our policy makers learn from our own internal 'success stories' and replicate them in the poverty pockets of the country.

The foremost of these is the general accelerated programme of irrigation development and fertilizer promotion under which the irrigated area has been increasing at the record rate of 2.5 million hectares during 1977-8 and 1978-9, the number of irrigation pumps by 4 to 6 lakhs a year, and fertilizer consumption at the rate of 21 per cent per year (CMIE 1979, 10.4) (Nearly 55 million hectares of known irrigation potential still remains to be utilized.) This rapid rate of irrigation-fertilizer growth must be maintained at all costs not only because it enhances our food security but also because it increases rural labour absorption directly by at least 0.44 million personyears per year. (An irrigated-fertilized hectare requires on the average 122 persondays of labour or 48 days more than dry hectare.) But it is necessary to ensure that small/marginal farmers get their due share of new canal water, pumpsets and fertilizer supply.

The second promising scheme is the Employment Guarantee Scheme (EGS) of Maharashtra which now generates 16 to 18 crores persondays of employment (or 5½ to 6 lakhs personyears of 300 days each) for the poorest rural people at a minimum wage. More than 80 per cent of the EGS budget is now spent on productive irrigation, conservation and afforestation works. For these works shelves of blueprints are now being increasingly prepared and kept at the district level in advance on the basis of technical surveys (Swarup 1980). The EGS approach is to my mind the most important single means of eradicating poverty; and EGS type schemes need to be extended in phases to all parts of the country and particularly to the high-poverty belts in the shortest possible time. For it is only under the EGS philosophy that the state accepts the moral, legal, technical, financial and organizational responsibility to provide guaranteed employment at poverty-line income to the poor within a definite time period. The work provided can all be directly or indirectly productive if strong, techno-economic project formulation bureaus are located in all districts/blocks. And the present unemployment (2 crores persondays) can all be absorbed at a (direct) cost of Rs 3000 crores a year which is less than one-fourth of the annual plan outlay.

For self-employment the Antyodaya approach of Rajasthan is the most promising. Under this scheme within 2 years 1.6 lakhs poorest familie were delivered income-yielding assets (pump, dairy animals, goats, sheep, bullock carts, camel carts, looms, sewing machines, retailing equipment, etc). This approach can be integrated in any area-development scheme and should in fact be adopted by lending agencies.

The three other promising schemes are the SFDA scheme, the food-for-work programme and operation flood. Under the SFDA scheme 6 million small/marginal farmers have received loans (assets) on a preferential basis; and in many districts where the schemes are well-administered hundreds of thousands of small farmers have risen up to the poverty-line. The administration of this scheme needs to be improved in many respects—I have made concrete proposals in this behalf (*Economic and Political Weekly*, 26 May 1979)—but it must be expanded to cover

4 million additional farmers every year so that in ten years or so the whole small/marginal farm sector is covered.

A conservative norm of employment generated under the food-for-work, programme is one personyear (full time equivalent) for a ton of grain, though official claims are higher. This norm implies that the utilization of about 2 million tonnes in 1979–80 would have generated 2 million personyears of employment. Even in normal years this programme can be kept at the 4 million tonnes level, for a government grain stock of 16 million tonnes is adequate; in drought-years the programme level can be raised. Thus this programme can be a substantial employment-generator. At the same time it releases the credit locked up in excess food storage; it helps create (or restore damaged) rural/public assets; and it improves the food intake of the poorest directly. Indirectly, it sets an effective floor to the rural wage rate and is the best cheap food supply system for the landless, a counterpart of the urban subsidized food supply system.

The famous dairy scheme Flood II which has been a proven success in Gujarat and Rajasthan is now programmed to cover 4 million milk producing families by 1978–9 and 10 million by 1985–6. The covered families, with a minimum land base, have been able to rise to the poverty line within three years.

These six schemes together have the potential of generating about 5 million personyears of employment every year, besides the employment which other labour-intensive sectoral programmes (fishing, forestry, small industry and minimum needs) may create.

### XIV. A CONCLUDING COMMENT

After a long period of trial and error it seems that we do have today the knowledge and field experience of about half-a-dozen successful approaches to the reduction of rural poverty and unemployment on a substantial scale. If the schemes based on these approaches are extended to the whole country, and especially the backward areas, and their administration improved, backwardness can be reduced.

In some parts of the country, of course, these techno-economic schemes cannot be launched or will not be effective without a restructuring of land and labour relations. For this restructuring we need not so much the mustering of the so-called 'political will' of the top rulers, as the universal politicization and unionization of the poor—the potential beneficiaries of all schemes. If the mass pressure of the poor rises, the will of the present rulers is bound to bend or rulers with the right will will replace them.

Just as technology is the key to the progress of production, trade unionism in the broadest sense (including geographical trade unionism of the neglected poor areas and class trade unionism of the hithereto unorganized poor classes outside the organized sector) is the key to the progress of redistribution. Therefore, the supreme task before all progressive forces—political parties, trade union workers, social workers, and the activist intelligentsia—is to raise the power of the poor. Without the universal politicization and unionization of poor areas and poor classes, there is little hope of any substantial redistribution of income or wealth in their favour.

### REFERENCES

Ahluwalia: M. S. Ahluwalia, 'Rural Poverty in India 1956–57 to 1973–74' in World Bank, India: Occasional Papers, Staff Working Paper No. 279, Washington D. C., May 1978.

Bhalla and Alagh: G. S. Bhalla and Y. K. Alagh, *Performance of Indian Agriculture: A Districtwise Study*, Sterling Publishers, New Delhi, 1979.

CDS: I. S. Gulati and K. K. George, 'Inter-State Redistribution Through Institutional Finance', Centre for Development Studies, Trivandrum, Working Paper No. 70.

CMIE: Centre for Monitoring Indian Economy, *Basic Statistics Relating to the Indian Economy, Vol. 2: States*, Bombay, November 1979.

FC: Government of India, *Report of the Finance Commission 1978*, New Delhi, 1978.

GOUP: State Planning Institute, Government of Uttar Pradesh, *Inter-State Disparities—Some Issues and Pointers for Policy Formulation*, Lucknow, January 1979.

Gulati and George: I. S. Gulati and K. K. George, 'Inter-State Redistribution Through Budgetary Transfers', *Economic and Political Weekly*, Vol. 13, No. 11, 1978.

ICSSR: Indian Council for Social Science Research, *Social Information of India: Trends and Structure*, Calcutta, 13 January 1979.

Mahajan: O. P. Mahajan, *Convergence in Regional Economic Development in India*, Kurukshetra University, Kurukshetra, June 1972.

Majumdar: Madhavi Majumdar, *Regional Income Change and Federal Policy in India 1950–51 to 1967–68: An Empirical Evaluation*, March 1978 (Mimeographed).

MAS: Government of India, Central Statistical Organisation, *Monthly Abstract of Statistics*, June 1979.

Mathur: Ashok Mathur, *Regional Growth and Income Disparities in India*, Centre for Regional Development, Jawaharlal Nehru University (Mimeographed, undated).

MFA: Government of India, Ministry of Food and Agriculture and Irrigation. *Guidelines for Intensive Development of Blocks Under the Programme for Integrated Rural Development*, Vol. II, New Delhi, 1978.

NIPF: Raja J. Chelliah *et al.*, 'Trends and Issues in Indian Federal Finance', National Institute of Public Finance and Policy, New Delhi, July 1978 (Mimeographed).

PC: Planning Commission, *Minimum Needs Programme*, New Delhi, 1978 (Mimeographed).

PC: Planning Commission, *Draft Sixth Five Year Plan 1978–83*, Revised, New Delhi, December 1979.

Ranis: Gustav Ranis, *Equality with Growth in Taiwan: How 'Special' is the 'Special Case'?*, Economic Growth Centre, Yale University, New Haven, July 1977 (Mimeographed).

Rao: D. C. Rao, 'Economic Growth and Equity in the Republic of Korea', *Wold Development*, Vol. 6, No. 3, 1978.

Swarup: Govind Swarup, 'Progress of Employment Guarantee Scheme', *Patriot*, 1 May 1980.

# Development in the Indian Economy Since Independence

A. M. KHUSRO

I will start with a bird's-eye view of the economy as one perceives it, as it has behaved in the past. I have observed from the vantage point of the University of Delhi and been close to policy makers and policy discussing circles, without actually being a part of it. This has provided me with an opportunity of a systematic exposition of the slow, sometimes perceptible and sometimes imperceptible, structural changes which have taken place in the Indian economy over the last thirty-five years or so.

Before going into what happened in the thirty-five years since 1951, I should really begin by asking what happened before. Prior to 1951 there was a slow increase of 1 per cent p.a. in the GNP over fifty years accompanied by a rather slow increase of 1.25 per cent in population over the same period. This resulted in a steady decline in the per capita income over fifty years. With the inception of planning, the declining per capita income got converted into a growing one.

In the fifties, in keeping with the general concern for growth of the newly independent nations, a number of new ideas on growth came to the fore. India was among the first to adapt and adopt them into growth models. To begin with the models were applied in their rudimentary form. Subsequently, they became more sophisticated with the Mahalonobis Model and the consistency exercises of the later Plans.

The major objectives of planning were: growth of the national product, increase in the Savings-Investment rate in the economy, employment generation and redistribution of national product.

With the passage of time, two more objectives were added.

The first was the derived objective of price stability which would depend on output being generated as planned and subject to the other inflationary forces being kept in abeyance. The second was the objective of self-reliance, which had two wings, export promotion and import substitution. In the early days, as we all know, there was export pessimism in the country. Nobody believed that experts could be given a big push as our export basket was heavily loaded with traditional items like jute, tea and cotton textiles. It was also reckoned that exports could be pushed only at lowered prices and we could end up being a net loser of foreign exchange. Therefore, the focus shifted to the saving of foreign exchange rather than earning it. In this way, the strategy of import-substitution came to the fore.

In my opinion each of these objectives failed to be achieved fully and each of these were achieved partially. The first four Five Year Plans aimed an annual 5 per cent growth of GNP which was never achieved; we always ended up with less. This is the failure of Indian Planning of the first twenty-three years, including the three years of Plan holiday.

Success consists in the fact that in no Plan was there a growth rate less than 3.5 per cent p.a. A steady growth of this magnitude was the characteristic feature of our first twenty-five years of planned development. In a sharp contrast the growth performance of the Fifth and Sixth Plans was nearly 5 per cent, notwithstanding the controversy surrounding the base years.

The second objective of investment went through fairly well. It is remarkable that 90 to 92 per cent of this investment was financed by resources generated from within and only 8 to 10 per cent came from abroad. The savings rate at times touched high levels of 22 to 23 per cent p.a., giving a margin for estimational errors, that would compare favourably with that of the developed economies like the United States and the United Kingdom.

On the fulfilment of the employment objective, there were both positive and negative features. In India's first Five Year Plan, we planned for about 7 million additional jobs and we ended up with only 5 million. In the second Plan, we could manage an additional 8 million against a target of 10 million and in the third Plan we achieved an additional 9 million against a target of 12 million. So the gap between the number of new entrants to the labour market and the number of additional jobs created widened. But, the fact remains, that the absolute number of additional jobs created equalled the populations of many European countries.

Then we come to price stability about which the less said the better. We never really managed any five year Plan except the Fifth one with a semblance of price stability. We always ran into 8 per cent—10 per cent inflation on an average and there was this phase in the early seventies when we were getting into the Latin American realms of price changes with 24 per cent price increase in 1973–4, mounted on a 20 per cent increase in 1972–3 and on a 18 per cent increase in 1971–2. For these three years we had a very bad time, everybody was shaken up with this alarming rise in prices. But there was a phase in the Fifth Plan when there was a semblance of price stability, following some good crops and serious recourse to macro-economic remedial measures such as controlling aggregate demand in the face of falling aggregate output.

Now we come to the objective of self-reliance through import substitution and export generation. Exports have remained sluggish throughout. This could be partly explained by the income inelasticity of the world demand for the traditional exports. Which are primary products subject to vast fluctuations and with the terms of trade moving steadily against them.

Regarding export of non-traditional items, we have succeeded over time in adding to the list. But this period, the past 36 years, was a building phase and the world had a much better experience with the manufacture of chemical, engineering goods and other new products. Also we were beginners and our products were very non-competitive. So exports remained sluggish and that objective of 5 per cent export growth was never met.

On import substitution, I think we had great success. We adopted a policy of import substitution in 1951 and the Latin American and many other developing countries had adopted a similar policy around the same time. We built tariff walls and they built tariff walls to protect the home industry against the external onslaught.

We protected and gave our manufacturers a chance to go

ahead to produce third-rate goods to begin with, going on with experience to produce second-rate goods and further to produce not many but some first-rate goods. A lot of failure to be reported here. Maybe we import substituted in many a wrong case in the sense that other countries may have had comparative advantage in producing those commodities. Nevertheless, we went ahead with the programme and in due course were producing a large range of commodities.

Well, this was it, the Latin American countries also raised tariff walls, but they allowed a lot of foreign companies to come into the country, avoid tariff and produce from within to reach the 'locals' giving the argument that the domestic entrepreneurs did not have enough experience. This in effect allowed these foreign companies to maintain contact with the metropolitan countries, get technologies and other imports from these. The self-reliance of the Latin American nations did not grow as fast as in the case of India. This strategy plunged them into huge debt obligations to the metropolitan countries. India's indebtedness, though large and rising is still at a manageable level. The debt–service ratio, ratio of debt obligations in relation to our export potential, estimated at 15 per cent, has remained on the low side. This I think is the major achievement of the planning era. In agriculture, in the beginning, 1951 to 1961, the Government was battering away with supply of inputs: irrigation, fertilizers and improved seeds. The farmers would not take them and say: 'Oh! well we are not used to irrigated cultivation, so we will only cultivate dry crops. Father had not used fertilizers and grandfather had not used these seeds. We do not know the meaning of wet cultivation. Therefore, we will not touch these seeds.' So, fertilizers kept piling up; irrigation potential kept piling up; new seed stocks kept piling up. Tata reported that agricultural implements were piling up. There were no takers. Until the end of the fifties and the beginning of the sixties people would not accept the new things on the input side. Meanwhile, the country was experiencing successes and failures in other areas. Land reforms were partially successful. Successful in some areas of U.P., Bombay, Hyderabad and Kerala. In other areas—multipurpose river valley projects, irrigation, fish culture, flood control, transportation etc.—there was not much success to report.

In community development, again the story is of partial success and partial failure. In the area of intensive agricultural development programme (IADP) of those days, the strategy was to focus on 7 to 15 districts and letting growth be generated, through extension services and intensive input usage. This would generate growth impulses in the surrounding areas. Community development programmes, land reforms, and river valley projects were all a mixture of failure and success. The cumulative effect of all this could be felt by the beginning of the sixties. Somehow, new attitudes got created even though earlier the farmers were not receptive to the new incentives.

Unlike many planned economies of the world where the strategy was to extract surplus from agriculture and put it into industrial and infrastructural development (slogan being 'Infrastructure first and consumer goods later'), the Indian planners adopted a totally different strategy, mainly because of the political set-up where on could not throttle consumption. We allowed consumer goods to be produced from the very beginning both in industry and in agriculture along with some push to capital goods and heavy machinery. Thus farmers began to get used to a wide range of consumer goods rather quickly as compared to the days where only three industrial items used to percolate to the agricultural society, namely, kerosene, matches, and mill-cloth.

Thirty years have gone and there has been a mass percolation of industrial consumer goods—watches, matches and mill cloth; edible oils and transistor radios; bicycle, bush-shirts and trousers. The list of industrial consumption goods in rural areas is very long and is almost the same as in the urban areas in comparable income brackets.

The result of all this was that farmers and the rural community slowly began to get drawn towards the purchase of industrial goods. But how do you purchase industrial goods unless you sell your own product and get cash in larger proportion? Marketed surplus had to increase.

Therefore, in the first ten years from 1951 to 1961, they brought more land under the plough to produce more, to sell more, to get more cash. Amazingly, in those ten years, 22 per cent addition took place in acreage under cultivation. Of course, in the next decade this land ran out and there was only 4 per cent increase in acreage in the sixties. So the idea of raising the yield per acre emerged. Once this idea entered which coincided with the emergence of technical changes in the world, the arrival of new seeds and new strategies of combining fertilizers, irrigation and new seeds in Indian agriculture was a logical corollary. This combination on the supply side and the emergence of new demand for industrial products led to a breakthrough which came to be known as the Green Revolution.

Alas the Green Revolution remained confined only to limited areas of Haryana, Punjab, Western U.P., parts of Tamil Nadu, parts of Andhra Pradesh and some other pockets. Rest of the sleeping giants of Madhya Pradesh, Rajasthan, Bihar, Orissa, Eastern U.P., West Bengal, Assam, etc. are still awaiting arousal. For a decade, the rate of growth of wheat output was 14 per cent per annum. It is not so now. So this is the story of Indian agriculture: a mixture of failures and successes.

In industry, from the beginning, the public and the private sectors were deemed to be the motive forces. Since the horizons of private businessmen were limited, it was thought and very correctly so, that the state had to come forward to build up the infrastructure. Around 1951 or so, an idea gained ground, which even the Keynesians became a party to, that India being an agricultural economy should remain agricultural. England and the other European nations should remain industrial and the two should exchange on the basis of the good old theory of comparative advantage. Nehru and others rejected this on the plea that it was based on static comparative advantage and argued for a rapid industrialization based on the concept of dynamic comparative advantage. Public sector became the main vehicle of growth, particularly in the area of 'commanding heights'. The infrastructure built up by the public sector in the country has been massive. What is more, the products of the infrastructure built in the public sector were made available to the private sector both in the farming sector and in the so-called functional industrial sector at abysmally low prices. So, the industrial and the agricultural sector flourished on the infrastructure built in the public sector. This can be viewed as a measure of the success of the public sector and the delivery of goods.

The failure of the public sector obviously emanates from its excessive bureaucratization. It was conceived that a government department cannot run enterprise successfully, and, therefore, a new cadre of experts and professionals had to be inducted into the public sector. This happened for a few years. Then quietly the bureaucrats took control of the public sector. The top layer of management in public sector came to be infested with civil servants. They made the public sector linked and responsible to bureaucracy rather than to the legislature where it rightfully belonged. Interference by the executive authority, namely, the Ministry and Department, into the affairs of the public sector increased and this showed itself in low profitability, low cost consciousness, and a massive under-utilization of capacity. This is the failure of the public sector which we are focussing on now. There is a gross underutilization of capital stock worth anywhere between Rs 30,000 to Rs 40,000 crores. Something drastic needs to be done. The performance of the private sector was noticeable in its wanton use of the infrastructure built in the public sector. They did very well for themselves generally. Investments in infrastructure was considered a taboo by the private sector because of the long gestations and low rates of return. In the early fifties no one except the Tatas came forward to build a one million tonne steel plant. Adherence to marginal cost pricing always kept prices of the public sector products at ridiculously low levels. The private sector flourished on account of the low priced inputs provided by the public sector. Its horizons expanded and it became an efficient producer of a whole range of goods of both kinds—capital and consumer—imbibing international technical know-how. This is the success story of the private sector. But the failure of the Indian private sector basically consists in its developing oligopolistic structures and behaviour. It is a beautiful textbook situation. In the oligopolistic private sector, the people appear to be competitors, but in effect, they are colluding with each other. I produce a four-seater car, you produce a five-seater car and someone else will produce a six-seater car. I sell in western India, you sell in southern India and the third person will sell in eastern India. The oligopolist because of the size believes that he can control the market if he takes major decisions regarding expansion or contraction. He firmly believes that any expansion will severely depress the prices. So he restricts output.

Hindustan Motors is a classic example, the price of an Ambassador car jumping from Rs 36,000 to as high as Rs 70,000 in a single year! How does one account for this? The oligopolist would always resist fresh competitors, instead they would browbeat one bureaucrat into giving them the licence to expand capacity and then sit over the licence. This is the order of the day. The situation can be remedied by introducing competitiveness where oligopoly exists, by enlarging the scope of the licensing system and by bringing in more producers and by allowing the existing producers to expand. This way they would be nearer the optimal size of production rather than get stuck at the high cost-high price configuration.

I am convinced that in a poor country like ours, only the products with economies of scale will sell in the poorer sections of the society. Handloom sarees and shirts will not sell in the rural areas though produced there because they do not have the economies of scale, whereas nylon sarees and dakron shirts will sell because of low overheads resulting from the scale factor. Similarly, leather chappals would be appropriate for the urban elite and for the export market, whereas plastic chappals would find a vast market in the rural areas. To achieve this the licensing policy should scuttle oligopolistic trends and expand scales. Foreign technology be brought in if necessary and homebred technology be encouraged in such a way that quality improves and exports are augmented. Indian exports are held up today because they are no longer predominantly traditional exports. In these products the other countries are way ahead of us. Our exports can be made competitive only by updating the technology. But this technology import has to be selective and judicious so as to give appropriate protection to home technologies. Appropriate tariff walls should be built so as to ensure unhindered growth of some selected technologies.

Before going into the redistribution and poverty alleviation objective, we should discuss the regime of administered prices coexisting with free market prices. The argument ran as follows. Indians were a huge mass of poverty-stricken people. They had to be provided with food and medicines. In order to make these accessible the prices had to be administratively reduced. The state even had to subsidize the producer. There was no escape from price controls in critical areas. It would have been politically and socially infeasible to do otherwise. This policy led to eyebrows being raised from various quarters, World Bank included. But the policy of administered prices has stood the test of time and the Bank withdrew its criticism. The success of the system was for everybody to see. Its major failure lay in the grain not reaching the rural poor. There is an urgent need of expanding the network of public distribution system in the rural areas.

But while all this is so good, who can deny that the control system multiplied and expanded into several commodities. Success of the food and drug price control system induced a multiplicity of controls covering a wide range of products. This led to the emergence of the dual market structure—the regulated market and the free market, with its consequent generation of illegal or black incomes. Successive governments have failed to curb the growth of black money. The major trouble with black incomes was not its encouragement to conspicuous consumption, but with its inability to get channelized into production and growth oriented investments. Black income cannot be invested in stocks and other securities which are the major instruments of the capital market. These incomes, therefore, came to be used in the formation of non-institutional assets like Jwewllery, land and housing. The supply of these non-institutional assets is fixed, there is no net addition, only the assets change hands. If you acquire land and build a house you are merely encroaching on these assets, only their prices have been growing. Additionally, black incomes having bypassed tax authorities could not even remotely promote redistribution of national income.

The scheme of voluntary disclosures failed in its desired objectives of mopping up these resources, and channellizing them into productive investment areas. Now the controls are receding into the background and the 1985 budget was an attempt to blunt the machine that generates black money. On the redistribution front, I think, it would be too much to expect that the process started right from the word 'go'. The reason for this is quite simple. Since 1951 our per capita income growth has never exceeded the lowly 1.2 per cent to 1.5 per cent per annum mark. This was too low for any percolation to the bottom layers taking place. We have the examples of Indonesia, Malayasia,

Thailand, Phillipines, etc. where per capita incomes rose by 3 per cent to 4 per cent p.a. and this really trickled down. No wonder Indian administration and the government had to run other programme for lifting up the poor. So the programme of Community Development, Intensive Agriculture Development Programme, River Valley Development Programmes and in later days IRDP and NREP came up. Some of these programmes were quite effective in alleviating poverty.

It is realistic to assume that the Indian Gross Domestic Product would continue to grow. In 1985 it grew by 4.5 per cent to 5 per cent. If it grows by about 5 per cent and the population growth comes down to 2 per cent p.a., then by the turn of the century we should have a per capita growth of more than 3 per cent p.a., which would be comparable to the East Asian countries mentioned earlier. Growth will trickle down and the anti-poverty strategy will work even better. I do not subscribe to the view that there is no correlation between growth and the poverty proportion. Growth will bring up the proportion of population above the poverty line. I am quite optimistic about it.

Lastly, I refuse to believe that food poverty is all important. That is not the only form of poverty. Health poverty is reasonably important. It impinges on food poverty. Education poverty is tolerably important. Literacy poverty is obviously important. Housing poverty is important. 'Non-access to industrial consumer goods' poverty is equally important because many of non-industrial goods have linkages with health improvement. I will, therefore, advocate a quality of life index rather than a calorie-based food index. The income elasticity of demand for non-food items is higher compared to that of food items even for population belonging to the bottom income brackets. Health, literacy and education are important components of a quality of life index. Taking literacy as an example, in the period 1901–51, something like this has happened. Population grew at the rate of 1.25 per cent p.a. Literacy percentage declined because of colonial domination and illiteracy percentage increased. We, therefore, have the phenomenon of absolute number of literates as well as illiterates rising. Call it Phase I.

Since independence, population has grown at 2.2 per cent p.a. Literacy percentage has begun to rise. In 1951, it was 17 per cent; in 1964, 24 per cent; in 1971, 29 per cent and in 1981, 34 per cent. Illiteracy percentages consequently have declined. Between 1951 and 1981, if you take 17 per cent of 350 million and 34 per cent of 685 million, you will find that literacy has gone up by more than 200 million, like the whole population of the United States. I have gone into these data. It turned out that among the literates we include the proper literates on the day of the census, but among the illiterates the 5-year-old, the 3-year-old children—to whom illiteracy is irrelevent—are not excluded. This number is close to 100 million and if we subtract it from the total population, the literacy percentage jumps up to 44 per cent. If these trends continue, the literacy curve will cross the illiteracy curve by the late eighties and a predominant share of India's population will be literate. This is Phase II.

Now we come to the interesting point. While the percentage of literacy has been rising and that of illiteracy falling, the absolute number of illiterates is rising. It is a matter of shame that even today 56 per cent of 750 million people are illiterate. Nothing I say here can dilute the fact that the mass of poverty is on the increase. The rate at which literacy has been rising in Phase II is faster than the rate at which illiteracy is rising. This is indeed redeeming. When you make projections on the basis of the conservative 2 per cent population growth, it becomes clear that by 1991 the literacy percentage would be above the illiteracy percentage. What is more, absolute number of illiterates would have begun to decline. That will happen by 1991 when Phase III would have begun. When we apply these yardsticks to the health access data we observe that already around 1980, the health access curve for the population surpassed the health non-access curve. The absolute number of people without access to health facilities has already started declining. This conclusion is based on a rather conservative figure of 30,000 individuals being catered to by a primary health centre.

So, a labour-surplus country like India with a high population has to pass through three phases. In the first phase, the population is increasing but increase in literate population is slower. In Phase II, literacy percentage increases, illiteracy percentage falls, absolute number of literates increases fast and absolute number of illiterates decreases slowly. Then we come to Phase III in which two things happen: the percentage of literacy becomes higher than the percentage of illiteracy and the absolute number of illiterates declines. India has moved from Phase I to Phase II and is now on the threshold of crossing into Phase III.

# The Uneasy Coalition of Economic Interests

DALIP S. SWAMY

If we look at the 30–5 years' Indian economic experience, we are struck with a very important aspect of economic growth. There has been some kind of reduction in the growth process after 1965 as compared to the period 1950–64. Whether we take the growth rate of agriculture or industry or public investment or private investment, we are struck with this important fact: the deceleration in the rate of growth of the Indian economy during the post-1964–5 period.

This leads us to the question: why has growth rate decelerated during the post-1964–5 period? Various explanations have been offered for this phenomenon. One explanation is the movement of terms of trade in favour of agriculture, which is not correct, at least for the post-1975 period. This can, therefore, be dismissed outright. Second explanation is the shrinkage of market. It is pointed out that during the post-1965 period, markets for industrial goods reached saturation levels and therefore the growth could not continue at the rate at which the Indian economy was able to perform before 1965. The market hypothesis does not appeal very much although one cannot dismiss it outright. The reason is that the basic cause behind the market stagnation hypothesis is that there has been a growing degree of inequality in urban and rural incomes and this growing degree of inequality has created markets for a very small segment of output, particularly for luxury output; consequently, the market for mass consumption has been shrinking. We really do not know whether the income inequalities are growing or declining. But obviously the Gini coefficient of urban income inequality and rural income inequality do not lend support to any hypothesis. Therefore, we cannot be sure that the income inequality has caused market stagnancy and market stagnancy has caused decline in economic performance during the post-1965 period.

Another important aspect which has something to do with the slow or stagnant performance of Indian economy during the post-1965 period is the increase in excess capacity in public sector and slowing down of the rate of investment in public sector. Along with the decline in investment in public sector the amount of subsidies as a proportion of GNP has been rising. The total subsidies were Rs 0.4 billion in 1950, Rs 0.5 billion in 1960, Rs 3.4 billion in 1970, and Rs 38.6 billion in 1982. If we calculate these subsidies, as a percentage of GNP, we find that there has been a sharp increase in the rate of subsidies in the Indian economy. Moreover, government expenditure on non-developmental activities, on defence, on administration, and so on, have increased seven times between 1950 and 1982–3, while the GNP increased only three times. Therefore, the rate of growth of non-developmental expenditure, defence and public administration is twice as large as the rate of growth of GNP.

When I put these aspects together, then an interesting story unfolds. The public investment is constricted possibly by the increasing claim on budgetary resources by a segment of the economy which is claiming subsidization and other segments which are claiming non-developmental expenditure: defence and public health. And this leads me to examine an important aspect of the political economy of our development process.

At the time of transfer of power in 1946–7, the dominant classes in India consisted of three important groups: one, industrial bourgeoisie; two, the rural landlords (not too many rich peasants existed at that time); and three, the group of administrators, civil servants, defence personnel, and so on.

Now in Marxist terminology, the third category cannot be defined as a class; it is a group. But in special circumstances this third group may act in an autonomous manner and to that extent it might be able to create an impact on the structure of the economy. In 1956, the Industrial Policy Resolution and the strategy of industrialization created a situation in which some kind of power and authority was vested into this group of administrators, the so-called State functionaries. They exercised the power of giving licenses to the industrial bourgeoisie and that of subsidization or infrastructure creation to the agricultural sector as well as industrial sector. For 10–15 years this power was exercised in a subdued manner. But as the coalition between the dominant agricultural class and the industrial class became non-reconciliatory, this third group began to exercise greater power and authority.

The upshot is that the planning process and the development of public sector have created a new rentier class. In order to direct scarce resources (capital, foreign exchange and raw materials) to the priority sectors the government organized a regulatory system of industrial licensing, price controls, taxes and subsidies. With the expansion of economic activities, power and authority of bureaucrats in the regulatory system inevitably increased. Public sector expansion, nationalization of financial, productive enterprises and defence have also expanded the economic prospects for this group. Under these conditions bureaucrats who manage licences, controls and taxes tend to assume the role of decision-makers. This illusory power and authority enabled them to extract rent from industrialists as well as landlords. Corruption was a device to circumvent the regulatory norms and procedures. The bureaucrats divided the industrialists and extracted rental income by favouring one group against the other. Sharp growth of business houses like DCM, Modis, Nanda and Reliance, illustrates this point. Selective favours make it somewhat difficult even for Chambers of Commerce to close their ranks against particular administrative policies. Thus, a group of bureaucrats, getting and claiming rent on the basis of human capital and illusory licence-giving power and authority, consolidated their position in the country.

Along with the parasitic bureaucrats emerged a group of political brokers who utilized their contacts with politicians for quick personal gains. Information in the modern world is money. Political brokers with access to crucial information in relation to government policies regarding licensing, taxes and controls, development schemes and tender selection of government contracts, etc., made money by selling the information to relevant parties. This group also acted as insurance agents to those unscrupulous traders and businessmen who evaded tax payments on their incomes.

The bureaucrats exacting rental income and the political brokers commercializing their contacts had one thing in common. They did not pay taxes on their illegitimate income. To this we can add another group of economic functionaries who did not pay taxes on their growing incomes. This group consisted of traders and industrialists who evaded taxes and rich agriculturists who were not covered by the tax system. The growth of these groups did not contribute to the economic power of the state. This weakness impinged on public investment for infrastructural facilities, which suffered to the extent of becoming the major bottleneck for industrial growth.

Thus, the composition of the ruling class has undergone some perceptible changes. At the time of independence, the ruling class was perceived to be a bourgeois–landlord combine. It had developed a cognizable distance from the imperialists as a result of the nationalist struggle. But soon it realized its economic and technical weakness and, therefore, consciously entered into collaboration with foreign capital of all types. These ties have been consistently strengthened since 1956, despite bargaining contradictions. While the bourgeoisie fathomed their distance and developed new relations with imperialists, they regarded the class of landlords to be redundant and dispensable. Therefore, whenever it was feasible, the government tried to dilute their power, gradually disassociating them from the decision-making exercises at the Centre and making them puppets in the states. The rich peasants, however, were to be appeased by providing them cheap credit and subsidies for agricultural inputs because they supplied surplus foodgrains to industrial centres. In addition to the rich peasants, the regulatory bureaucracy and political brokers also tended to become autonomous, defying to subserve the interests of the bourgeoisie.

The rise of rich peasantry and regulatory bureaucracy and the dilution of economic power of landlords had become a part of the new political reality in the 1980s. These 'proprietory' classes fight and bargain with industrial bourgeoisie for their share in the spoils of the system and often strike compromises in the form of 'log-rolling' in the usual fashion of pressure group politics. As a result, an elaborate network of patronage and subsidies and an oversized service sector have come into being. The share of these groups can be gauged by the fact that subsidies of all government units plus losses in public sector, electricity corporation, transport, etc. have increased from 40 crores in 1950 to Rs 3,860 crores in 1982. At the same time, defence and public expenditure have increased at twice the rate at which the country's Gross National Product has grown. These subsidies and bureaucratic spendings have no correlation with investment, or output, or export performance. They bloat up conspicuous consumption. The growth of these groups have raised the cost of political brokerage, and with it the economy's surplus is dissipating into luxury living.

The marginalized section of population and the unemployed who clamour for the crumbs at the gates just outside the periphery of the ruling class are to be controlled through police and paramilitary forces, the expenditure on which has grown at the rate of 9.5 per cent per year since 1960.

This scenario has made up the fiscal crisis of the State. The government's non-developmental expenditure for keeping the new groups in the ruling class happy, for coaxing and coercing the intermediate groups of middle class and small industrialists and for guarding the fortress, have been rising beyond capacity. The government revenue has failed to grow at the required rate due to the resistance of the new groups to pay taxes. The net result is the blocking of the accumulation function of the State which was considered necessary in 1956.

What is the State doing to tackle this crisis? One solution is to completely reorient the strategy of industrialization, which has created this mess. This alternative would require a moratorium on the production of luxury goods. Top priority should be assigned to major irrigation schemes, power generation, road construction in rural areas and small-scale industries in towns. Such a change in investment priorities would obviously require a revolutionary break from the past. It will hurt the interests of big industrialists whose power has been consolidated over the years. Above all, it will be against foreign capital, which is looking for new opportunities to dump its outdated factories and technology in India. Hence, the alternative of self-reliant, labour-intensive strategy of industrialization is not a serious proposition at present.

The other alternative is a marginal change in the system of political management, while continuing the ongoing process of industrialization. This alternative is being pursued now. The details of this scheme will unfold over the years, but the following seems to be the major aspects of the new strategy. The emergence of rich peasantry, bureaucrat rentiers and political brokers have silted up the channels of surplus mobilization and public investment. Till now it was difficult to dredge the silted channels because of higher risk of dismantling the patronage structure carefully cultivated over the years by the government which represented a coalition of interests. That coalition of interests seems to have gone into the background now. Industrial bourgeoisie have apparently dominated the government, who now feel somewhat confident to tackle the upstart politicians, corrupt bureaucrats, and so on. The rich peasants are being cut to their size. They have been suffering for a decade on account of paying relatively higher prices for agricultural inputs-diesel, tractors, fertilizers, etc.—as compared to the prices of their produce. The landlord class had outlived their relevance in the 1950s; the rich peasantry lost its charm in the 1970s. Some landlords even now continue to wield power and authority, but their class has lost prominence. Similarly in future some rich peasants may remain inside the power circle, but their class will be ejected from the ruling coalition. The industrialization process, on the other hand, will be more capital- and energy-intensive. It will require more, not less of foreign capital. The rentier class will also be cut to their size. Dismantling of licensing system, liberalization of imports, elimination of price controls, raising of MRTP limits, etc. are the important milestones on the road leading the bureaucrat-rentiers to a dead end.

Ever since the Second Five Year Plan economic crisis has been tackled by the state in a manner that detached the dominant industrial class from the indigenous groups and integrated it (the dominant industrial class) with foreign capital. In a system where the tasks of bourgeois democracy have not yet been completed and semi-feudal conditions still prevail in the countryside, the process of detachment from the native classes and integration and consolidation with international capital is accomplished by centralization of decision-making. Until 1977 the trend of growing centralization of power and authority had clearly feudal manifestations with the democratic institutions being reduced to rubber stamps.

In the 1980s the feudal manifestations of the centralization process may be given up in favour of capitalist manifestations. Professionals may be encouraged, computers may store and analyse information, major developmental schemes may originate through the contracts with foreign aid-giving agencies and the Centre will thrust such schemes on the states through bureaucratic channels.

Thus, the trends towards greater dependence on foreign capital and centralization of decision-making have become irreversible. With the extension of these trends, social contradictions will sharpen in future. Increasing dependence on foreign capital has already made production and employment vulnerable to outside forces. Increase in centralization has become a source of corrosive tensions in the federal structure in relation to the states. In the next decade the new coalition between the industrial bourgeoisie and international capital will have to reckon with the challenges from the intermediate classes and the proletariat. In order to consolidate its position the former will increasingly resort to repressive measures and the latter will have to organize to defend their existence. Events are driving the nation in the direction of a protracted class war. Social scientists cannot afford to remain indifferent to these developments; they will have to choose their friends and enemies.

# Indian Economy: Performance and Policy

KAUSHIK BASU

I begin with an evaluation of the Indian economy's performance with respect to growth and the provision of basic needs. A question which has been raised is: Have we reached a stage of economic achievement where there is reason for joy? This was answered in the affirmative and it was argued that it was time we jettisoned our pessimism.

I want to examine this question a bit closely. There is one piece of statistical information which has been considered a lot. This is the growth rate. It has been pointed out that in the last five years, the five years of the Sixth Plan, the growth rate has been above 5 per cent which is very good performance. What we must not forget, however, is that the best thing that can happen to a five-year plan is for its base period to do very badly. That takes care of many targets in a very simple way. This is what did happen partly this time because the base year performance of this five-year plan was particularly bad.

Recently there has been a fairly detailed study by the National Council of Applied Economic Research (NCAER) and they have come to the conclusion that there was a break around 1972–3 which divides India's growth experience. It was 3.5 per cent before this time and after that it has been around 4.1 per cent, that is, there has been a small but significant change. I shall nevertheless argue that there are several reasons for dissatisfaction with our performance thus far. Let me begin by disposing off a relatively minor point. The Gini-coefficient cropped up quite a few times in today's discussion. The general feeling was that the Gini-coefficient has either marginally improved or it has remained more or less the same. So inequality, it seems, has not increased in India. But what we must appreciate is that there are two kinds of Gini-coefficients which we can compute. There is the white Gini-coefficient and there is the grey one. The white Gini-coefficient is one which takes into account only the white income in the country; and we shall call a Gini-coefficient grey if it takes into account both the white and black incomes. Now, while there is much controversy about the extent of black money in the economy, there is considerable consensus about its positive growth. Virtually all statistics show that black income has gone up steadily over the last twenty years. It is also quite clear that black income accrues to a fairly high-income group. These two facts imply that the grey Gini-coefficient would show a worsening *vis-à-vis* the white one. Since the white Gini-coefficient has remained constant or *marginally* improved it is likely that the grey Gini, which is the real Gini-coefficient in the country, has deteriorated.

I shall not go into statistics about poverty, but instead use the same kind of information that Professor Khusro has used in his paper. If you look at poverty across the country it is not clear where the proverbial silver lining is. While it is true that we have done well compared to the situation that prevailed thirty years ago, the overall picture is still pretty bleak. Moreover, if we broaden our view from economic poverty to standards of living and basic needs in general, we can look at several indicators. An important one is infant mortality; and, judging by this, India's performance is quite disappointing. Our infant mortality is 125, which means that out of one thousand live births, 125 die in the first year. How does it compare with developed countries? In most developed countries the infant mortality rate is roughly of the order of 8 to 12. In Japan it is about 9, in England it is about 8.

One may point out that India is a poor country and we cannot really provide health facilities of a high order. But we can think of other poor countries which have performed well in terms of basic needs. Prominent examples include Sri Lanka, Cuba and Costa Rica. Looking at Sri Lanka's health statistics, one finds that infant mortality is around 37. So India's 125 cannot be explained in terms of income and poverty. This is a kind of characteristic which can be improved even in a poor country. In fact, one does not have to go outside India to find examples. Even within India, Kerala has statistics which rival advanced countries, and Kerala is still a poor state. Turning to life expectancy, we find that in India life expectancy at birth is 52 whereas in an advanced country it is around 75. Again Sri Lanka with life expectancy at 66 is an 'outlier'. So there is no reason for complacency in India.

I now want to look at another worrying feature of our economy's development experience. This is the experience of the late seventies. In the early seventies, it was believed that for a country to take off there were a couple of well-defined things that it needed. Of these, a high savings rate was considered crucial. We were told that a savings rate of 15 per cent or above is very good. Currently, India saves around 20 per cent of her income.

Also important for growth is comfortable foreign exchange reserves. In the early seventies our foreign exchange position was very poor. It was about Rs 600 crores in 1973–4. Then it started doubling each year for a couple of years and was fairly comfortable by Indian standards by the late seventies.

Finally, the food stock position was very heartening in the late seventies. The Government held foodgrain stocks of the order of 15 million tonnes. So, in terms of these crucial parameters we were doing well. These, however, are all instruments. We must realize that food stocks with the Government is not something which the people eat, the savings rate is not something which you wear and one cannot sleep under the roof of foreign exchange. These are just the instruments, which have to be translated to basic needs. That did not happen in India. This is a puzzle not only about the Indian performance but in what it says about economic theory and development economics.

What had gone wrong? I cannot pretend to know the answer, but one factor which must have been prominent is the infrastructural bottlenecks which plagued the Indian economy in the late seventies. Acute power shortages were occurring all over India. Railway freight carrying had reached a low level. Coal production was short. There was also shortage in cement and steel. So, on several infrastructural fronts we were doing badly. Infrastructural bottlenecks are especially problematic because they feed on one another. If the railways start doing badly, then coal does not get transported from the pithead to where it is needed. When coal is not taken to where it is needed, electricity generation suffers. If electricity and coal movement suffer, then the railway performs poorly and the chain is complete.

Turning to present times we find that once again we are moving towards a similar situation. Our savings rate is a comfortable 23 per cent or 24 per cent. The foodgrain position is better than ever been before. Only the foreign exchange position is not that good. All this indicates a scope for faster development.

We should study the late seventies situation and try to avoid errors this time. It is quite clear that we have to be well prepared with infrastructure and the kinds of things which the public sector provides the Indian economy if we are to make the most of this opportunity.

How has our recent policy-making responded to this challenge? I analyse this by examining the most important of the major policy instruments that we have in the country: the Union Budget.

II

From the point of view of equity and poverty-removal this year's Budget offers little.[1] The elitist bias of the Budget is transparent when one looks at the huge cut in the wealth tax (the maximum marginal rate being reduced from 5 per cent to 2 per cent) and the total abolition of estate duty. It has been argued that estate duty nets in very little anyway. This is a poor argument because for any revenue or tax we could define categories sufficiently finely, e.g., instead of talking of excise duty, we could talk of excise duty from item A, excise duty from item B, etc., so that from each item revenue collection is small. If for this reason it is abolished, we could soon have no

---

[1] Parts of the discussion that follow here were published in *Economic and Political Weekly* (vol. 20, 20 April 1985) under the title 'India's Fiscal Policy: Lobbies and Acquiescence'.

revenues! Moreover the purpose of estate duty is not just revenue collection but equity as well; so that human beings start off life a little less unequally. Similar arguments apply to the wealth tax.

The Budget's direct contribution to anti-poverty programmes is small. The outlay for the National Rural Employment Programme (earlier known as Food For Work), for instance, is Rs 230 crores, that is, the same amount as was allocated last year. In fact, the total amount of all outlay for poverty alleviation and rural employment programmes will be slightly smaller than in 1984–5. Now, there are certain kinds of outlays which, because of built-in factors, go up if prices rise. Poverty programmes are not like that. Hence, every bit of inflation that occurs will cut into the 'real' outlay for poverty programmes. It is therefore likely that these special programmes, which on most normative grounds ought to be stepped up substantially, will stand diminished. It is this, coupled with the wide concessions to the urban rich, which makes the Budget a biased one.

Not just with respect to these programmes, but in many ways the Budget collides head-on with the 'Approach to the Seventh Five Year Plan' (henceforth, *Approach*). This is particularly bewildering given that this is the first Budget during this plan period. First of all, the Plan outlay in this Budget is small, only 6.5 per cent higher than the outlay for 1984–5, which means that even a normal round of inflation would render this year's outlay smaller than last year's in real terms.

Consider the small allocation for employment creation and poverty removal. One way of defending this is to argue that this year's Budget will help growth (as a matter of fact I do believe it will) and this will have a trickle-down effect. The validity of the 'trickle-down' theory is doubtful but it is entirely possible that those who drafted this Budget genuinely adhere to it. What is curious is the way it contradicts the objectives as set out in the *Approach* (p. 1): 'There must be a sharper focus on employment and poverty alleviation. Instead of relying on general economic growth for raising employment opportunities, it is necessary to treat employment as a direct focal point of policy.'

Regarding the size of allocation for poverty removal and

employment programmes, this is what the *Approach* (p. 5) has to say: 'The Sixth Plan envisaged the reduction of the percentage of people below the poverty line to less than 10 by 1994–5. The attainment of this goal will require a larger investment in the programmes aimed at giving self-employment and wage-employment to the poorer sections of the community'.

One reason which is being cited for the pruning, in real terms, of the NREP is that this project has not been running smoothly and there has been misappropriation of funds. So instead of rectifying these problems the Budget gives in to these forces of misappropriation and cuts down allocation. Also, in case there are difficulties with a particular programme, we should think of alternative methods of subsidizing the poor and creating jobs, instead of citing these difficulties and promptly switching these funds over all the way to the other extreme—giving tax concessions to the rich.

This is unfortunate because this Government, unlike its predecessors, seems serious about cutting down corruption and has taken some laudable steps in the first few months of its governance. Its fiscal policy, as revealed in this maiden Budget, however, lacks courage as it merely appeases the powerful urban lobbies. The sharp lowering of wealth tax and estate duty is a clear case of acquiscence in the face of elitist compulsions. Income tax rates, it has been alleged, have been lowered to curb black money. But there is no evidence that lower rates lead to better compliance, excepting in a purely definitional sense. That is, even if a person has the same amount of undisclosed income, he will have less black money because the tax burden is now smaller.

There are two ways of improving law abidance: (i) better policing and (ii) changing the law to accommodate what is happening anyway. There are indeed situations where option (ii) plays a role but if a government relies on it too often, as this Budget does, it would be like the commands of the king in Saint Exupery's 'Little Prince' (chapter X):

'May I sit down?' came a timid enquiry from the little prince.
'I order you to do so', the king answered. . . .
'Sire', he said to him, 'I beg that you will excuse my asking you a question . . .'

'I order you to ask me a question', the king hastened to assure him.

And when asked to display his powers by ordering a sunset, the king boasted that he could do it but there was a right time for such things and leafing through a bulky almanac, he added:

'That will be about-about-that will be this evening about twenty minutes to eight. And you will see how well I am obeyed!'

# Key Components of the Strategy of Growth in India

RANJIT SAU

India has just entered the period of the Seventh Five Year Plan. The plan itself is in the process of finalization. The basic strategy of development is being worked out. An intense debate is going on in respect of vital matters such as the means of generating employment opportunities, the role of imports, the place of small-scale enterprises, the way to mobilize resources, and so on. All this reminds us of those hectic days in the mid-fifties when the Second Five Year Plan was being formulated in the midst of great enthusiasm, expectations, and challenges. After a long pause of scepticism and disillusionment there is again an air of great concern and determination for development planning.

There are several areas which cry out for immediate action. India is in the grip of a prolonged *power-famine*. The loss of output, employment, and foreign exchange due to the shortage of electricity is colossal. Perhaps the problem deserves to be handled on 'war footing'. The poor state of Indian railways, burdened with old rails and rusting wagons as it is, cannot escape anybody's attention. Telephones do not work; the agony turns into a comic relief when we are advised by a minister to return the instrument if we do not like to have an all-too-frequently dead receiver. The 'supply-side' bottleneck, in this sense, has been very severe. What is worse is the stoic attitude to it; we seem to have resigned to all this in a sublime philosophical mood.

In addition to this sort of urgent and glaring issues there is another class which also merits immediate consideration. The government has to raise revenue; procurement prices of wheat and rice have to be fixed; trade policy for the next year has to be announced and so on. Such matters involve a wider policy perspective and a longer time horizon in comparison with the former items. And then there is a third level at which dwell more fundamental and strategic concerns of development planning that define the broad contours within which other policy decisions are taken. This paper deals with four specific elements of growth strategy falling in this category. These are as follows:

*i.* district-wise industrialization—the policy of 'each district to have at least one major industry';
*ii.* modernization and technological advancement throughout the economy;
*iii.* greater resort to imports as a means of creating a competitive environment; and
*iv.* regeneration and optimal utilization of land resources.

We have gathered these four parts from the current series of policy statements by the Government of India. They seem to constitute the core of the growth strategy that is emerging unmistakably at the hand of the young Prime Minister. They must be a great source of delightful challenges to economists, for these propositions have profound theoretical connotations apart from their enormous practical significance.

### State Public Sector

A while ago, in a state assembly election campaign the Prime Minister reportedly announced a new policy of decentralized industrialization in the shape of 'each district to have at least one major industry'. So far, in the formulation of regional development plans considerable stress has been put on the local resource-based industrial projects. It has been, in essence, a Hecksher-Ohlin type of comparative-advantage-oriented policy of 'export' promotion across regions, tempered at the margin, by a measure of freight and price equalization of a few critical inputs like coal and steel. As a result, regional concentration of industries has been accentuated, and some areas have suffered industrial decay or almost complete deprivation. All this is now going to be modified, as the Prime Minister's announcement indicates, by an approach that would locate at least one *major* industry in each district. In a sense, the new thrust would rely on regional 'import substitution' where the scope for 'export promotion' on the basis of local resource endowment is limited. This, we believe, is a correct step in the present juncture, for the following reasons.

Contrary to the 'vicious circle of poverty' thesis of Nurkse, the propensity to save is, historically, found to be stronger than the available inducement to invest. As Keynes (1936: 347–8) puts it:

> There has been a chronic tendency throughout human history for the propensity to save to be stronger than the inducement to invest. The weakness of the inducement to invest has been at all times the key to the economic problem. The desire of the individual to augment his personal wealth by abstaining from consumption has usually been stronger than the inducement to the entrepreneur to augment the national wealth by employing labour on the construction of durable assets.

In India, too, one can argue, the *nouveau riche* farmers and several others have gathered a good bit of saving that is waiting, scattered over thousands of towns and villages all over the country, for a catalyst to show the path toward productive investment. If at least one major industry is set up in each and every district it would certainly create a conducive environment for small potential capitalists to come forward with their accumulated funds for creation of durable assets and employment opportunities.

There is at least one more justification for the policy of 'each district to have at least one major industry' The rural–urban hiatus in terms of per capita income and standard of living is well known. Agriculture alone cannot provide, beyond a point, enough scope for investment and greater earnings. Now there are two ways of improving rural income under such circumstances: either move the terms of trade in favour of agriculture, or set up new industries in rural areas (that would also, incidentally, reduce or avoid the costs of urbanization and migration). It is said that South Korea, for example, has adopted the former course, while Taiwan has opted for the latter (Scitovsky 1984). Since continuous raising of agricultural prices or subsidization would have many unwelcome consequences, it would be a better idea to set up industrial projects in every district to create additional avenues for income and employment in towns and villages. No doubt, this proposal may, on occasions, militate against the benefits that usually accrue from economies of scale. It is a question of clearly perceiving the trade-off, and weighing the pros and cons. On the whole, the strategy of *regional import substitution*, at least for a while, may pay off, considering the overall situation of the country at the moment.

But who will take the initiative in setting up at least one *major* industry in each district? In the given circumstances it appears only the public sector can shoulder this responsibility. In line with the Prime Minister's policy we believe that a similar stand should be taken with regard to *small* and *medium* industries as well. State governments may be called upon to launch a *State Public Sector* for this purpose. In India there is a sort of division of labour between the Centre and the States: the Centre is mainly responsible for industrial plan projects, while most of the agricultural plan projects fall in the purview of States. Perhaps the time has come for the State governments to be assigned a more active role in the sphere of industrialization—specifically in respect of small and medium industries,[1] while

---

[1] It may be mentioned that in a memorandum dated 24 January 1984, submitted to the Minister of Finance, Government of India, we suggested a similar policy. The memorandum was a follow-up note at the minister's suggestion after a meeting with him at his invitation. It is reproduced below in part for it has certain relevance now.

The rate of saving in India is not too low; but investment seems to be lagging behind. To increase the growth rate of the economy, the saving has to be stepped up, and the savings must be transformed into productive investment.

Much of the savings in India originate in the household sector, and remain scattered throughout the country. Financial institutions like commercial banks and the LIC mobilize part of the savings for capital formation. Still there remains a sizable part of the savings that has to be activated into productive investment. In recent years small and medium scale industrial units have multiplied in number; but most of them are concentrated in and around urban areas. Besides, their financial performance seems to indicate a lack of viability and stability in many cases. The extent and frequency of fluctuation in the Indian economy has increased,

the conventional *public sector* continues to be in charge of relatively large industrial projects in the plan.

### Forward-Biased Labour Intensity

The official call for rapid modernization and technological advancement in industry, agriculture, trade and commerce raises the dilemma that once perturbed David Ricardo, among others, when he saw, about two centuries ago, the arrival of newly invested machines in the course of industrial revolution in Britain having negative impacts on employment.[2] The

---

and with it the position of the smaller units has become all the more vulnerable.

In order to utilize the investment potentials that are found in household savings in thousands of villages around the country the government may consider creating an appropriate environment which would stimulate small potential entrepreneurs to undertake industrial projects. These entrepreneurs suffer from what may be called an *isolation paradox*. In isolation they do not dare invest their funds in industrial activities which have some risks at least initially. If the government sets up some model industrial units, I believe it would create a conducive environment for potential entrepreneurs to come forward.

I therefore propose that the public sector should, on its own initiative, take up a programme of establishing *at least one medium or small scale industrial unit in every district every year*, so that in five years there would be at least five such units in each district of India. This would have a catalytic effect, and rural entrepreneurs would come forward with their savings for investment in industrial projects, which should be supported by financial assistance through term lending institutions.

For administrative purposes this proposed public sector in small and medium scale industrial enterprises may be kept under the jurisdiction of state governments. The financial and other implications of the proposed *State Public Sector* in small and medium scale industries can be worked out, once the basic approach is found worthwhile. It is believed it would ensure rapid economic growth by balancing investment with savings, increase industrial production and rural educated employment, facilitate regional balance, and, on the whole, create a favourable atmosphere for rural transformation. (Emphasis in the original.)

We mooted this proposal earlier in a note privately circulated in 1978, and also orally presented it later in a Seminar in Lucknow.

[2] Throughout the nineteenth century the relation between the application of modern machines and the volume of employment was a subject of

classical Ricardo-machinery-effect has become a live issue in India today. It is a genuine problem at the aggregative level, and more so at the micro level. However, it appears this negative effect can be neutralized, or its duration shortened, by a suitable choice of technology and industrial mix. Below we suggest an approach in this connection, which may be called the strategy of *forward-biased labour* intensity, in the absence of a more appropriate name.

Consider a simple industrial project. It takes a certain amount of time for its construction works; and then it is operated at a fixed level with the gross output of one unit per period. Let the life-span of the project be infinity, for the sake of simplifying the algebra. For further simplification suppose the construction period is one period. If $a$ is the input necessary for construction, $b$ the input per period of operation, $w$ the price of input in terms of the output, and $r$ the internal rate of return, then we get:

$$-a\,w + (1 - bw)/r = 0$$
$$\text{or } 1/w = b + a\,r \tag{1}$$

we can think of $a$ and $b$ as inputs of labour in the main, and, so, $w$ is the wage rate measured in terms of the output of the project. Equation (1) gives an upward-sloping straightline, such as $CC$ in Fig. 1 (Hicks 1973: 81–8).

Now, take an alternative project with lower capital cost, $a'$, but higher operating cost, $b'$, represented by $C'C'$ in Fig. 1. There is one rate of interest, $r$, at which both the projects are equally

---

heated exchange. It was known as the Compensation Controversy. David Ricardo startled and annoyed many of his friends by his conclusion that machines destroyed jobs in the short run, in particular. John Stuart Mill dismissed the so-called Ricardo effect as rare in practice, or too feeble in magnitude soon to be swamped by the positive impacts of faster capital formation. By contrast, Marx saw in machines the seeds of the 'reserve army of labour', that was supposed to swell in ranks over time (Hicks 1977: 184–90).

After a long silence in the literature the question was re-opened systematically by John Hicks in 1932 and received at that time an untenable formulation at his hand. Subsequently, Joan Robinson, Paul Samuelson, Charles Kennedy, and again John Hicks, among others, have dealt with it. The topic also appeared, in a big way, in the debate on the choice of technique in development planning.

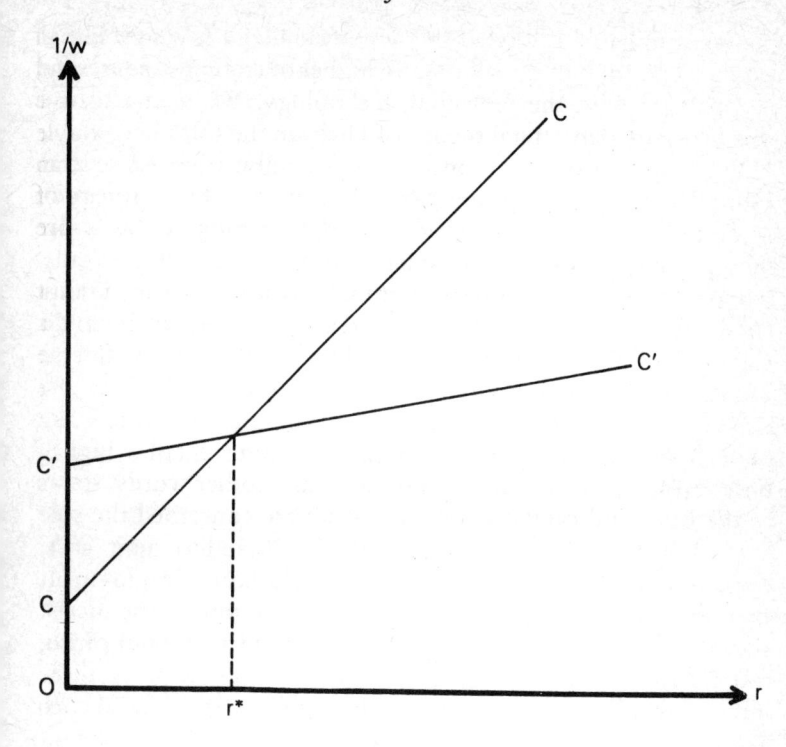

*Figure 1*

worthwhile; but at higher interest rates the latter project is preferable. To look at it another way, there is one wage rate at which both projects are equivalent. At lower wage rates the latter project, represented by $C'C'$, is preferable. From this it may be argued that so long as the wage rate is 'low' the projects with lower initial capital cost, but inevitably higher operating cost, are to be preferred to those alternatives which have the opposite time profile of costs (high capital cost, low operating cost).

Hicks (1973: 97–9; 1977: 184–90) contends that the negative Ricardo-effect is particularly strong in those cases where the new technology incurs heavy initial capital expenditures, though it saves on the operating costs as the redeeming feature (Hicks calls it a 'forward-biased' technological progress). The negative Ricardo-machinery-effect on employment is, of course, mitigated if instead the new technology saves on initial capital cost, though it may require higher operating expenses, in comparison with the prevailing technology. We intend to use this neo-Austrian capital theory of Hicks in the following way.

We conceive of the economy as a combination of several *vertically integrated* production processes. The Ricardo-machinery-effect can be met if the new technology, that is, the new production process considered in its entirety of vertically integrated form, economizes on initial investment costs. Translated into more operational terms and across industries, it would mean that the new technology would have little or no adverse impact on total employment in the economy if *the basic and capital goods* industries succeed in reducing unit cost in the wake of technological change even though it might entail a higher unit cost in the later 'stage' of production. In other words, so far as the basic and capital goods industries are concerned the sole aim of technological change would be to reduce unit cost, regardless of the direct effect on the volume of employment therein. Industries like steel, power, railways, mines, chemicals, should go for cost-reducing modern technology without caring too much for direct labour absorption. Since most of these industries fall in the domain of the public sector the above-mentioned principle is of special relevance to the government, busy as it is now with the drafting of the Seventh Five Year Plan. The principle also makes sense in the framework of Sraffa's system, where the rate of profit is determined by the condition of production in the 'basic' industries only.

The scope for labour absorption should be sought, according to this theory, in the technology frontier pertaining to the non-basic industries such as non-essential consumer goods, which come in the later stage of production. It is in this sense that we call it a strategy of *forward-biased labour intensity*.[3]

[3] In his Parliament speech the Prime Minister is reported to have said: 'Industry is not necessarily the best place for employment. Sometimes, it is the most inefficient place for employment' (*The Telegraph*, Calcutta, 16 March 1985). In an interview he had said: 'Jobs today are not available in industry. . . . We need to reorient, and to generate employment where it is in today's world in services' (*Sunday*, Calcutta, 10–16 March 1985). It is not clear to us what the Prime Minister exactly intends to convey through this statement, and where precisely he draws the line between industry and

## Growth is Beautiful

The renewed enthusiasm for opening up the Indian market all the more to the opportunities and tensions of the world economy outside constitutes another major element in the evolving growth strategy. It is motivated, in part, by a widespread feeling that India's industries have enjoyed the benefits of a sheltered market, perhaps a bit too long. It is time that they ceased to be treated as infants, and they strived to earn their legitimate place in the world map.

Lack of competition, no doubt, has given India's industries a privilege to be careless about cost and efficiency. There are many instances where with little effort and expense a sizeable amount of cost saving can be effected through replacement of worn-out machinery, recycling of wastes and by-products, and economic use of utilities like water and power. But now the industry simply does not care, presumably because there is practically no competitive threat (Sau 1984). Liberalization of imports is certainly one of the ways to make them wake up. Furthermore, it is pointless to try to reinvent the wheel when advanced technology is available in the world market, and can be imported, at a price. The question one can ask here with respect to the matter of competition at home is: is the greater and easier flow of imports the only channel of generating a competitive atmosphere in India's industry? Can a competitive spirit be generated from within?

Analysing the financial data of public limited companies during the three decade period, 1950-80, it is found that small companies (as per the definition of the Reserve Bank of India) are way behind the medium and large ones in terms of both the average rate of profit and its stability over time, as shown in Fig. 2. It appears there is a wide gulf between small and big companies in India. There is, of course, no one-to-one correspondence between the size of companies and the 'size' of the owner capitalists; quite a few small companies, for instance,

---

services. But if he means that the basic and key industries should be spared of the special burden of job creation and that employment opportunities should be sought rather in downstream projects, the thesis can perhaps be justified in the light of the neo-Austrian capital theory enunciated above.

[Figure: rate of profit (%) vs Years, showing Large companies, Medium and large companies, and Small companies curves]

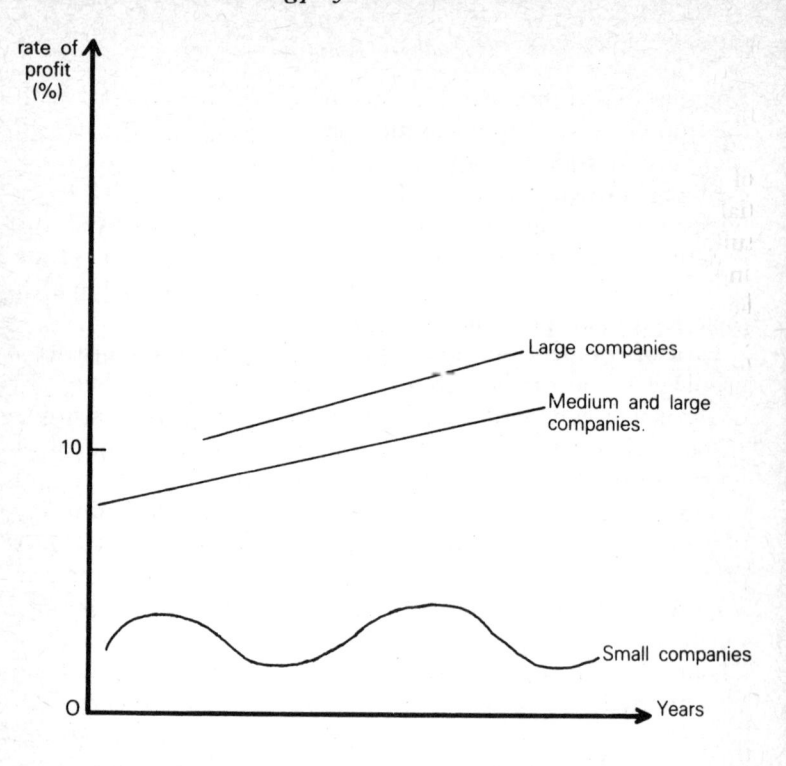

*Figure 2*

are presumably *benami* possessions of large monopolists. Yet the fact remains that, first, small capitalists, by definition, can own only relatively small companies, and second, the prospect for graduation of a small company into a medium and large one, as a rule, remains rather bleak, given the vast distance of profitability and security. To put it differently, in India there is little scope for upward *mobility* of small capitalists, unlike in countries such as Britain, Germany and Russia during the corresponding stage in their history. Small capitalists in India do not stand up as a potential threat to bigger capitalists who are at present operating in an oligopolistic market where collusion is easy, and manipulation of strings with the government bureaucracy is frequently heard of. This milieu vitiates the ambitions of small capitalists; what is more, it discourages landlords and capitalist farmers from joining the ranks of industrial capitalists. The structure of capitalist class in India reproduces itself with deep chasm within; it is not conducive to the capitalist transition of the Indian economy.

In some parts of the country agriculture has reached a plateau of prosperity. The farmers have meanwhile gathered a substantial amount of investible resources; but they are not finding suitable outlets. Small enterprises are inadequately profitable and highly risky as shown in Fig. 2; and hence rich farmers hesitate to invest their funds in those industrial ventures that are characteristically not promising in the long run. The net result is frustration in the wake of success in what may be called 'primitive accumulation' in the sense of Marx. Tensions which are being reported from several corners of the country are of two types: some are the after-effects of a successful green revolution in agriculture, while others are the consequences of underdevelopment that accompanies capitalist development in a country. The new scheme of at least one major industry in each district is likely to have some beneficial impact in this context.

One has to distinguish between the following: (a) the small-scale sector, (b) a small-scale industry, (c) a small-scale enterprise, and (d) a small entrepreneur. An entrepreneur with modest resources deserves support and incentive by all means so that he can launch and operate an industrial unit. But it should not be made attractive for him to stay small all his life. Small capitalists should be given an initial impetus, but they should be encouraged to grow to reap the benefits of large scale production in due course. Only then a spirit of competition and an urge to grow would permeate the entire economy. The threat of imports would then work as only an additional reason for competitive behaviour. By contrast, in the absence of an *internal* pressure and inducement for industry to improve efficiency and productivity, the external threat of easier imports may only lead to a massive uprooting of India's industry, and hence it would be self-defeating.

*Vanishing Frontier Lands*

In an address to the nation broadcast on radio and television on 5 January 1985, the Prime Minister announced the intention to set up a Wasteland Development Corporation charged with

## TABLE 1
### Pattern of Land Utilization in India
(Million hectares)

| Year | Total reported area | Forests | Not available for cultivation | Permanent pastures and others grazing lands | Land under miscellaneous tree crops (not included in col. 10) | Culturable waste land | Fallow land — Current fallows | Fallow land — Others | Net area sown |
|---|---|---|---|---|---|---|---|---|---|
| 1 | 2 | 3 | 4 | 5 | 6 | 7 | 8 | 9 | 10 |
| 1950 | 284.3 | 40.5 | 47.5 | 6.7 | 19.8 | 22.9 | 10.7 | 17.4 | 118.7 |
| 1960 | 298.5 | 54.1 | 50.8 | 14.0 | 4.5 | 19.2 | 11.6 | 11.2 | 113.2 |
| 1965 | 305.5 | 61.5 | 49.5 | 14.8 | 4.1 | 17.0 | 13.2 | 9.3 | 136.2 |
| 1975 | 304.5 | 66.9 | 39.5 | 12.6 | 4.0 | 17.4 | 12.5 | 9.5 | 142.2 |

*Notes on columns:*

1. Crop-year beginning July.
3. Includes area actually forested or lands classed or administered as forests under any legal enactment dealing with forests whether wooded or maintained as potential forest land.

4. The land which is absolutely barren or uncultivable or covered by buildings, waters, roads, railways, mountains, deserts, or otherwise appropriated for non-agricultural purposes.
5. Cover all grazing lands whether they are permanent pastures or meadows or not, and village common and grazing lands within forest areas.
6. Includes all cultivable land, not included under area sown, but put to some agricultural use.
7. Includes all lands available for cultivation but not taken up for cultivation, or taken up for cultivation once but not cultivated during the year and the last five years or more in succession.
8. Fallow land implies all lands which were taken up for cultivation but are temporarily out of cultivation for a period not less than one year and not more than five years. Lands lying fallow for a period of one year are included in this column; fallow for more than one year is included in col. (9).

Source: Government of India, *Statistical Abstract*, 1979, pp. 40–4.

the task of reclaiming five million hectares a year for cultivation of fodder, fuel-wood, and trees. He also mentioned a proposal to appoint a high-power Central Ganga Authority which would cleanse the much-polluted riverine system. Since then the Corporation and the Authority have been constituted. It is, indeed, a momentous step in the right direction. Natural resources of a country like India urgently require revitalization and optimum utilization. Land resources, in fact, have been exploited for centuries without much care or consideration for overall national interests. These precious resources are at some places over-exploited to the point of exhaustion, at others inoptimally under-utilized.[4] India, with her 700 million population, growing to reach the mark of billion soon, can ill afford the luxury of plundering or wasting the veritable gifts of nature. Dynamically efficient revitalization and exploitation of land resources must be a prime ingredient of India's development strategy.

The ancient civilization of India, as recorded in the Vedas, Upanishads, and Puranas, found its cradle in forests, valleys, hills and mountains. The march of time has seen drastic alterations in India's topography (Habib 1982; Sen 1955). The pattern of land utilization in the contemporary period, as given in Table 1, col. 4, shows how the area under human habitation and natural barriers like mountains and waters is getting eroded, to make room, presumably, for cultivation (col. 10). Forest land (col. 3) is increasing, at least on paper; but there are grave doubts about the meaning of this particular piece of statistics. It is widely held that forests are being denuded and encroached upon remorselessly. In any case, forest land in India is considered grossly inadequate for ecological equilibrium, and too little by international standards. The remaining areas, enumerated in cols. 5 to 9, are of a type that merits special attention here. The Waste Land Development Corporation would presumably be concerned with the land as of col. 7 only.

[4] Under-utilization of agricultural land, in particular, has been noted long ago. In a sense, there is an 'excess capacity' of cultivable land in India which could be multiple cropped to augment output (Sau 1973: 58–9). However, straining the land too much, we must not forget, it could, in some conditions, produce serious ecological imbalance (Jodha 1980).

But it may be reasoned that the entire spectrum of non-cultivated land, shown under cols. 5 to 9, merits comprehensive planning. It has, by and large, the potentiality of being harnessed either for raising forests or for cultivation of fodder and fuel-wood or some such useful, though inferior, crop. It is, of course, a matter of technology; but hardly can it be left to technologists alone. For there is a fundamental principle of economics in it.

Domestic as well as international forces have bearing upon the actual pattern of land utilization in a country (Feder 1979). For an illustrative exercise of *optimal* utilization of land, particularly of the 'marginal land', let us classify the total area under the following four heads:

1. Farm (col. 10 in Table 1),
2. Forest (col. 3),
3. 'Frontier lands' (cols. 5 to 9), and
4. Others (col. 4).

We introduce the expansion 'frontier lands' with the implicit suggestion that such land resources are being currently left more or less inactive, while they may be amenable to appropriate productive use, even within the limits of prevailing technology. These lands are scattered all over the country. As Table 1, cols. 5 to 9 have it, frontier lands are a depleting category in India; the figures (in million hectares) are as follows:

| | | |
|---|---|---|
| 1950 | ... | 77.5 |
| 1960 | ... | 60.0 |
| 1965 | ... | 58.4 |
| 1975 | ... | 56.0 |

The downward trend lends evidence to the hypothesis that much of it, if not all, has productive potentiality, albeit meagre in comparison with some other types of land.

The analytical problem that we pose for the economist is this. Suppose farms produce wheat; forests, trees; and the frontier lands can be developed to produce fodder and fuel-wood. Total land under these three categories is given. Land is obviously heterogeneous. How should the total area be allocated among the crops? This is a standard exercise in elementary economics. We can further simplify it. We know *a priori* that the existing area under forest is inadequate for the country, and that the land on which it stands has the comparative advantage in forestry than in other alternative crops. That is to say, we can only further add to the forest area, not subtract from it. A similar assumption is made for the *existing* farm land. Now, suppose we count fodder as an 'inferior' variety of wheat, and fuel-wood as an 'inferior' variety of tree. The agenda is then reduced to that of an optimal allocation only of the given 'frontier lands' between farm and forest. In that case, a farm produces wheat or fodder; and a forest, tree or fuel–wood. We shall proceed with this simplified framework.

The Wasteland Development Corporation, which we imagine is going to have an assignment vital for the nation, would face an analogous problem. Substantial amounts of funds are to be spent on this account over the years. And its efforts would have a tremendous bearing upon the country's agriculture in particular, and villages in general. Actually the matter is somewhat more complex. For there are external economies and a symbiotic bond between farms and forests. Traditional economics of resource allocation is doubly handicapped in this situation. First, it has an inherent bias, in a situation of high interest rate, against certain kinds of projects. Second, it is, as such, unaccustomed to the kind of relationship that prevails between farms and forests. Should the conventional methods be uncritically applied here, I am afraid, this venture would become crippled from the very start. Below, we shall present an improvised model for programme assessment that meets part of the difficulties inherent under the given circumstances.

To fix our ideas a little more concretely, let the 'frontier lands' be rounded off at 60 million hectares. How much of it should be converted into forest, and how much into farm—both inevitably of 'inferior' type? This is the question. Keeping in view the figures of Table 1 we might also say that at the moment forests cover another 60 million hectares, and farms 140 million hectares. It is a game of distributing 60 million hectares only, between two claimants—farm and forest.

Austrian capital theorists have been very fond of raising trees in their models,[5] which clearly demonstrate that turning a

---

[5] For the economics of forestry, see Dasgupta 1982: 178–92; Samuelson

wasteland into a forest would be a fairly time-consuming affair with a sizeable capital cost. Also the Austrian theories are apt to point out that there is little or no operating cost in this enterprise. High initial investment and low recurring cost are the characteristic features of forestry, while a project for raising fodder on the erstwhile wasteland would have opposite features, relatively moderate capital expenditure and bigger annual operating costs. If the time horizon of the planner is rather short the dice, therefore, gets loaded against forestation right from the beginning.

What is more, a high interest rate is unfavourable to forestry on the present value criterion. We can illustrate the point with reference to Fig. 1. A forestation project requires a heavy initial capital cost over a rather long period and only a moderate operating cost per year thereafter. So we can associate $CC$ with an aforestation project, $C'C'$ with a fodder project as an alternative to it. Now, interest rate being rather high in the country, the long-gestation capital-intensive forestation project will evidently fail the test of present value criterion in comparison with the short-gestation fodder project.

## Two Functions

We can put the question in another analytical box. Let the total area under farm, frontier lands, and forests be given. Suppose we can arrange the land into several plots in a descending order of productivity with respect to the farm product; for simplicity it is assumed that the same ranking holds, now in the reverse order, with reference to forest product. The problem is to allocate the frontier lands between farm and forest, so that fodder and fuel-wood can be raised in these presently inactive areas.

In Fig. 3, $OO'$ is the total land duly arranged. At the moment, $OF$ is under farm, $O'G$ under forest, and the remaining $FG$ is what we have called frontier land, that is to be given over to fodder and fuel-wood cultivation. $AA$ and $BB$ are productivity curves respectively of farming and forestry,

1937; 1976. For location theory of the pioneer, von Thunen, see Samuelson 1983.

*Figure 3*

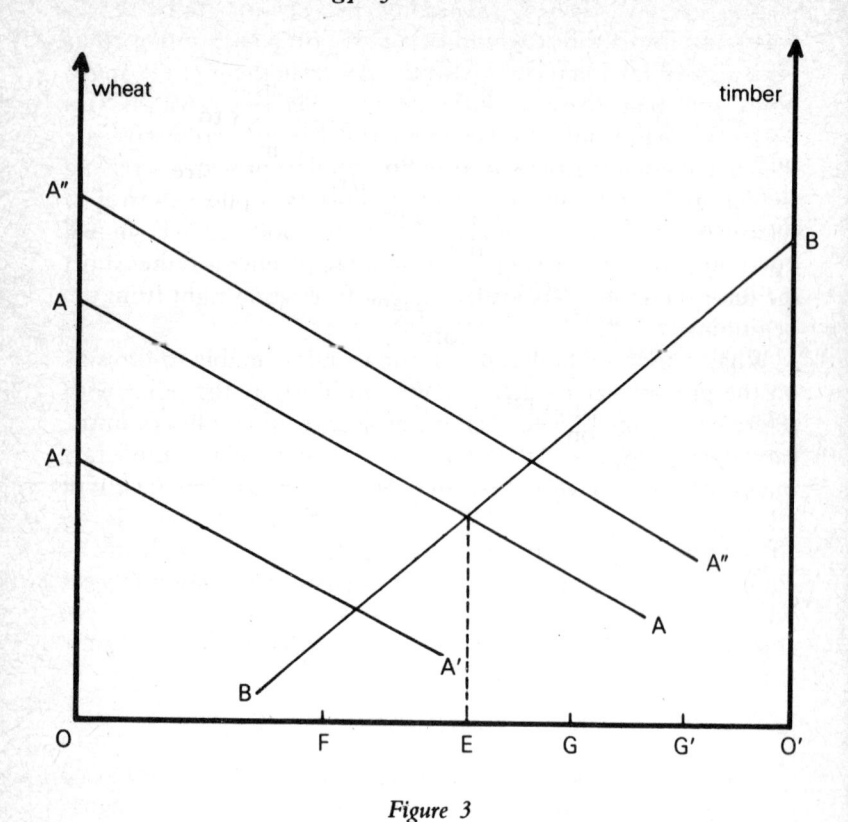

where fodder and fuel-wood are treated as inferior varieties of wheat and timber. Evidently, output would be maximized if *FE* is absorbed as farms and *EG* as forests.

Forests have both *protective* as well as *productive* functions. From both these points of view a stage has come for India when forests and agriculture are no longer competitive but primarily complementary (Sen 1955: 533). That is to say, farm productivity in India has now come to depend upon the existing volume of forest resources which determine rainfall, soil moisture and other ecological qualities. This fact can be taken note of by making the curve of farm productivity in Fig. 3 sensitive to the land under forests. *AA* is the farm productivity curve when the forest land is given by $O'E$. We can draw such curves for alternative volumes of forest land. Suppose $A'A'$ is such a curve with forest land of $O'G'$, and it shifts to $A''A''$ if forest land raises to $O'F$. The allocation problem can be solved, after several interations, with standard economic tools. From Fig. 3 it is easy to construct a transformation curve between wheat (including fodder) and timber (including fuel-wood) as shown in Fig. 4. Given the relative prices of wheat, fodder, fuel-wood and timber, the equilibrium would be reached at a point like $M$ where the slope of the tangent reflects the given configuration of relative prices.

Can the method of finding the solution under such circumstances be operationalized? Can it be made effective through a series of parameters that are to be handed down to planners and programme evaluators? The concept of production function, we know, has found a prominent place in the literature on natural

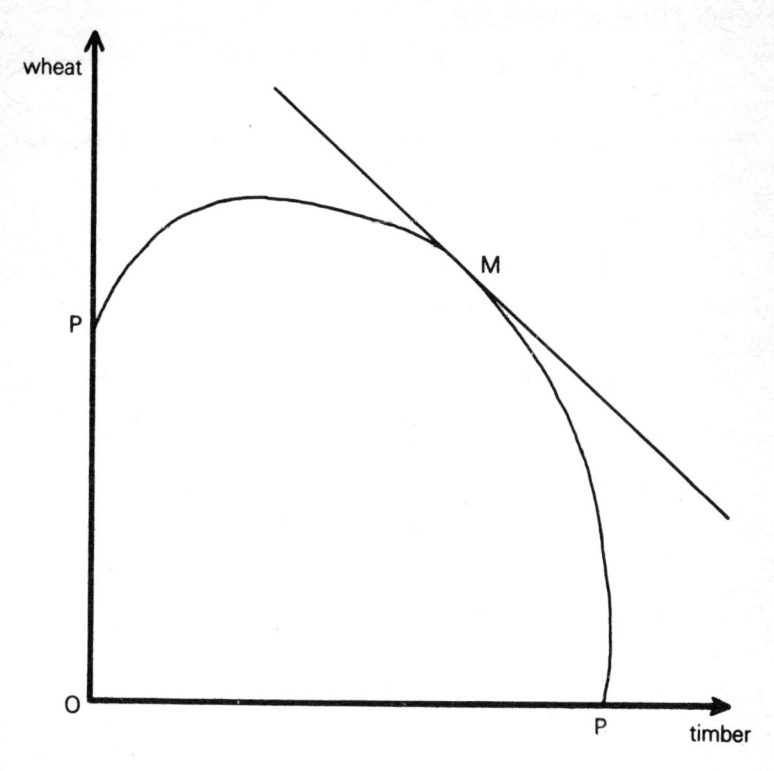

*Figure 4*

resource management and control.[6] As a tentative approach to theoretically capture the external economies emanating from forests and reaching into agricultural fields we resort to that widely used device which has of course attracted a fair share of criticism. The battle of production function between two Cambridges—on two sides of the Atlantic—has set many a river on fire. Nevertheless, we dare postulate production functions as follows:

$$W = W(X,Y) \qquad (2)$$
$$T = T(Y) \qquad (3)$$

Where $W$ and $T$ are wheat and tree outputs respectively, and $X$ is the area under wheat (including fodder), and $Y$ the area under forests. The presence of $Y$ in (2) is a recognition of *external economies* of forest *vis-à-vis* agriculture. We adopt the following symbols for convenience:

$$W_1 = dW/dX; \qquad W_2 = dW/dY.$$
$$T_1 = dt/dy.$$

Of course, the three derivatives are positive. The problem is to maximize:

$$W(X,Y) + T(Y) \qquad (4)$$

Subject to the constraint that the aggregate land ($L$) of three categories—farm, forest, and frontier—is fixed, to be distributed between the first two categories in the optimal solution.[7]

$$L = X + Y \qquad (5)$$

The first-order conditions are:

$$W_1 = T_1 + W_2 = \lambda \qquad (6)$$

where $\lambda$ is the Lagrange multiplier.

---

[6] Dasgupta (1982) gives several examples. The production function for lobster catch, for instance, is estimated by Henderson and Tugwell as follows;

$$X = 2.26 \, S^{0.44} \, E^{0.44}$$

Where $X$ is the catch, $S$ the stock of lobster, and $E$ is number of traps.

[7] To complete the story we have to further specify that $X$ and $Y$ do not fall below their initial values.

We now proceed to make a further assumption that may cause many an eyebrow to rise. We take it that production function (2) is homogeneous of degree one; so:

$$W = W_1 X + W_2 Y$$

Therefore, $W_2 = (W - W_1 X)/Y$ \hfill (7)

Condition (6) can be rewritten as:

$$T_1 = W_1 - W_2 \qquad (8)$$

or, in view of (7) and (8) we get:

$$T_1 = (1 - X/Y).W_1 - W/Y \qquad (9)$$

This gives us a formula for optimal allocation of frontier land which is rather easy to use. Note that in India actual ratio $X/Y$ is currently about 2.33. If 60 million hectares of frontier land is equally divided into two parts the $X/Y$ ratio would become 1.9. So we may approximately put it at 2.0 for the guidance of land resource planning. Now, note that $W/Y$ is simply the average wheat output (including wheat equivalent of fodder crop), reckoned per unit of forestland, while $W_1$ is essentially the output in the marginal agricultural farm, which may not be difficult to estimate. A complex incidence of external economies can thus be incorporated operationally in a relatively simple formula, provided the underlying assumptions are granted.

Equation (8) has an interesting implication. Consider two alternative projects of wasteland development, one has fodder as the output, the other fuel-wood, or forestry. The latter project, it says, should be accepted even if its net (direct) output falls short of that of the former project, indeed, by not more than a certain amount, namely, $W_2$. To put it differently, *the common principle of equating (direct) yield of two such projects at the margin suffers from an unwarranted bias against forestry.*

## Concluding Remarks

The recent elections for the Parliament and State assemblies have reconfirmed the voters' clear preference, in true spirit of democracy and federalism, for a multi-party system in the country. It so happens that the 'core' States (geographically speaking) have revealed a certain political orientation at the level of the legislative assembly, while those in the 'periphery' (geographically speaking) have demonstrated a more diversified pattern; on the other hand, in the matter of national politics they are unequivocally unanimous. We must carefully understand the message of the people. The Prime Minister's own twin proposals—wasteland development and districtwise industrialization—would require a greater degree of mutual trust, cooperation and respect between the Centre and the States. Resources of the country are not under the monopoly of any one political party; they belong to the people irrespective of their electoral preferences. The Centre–State relation has a very crucial role to play in the newly emerging strategy of development in India.[8]

Poverty and unemployment are the two major problems in the country. The true index of the success of a development strategy lies in the extent by which these two maladies are reduced. It is the lesson of the past three decades that modern technology can be harnessed for the benefit of the economy as a whole. Man is no longer helpless, economically speaking, in front of the machine; for the Ricardo-effect can be neutralized through proper management of the economy. India has the added advantage of a vast area of hitherto inactive land, some 60 million hectares of it, which can be opened up for productive use. If past data are any indication, this land is going to be anyway encroached upon sooner or later by the advancing column of land grabbers. It is high time that a scientific, well-coordinated long range plan was launched to save the country from that peril. *The wasteland, adequately developed, can even provide settlement for landless agricultural labourers.* For example, one million hectares, out of the total 60 million, can absorb an equal number of landless families. And it would bring tremendous political dividend. Not that this kind of land

---

[8] It is well known that the delay in the implementation of the recommendations of the Eighth Finance Commission hit one State, in particular, very hard. West Bengal was deprived of funds to the tune of as much as Rs 325 crores in one year, 1984–5. The attitude of the then Union Government as reflected in this episode was inimical to a healthy Centre-State relation. The new government in New Delhi, it is hoped, will eschew the path of such confrontation with the States.

development programme is being thought of for the first time in history. There are several instances of similar campaigns within recent memory in India and in certain neighbouring countries; and, we know, the actual records of achievement in these episodes had not been always very commendable. No massive programme, involving something like 60 million hectares of land, can succeed without popular support and vigorous participation. It is here that the political leadership of the country can make a historic contribution.

### REFERENCES

Dasgupta, P., *The Control of Resources*, Oxford, Basil Blackwell, 1982.

Feder, E., 'Agricultural Resources in Underdeveloped Countries: Competition between Man and Animal', *Economic and Political Weekly*, Special Number, August 1979.

Habib, I., 'The Geographical Background' in T. Raychaudhuri and I. Habib (eds), *The Cambridge Economic History of India*, vol. 1, 1982.

Hicks, J. R., *Capital and Time: A Neo-Austrian Theory*, Oxford, Clarendon Press, 1973.

Jodha, N. S., 'The Process of Desertification and the Choice of Interventions', *Economic and Political Weekly*, August 1980.

Keynes, J. M., *The General Theory of Employment Interest and Money*, London, Macmillan, 1936.

Samuelson, P. A., 'Some Aspects of the Pure Theory of Capital', *Quarterly Journal of Economics*, May 1937; reprinted in *The Collected Scientific Papers of Paul A. Samuelson*, vol. 1, ed. J. E. Stiglits, MIT Press, 1966.

———, 'Economics of Forestry in an Evolving Society', *Economic Inquiry*, vol. 14, pp. 466–92, 1976.

———, 'Thunen at two hundred', *Journal of Economic Literature*, December 1983.

Sau, R., *Indian Economic Growth*, Calcutta, Orient Longman, 1973.

———, 'Structural Change and Economic Development in

International Perspective', Presented in the Silver Jubilee Seminar, Institute of Economic Growth, Delhi, April 1984.

——, 'Development of Capitalism in India', *Economic and Political Weekly*, Review of Political Economy, 1984a.

Scitovsky, T., 'Comment on Adelman', *World Development*, vol. 12, no. 9, September 1984.

Sen, S. R., 'Forestry and Agriculture in India', *The International Journal of Agrarian Affairs*, June 1955; reprinted in A. M. Khusro (ed.), *Readings in Agricultural Development*, Bombay, Allied Publishers, 1968.

Sraffa, P., *Production of Commodities by Means of Commodities*, Cambridge University Press, 1960.

# Some Reflections on the New Strategy

PREM SHANKAR JHA

A discussion of the past growth strategy may be interesting academically but not very useful otherwise. So I would discuss strategy for the future only, and for this I am grateful to Ranjit Sau for outlining the four components of a future strategy. First of all, we are talking about the need to decentralize, at least to have one important industry in each district. No one can seriously challenge this proposition and we have to think of a spatial policy of industrialization along these lines. Our industrialization has so far been governed almost entirely by considerations of the sources of raw materials and energy. One must look at the energy availability pattern to understand the pattern of industrial development, as exemplified by the early industrialization in the Bengal–Bihar coal belt and also the latter industrialization in that region. The truth is that coal has been the main source of energy, and oil the main motive force for industrialization in the last thirty years.

The problem with decentralization is that unless one plans this very carefully on the basis of a kind of comparative advantage, one is bound to get into enormous difficulties, political as well as economic. The public sector did try in its engineering plans to go in for a decentralized pattern of industrialization. Problems were realized at the time of implementation. The public sector required large proportion of skilled workers, but they were not available in the backward areas where the public sector units were located. Such was the experience with the MIG factory at Koraput, the Heavy Engineering Corporation (HEC) at Ranchi and the Mining and

Allied Machinery Corporation (MAMC) at Durgapur. When the MAMC was set up at Durgapur, it was a largely tribal-inhabited forest area. The result was that they could not find any skilled workers locally. So they advertised in the State newspapers. They found that they could not get enough workers in the State. So they advertised nation-wide, and even then there was no adequate response. So the public sector (MAMC) management went about setting up its own worker-training centres. A very serious, rather endemic, problem arose at Ranchi. Tribal people were displaced from their land in thousands and promised jobs, but the kind of jobs that were created have not been filled till today.

This kind of idea of implanting growth centres is not easy to put into practice. It has to be done very carefully on the basis of spotting areas where growth impulses are already present, e.g. agricultural growth impulses. If you look at the way the new industrial townships have developed throughout Western U.P., Punjab and Haryana, the pattern becomes quite clear. First the marketing centres come up, then the agro-processing centre, after that there is some development of major industries and, finally, full-fledged industrial units come up. Further, if you look at the map of cities of various sizes in India and compare that with agricultural development, you will find in fact that the maximum number of cities of 5 to 10 thousand population have sprung up precisely in the areas where there had been some kind of agricultural breakthrough. A mechanistic approach is really not possible. We really have to go back to increasing agricultural productivity first. There is a study on Katihar (in Bihar) and it came to the conclusion that this is one city which is permanently threatened with inundation. It is in a bowl. The best thing they could do was to actually build a drainage system, a whole network of tanks, and to set up fisheries. It is fishery that provided the growth impulse in that small town of Katihar, which nothing else had been able to give so far. In fact, a lot of imagination is required for this. However, one cannot get away from the main thing, that you must start by increasing productivity (in absolute terms). The kind of investment that was made in the public sector MIG project must be avoided, where three components of the MIG factory were put in three backward areas in three parts of the country and then every

MIG had to be assembled by bringing the parts from all the three places. It was absurd because this is the kind of industrialization that puts a strain on your transport system, which being extremely capital-intensive, may well not be able to bear much strain.

Therefore, decentralization of industries has to be in areas where some growth impulses have already manifested themselves. One other possibility is energy. We are on the brink of an energy transition in this country. We will soon have to find significant areas of renewable energy sources, to replace fossil fuel. To the extent we succeed in doing this, the renewable energy sources would naturally lead to decentralization. Any renewable energy production unit, whether it is power generation from paddy straw (which is being burnt in the fields in Punjab and U.P. and going waste in millions of tonnes a year), or it is fuel-wood based, will naturally be decentralized. You will, therefore, get a decentralized industrial pattern developing as a result of the compulsions of energy and technology, not quite in the manner you got support-based industrialization or Bengal–Bihar industrialization developing in the earlier phase when coal and oil were the principal means of energy. I certainly anticipate this to happen in the future. The thrust on renewable energy will need to be greatly increased because of the kind of social benefits that emanate from it. This is one important aspect of the New Strategy.

Coming to technology, I would like to say that I completely agree with Sau. I should also point out that when he is talking about industrialization he has a rather special definition of industry: a vertically integrated industrial set-up which starts from the very base and goes right through to the final product. An industry would thus include a fertilizer plant, perhaps an oil refinery, agriculture and then possibly power and other inputs. The totality of this would be defined as an industry. If you define an industry in this way as a source of a completely vertically integrated column of activity in an economy, then what Sau is talking about makes sense. Trying to go for employment intensity at the base, whether it is in energy, petrochemical, basic metal or ceramic, would be disastrous. I think it is the employment-generating effect of the final products of this industry that is important.

I will only add a word of caution. While it is possible to draw up a blueprint like this, I do not really see it happening easily as a transition. From the kind of completely *ad hoc* technology imports till now, we have to move to a systematic well thought-out technology policy. What we are facing today is, I think, a kind of a threat from two sources. In the late fifties and early sixties, we went in for a series of specific technology collaboration agreements. In fact, thousands of them to produce specific products. Now over the last two and a half decades these products have become obsolete. The technology involved in them has become obsolete. The materials being used have become atrociously expensive.

As a consequence of this kind of obsolescence, the equipment we are making in the country now is not even manufactured abroad. The equipment cost may be low, the design cost may be low, but the raw material cost is very high. If you are then not able to compete with imported equipment, what follows is that instead of wanting to bring in new technology, people are once again putting enormous pressure on the Government to bring in the new technology in the form of the products themselves. Thus if our power-generating technology becomes obsolete, there is pressure to import 500 kwh power-generating sets. What you are really facing today is a situation in which on the one hand those who use the domestic equipment, become uncompetitive and those who are able to get imported equipment are actually running the country's own capital goods industry into the ground. We therefore face a kind of capital goods decentralization situation here, which is extremely dangerous.

On the question of import liberalization, if one relies solely upon imports to give a competitive edge to the Indian economy, we will destroy Indian industry. There are two reasons for this. One is technology that we mentioned above and the other is the structure of domestic taxation. Now in 1984–5, the excise duties amount to about Rs 11,700 crores and customs duty to about Rs 7000 crores. I am not for the moment worried how this affects each single industry or product. If you think of industry conceptually as one joint firm, then a situation exists in which there is a net negative protection to Indian industry worth Rs 4000 crores. Put in another way, customs duty is equal to 18 per cent of value added by industries, but excise duty is equal to about 32 per cent. So you have on the aggregate a net negative protection of 14 per cent. If in this situation you start talking about import liberalization without first changing the fiscal structure inside the country, then you are destroying your industry. It is not just a matter of technology. It is the way that you have built your fiscal system in order to extricate revenues to meet Government expenditure.

Any time it is suggested that excise duties be lowered there is a scream from the Expenditure Department of the Ministry of Finance because it is a budget asset. This argument has been used now for the past one decade at least to justify increasing the rate of indirect taxation of commodities continually. We have neither been able to control the budget deficit nor have we raised any real revenues through increased taxation.

I agree with Sau that there are other ways of increasing the competitiveness within the economy and that import liberalization must come last, not first. What is needed is a drastic cut in the average rate of domestic indirect taxation, preferably starting with maximum cuts on duties on raw materials and on some manufactured goods going into the production process and selective cuts on certain final goods also. After this is done, and only if this is done, can we think in terms of import liberalization. One other thing that we have also to keep in mind is that if you want domestic competition to increase, you must completely remove industrial licensing. What industrial licensing has done to this country is to break up the already small market for a product into further non-competitive segments. Further, it makes it impossible for an efficient company to edge out an inefficient one.

We have raised any number of shibboleths for this: commanding heights of the economy, concentration of economic power, etc. But the plain truth of the matter is we have sheltered the inefficient producer at the cost of the consumer. We have sheltered the well off at the cost of the really poor in the society and this must end.

Lastly, the most important point that Sau has made is about the degradation of the land. We have destroyed our forests. We have subjected our land to erosion. We have subjected our rivers and land to terrible problems of flooding and inundation. The climate is changing in large parts of the country. What we are now faced with is not just a commercial energy problem, it is a more serious non-commercial energy problem.

Broadly speaking, India has 300 million hectares of land and about 120 million hectares is cultivated; about 30 to 40 million hectares are permanently fallow. The land under forests is normally about 70 million hectares but in fact only about 30 and 40 million hectares of so-called forest land is actually administered by the Forest Department. They do not have a single tree anymore. About 50 million hectares of land under agriculture should never have been brought under the plough at all. All in all, there is about 100 million hectares of land that needs regeneration in this country. This is the minimum. There are of course estimates that the amount of land that is ecologically degraded is actually 175 million hectares out of 300 million hectares. This is both a problem as well as a potential. I think the most obvious thing to do is to bring huge areas under tree. Further, since you have both a commercial energy crisis and non-commercial energy crisis, it is a problem of shifting your energy base from non-renewable sources like oil to renewable sources of energy. As trees are our most abundant bio mass, what we need is a very serious afforestation programme. In this I must say I do welcome the Prime Minister's statement that 5 million hectares of land is to be brought under trees every year. I do not know whether this figure is achievable, but even if we achieve 2 million hectares with public and private initiative, I think we will be turning the corner by the end of the century.

# Contours of a Reorientation

V. S. MINOCHA

As a disclaimer it must be mentioned at the outset that this write-up is not intended to be a full-fledged paper on a theme which, in fact, warrants a tract of a respectable size. It has the modest aim of raising some issues for discussion.

It is pedantic ritualism to say that the strategy of growth fondly adopted by the Indian planners has had the keynote of emphasizing the so-called heavy industry. Of course, a more correct description is that there has been a three-fold emphasis: agriculture, infrastructure and producer goods industries. No specific ranking of these three is intended in the way they are listed here.

It is equally facile to recall that the rationale of this strategy can be found in the continental size of the economy (reflecting both diversity of resources and adequacy of demand) and in the realistic assumptions of foreign exchange shortage being the main constraint in the process of growth, taking a long view from the vantage point of the early fifties.

All this is well known and a much discussed theme. What calls for attention are a few hidden aspects of the theme that have somehow remained a little obscure. For example:

1. The Indian strategy of growth, so easily identified, is better appreciated as an approach to the consolidation of a process that had begun during the inter-war period and was very much accelerated as a side-effect of the Second World War. This is not to downgrade the importance of modelling for planned economic development. On the contrary, the realism and relevance of that modelling can be easily observed in the perspective of historical continuity in the process of development through industrialization.

2. Another factor of importance in that historical continuity is the

role of protectionism in stimulating industrialization within the economy. This is generally described as industrialization through import substitution. But, what is wrongly read into it is the inference that this amounts to an inward-looking approach to development. That is absolutely wrong because a truly inward-looking approach to development would imply self-sufficiency rather than self-reliance and would be reflected in a clear and continuous decline rather than a mere change in the composition of an increasing volume and value of the country's imports. These contrasts have only to be mentioned to demonstrate that India has adopted an outward-looking and not an inward-looking approach to development. In fact, from a different angle it can be argued that India is unnecessarily sticking to the acquired habit of looking outward (not only in the economic sphere).

3. If import substitution must not be confused with inward-looking approach to development, it is too simplistic and even misleading to argue that an outward-looking approach is nothing more than export augmentation. That a vigorous, even aggressive, export drive is called for at this stage of India's economic development is not denied. But its rationale is not that an outward-looking approach is required to replace the earlier inward-looking approach. Rather, both import substitution and export promotion are to be appreciated as two phases of one and the same sequence of India's drive towards a modern self-reliant economy. Self-reliance as against self-sufficiency has the connotation of a country deriving full advantage of international division of labour in a manner that acquisition of goods and services from outside for internal use (consumption as well as investment) is backed by adequate purchasing power earned through exports or borrowed with honour. This has important bearing on issues like India playing host to direct foreign investment and the choice between import of technical services and developing them within the economy.

4. The reference to 'a modern self-reliant economy' in the preceding paragraph is meant to indicate that the process of development through industrialization has in it the important component of building up a nation-state. This aspect is generally not discussed following the maxim that basic drives and passions are to be experienced and not described. Here again, historical continuity with the independence movement can be easily seen and appreciated. Also, what it means is that India as a modern nation-in-making is, as it were, striving through encounters with economically superior and politically more powerful nations to come up and have the pride of being their equal. It could be said within the permissible

limits of exaggeration that nationalism has been the only operative ideology.

5. As an inevitable concomitant of the process of development through industrialization what has always been intended as part of the strategy is the sharpening of economic dualism between modern and traditional sectors. Sharpening here means extension of the modern and shrinkage of the traditional sector. This dichotomy, needless to say, is not a commodity-wise classification but is essentially based on differences in organizational pattern and general productivity level. Thus, modern-traditional dichotomy must not be confused with industry-agriculture sectorization. It is only because capitalism and capitalist have become dirty words that Arthur Lewis's original distinction between capitalist and subsistence sectors has been avoided. Otherwise, it would have been said candidly that the Indian strategy of growth has in its essence aimed at nurturing capitalism—pure and simple—so as to demonstrate how the magic of private property works (*à la* Ranade) in relation to building up a modern nation-state. Would that have been too blunt a remark?

In the caption given to the write-up mention is made of reorientation and not, for example, the need for scrapping or radical change. The plea, in other words, is for continuation, consolidation and, if necessary, modification of the long-term strategy followed so far. Let the time-horizon for the pursuit of this enquiry be the next three Five Year Plans against the backdrop of the six Five Year Plans that have been completed by now. What specific problems are likely to emerge over this long-span and what can be suggested for resolving them?

Here, it is necessary to remember that, in general, any discussion of growth strategy is necessarily focussed on balancing the various options that the government has in dealing with the relevant issues. Thus, the unbalanced growth strategy (Hirschman) is essentially a plea on good reasoning for a selective approach to public investment in contrast to diversified pattern, again on public investment, advocated by the balanced growth school. This is only an illustration because the strategy of growth even understood as a consistent set of governmental measures means a lot more than planning for production and distribution of goods; also more than investment for the sake of increasing productive capacity. A meaningful growth strategy must also, nay will primarily, aim at the producer and not merely the product.

In a nutshell, the strategy of growth followed so far and projected for the foreseeable future has the primary goal of stimulating and promoting business entrepreneurship in the Schumpeterian sense of 'carrying out of new combinations' of resources known to be relevant for producing economic goods. It bears repetition to say that business entrepreneurship is not specific to trade and industry, it is equally relevant in agriculture. An all-pervasive change is what has been aimed at. To make economic change an on-going process what sort of reorientation of the strategy is called for?

Obviously, the foremost worry at this stage is how to not only maintain but also accelerate the tempo of economic change. Details apart, it can be taken as a safe assumption that there has, indeed, been a marked change in the Indian economy since Independence (in fact, since the Second World War). Let only a couple of facts be highlighted as summary indicators. There is, for instance, the fact that the share of agriculture in gross domestic product is now less than 40 per cent, compared to the early post-Independence ratio that used to be upward of 50 per cent. Then, there is the remarkable push-up in the rate of domestic saving (assumed as 26 per cent p.a. in the Seventh Plan Approach document) and the related fact that an increasingly larger proportion of gross capital formation is matched by domestic saving.

Such facts may, however, give a wrong twist to the concern with maintaining the tempo of development. In view of the significant contribution made by public investment to the pace and character of development so far, it can be too easily argued that what is called for even now is further acceleration in the rate of public investment. This is a wrong inference and, therefore, an inappropriate plea because (*a*) it fails to identify the major problem at this juncture which on any reckoning is how to achieve better utilization of given capacity rather than how to create additional capacity (though the latter problem is not altogether absent), and (*b*) it obscures the fact that when the hairy shell of socialist clap-trap is removed the crucial role of public sector in India can be easily seen as that of a prop to private business sector and that this support has been over-extended. In other words, the main reorientation of the growth strategy has to be in the direction of making the private business sector less dependent on the state exchequer and the linkages with public sector.

The so-called liberalization of trade and tax policies is a clear pointer of transition being made to this sort of strategy which, of course, is a welcome sign. What is a little perturbing is that the response from the private business sector as reflected, for example, in the excitement over this year's budget is more in the nature of euphoria over the gains obtained rather than gearing up for a more competitive economy. The trees are counted but the wood is missed—which is very uncharacteristic of the Schumpeterian entrepreneur. It shows once again that over-extension of government support for the sake of promoting business entrepreneurship can be self-defeating. It is perhaps necessary to guard against yesterday's critics of 'socialism' (read public sector and government regulation) to make a turn-about tomorrow and clamour for undeserved state patronage.

Liberalization, it must be made clear, implies adopting a certain kind of control mechanism which is considered more effective than the alternatives and not moving towards an uncontrolled economy. More specifically, what is required as a strategic change in policy is to revamp the financial system including the nationalized banking segment such that it assumes—rather resumes—the disciplining role of the scrutinizer. That the financial intermediation ratio has increased tremendously and there is no let-up in that rising trend, are clear indicators that the country's financial system is well placed to play that role and thereby induce cost effectiveness, which is another name for financial discipline, and a greater utilization of output capacity.

A related plea is for restructuring the regulatory framework of business in such a manner that the loss of capital is seen by the entrepreneur as a real threat in case of business failure. It is vicious veneering to describe business failure as sickness. It is also well to remember that the first principle of business is not to earn or maximize profit but to keep the capital intact. Therefore, nothing worries the business entrepreneur more than the situation in which he is in danger of losing his capital (which to him is more than losing his face). That is why he has the sure instinct of clinging to the elder person, the leader, the bureaucratic machinery, the made-up ideology and what not for the sake of replenishing the sand he knows is slipping through his fingers. The real case for liberal economic policies is to make the business entrepreneur more and more fend for himself. Thus, the drive for export promotion should really focus on how to make the producers with potential exportable surplus realize that to export makes good business sense.

The key idea in this context is to appreciate that what is required is reshuffling of resources and not allocation of new resources. If this had been built into the growth strategy, there would have been a lot more of auctions, mergers and takeovers of losing business units than has been the case. (Let it be marked that reference is to losing units.) The horizontal conflicts among business entrepreneurs ought to be resolved in a manner that draws very little from the public funds. The role of the government should really be confined to that of a refree.

What about the losing units in the public sector? Obviously, the control mechanism relevant for the private sector will be absolutely inapplicable in the case of the public sector. The criteria that guide the setting up and functioning of the public sector requires close scrutiny as it is not a holy cow. It is also known for its inadequacies and inefficiencies, which are more serious than those pertaining to the private sector not because they are more numerous or more glaring but because they have more far-reaching consequences. If linkage effects (especially the forward linkage effects) constitute an important reason for setting up the public sector, its ill-functioning leads to adverse results again for the same reason. The point, however, is that the threat mechanism of capital loss is just not relevant in the case of public sector units. (Loss of face; maybe yes.) Thus, an important component of the new strategy of growth will have to be a well-thought-out, vigorous drive to make public sector management a model of professional management.

It is implicit in these suggestions that the growth strategy needs to be structured now with emphasis on things other than allocation of investment resources. More than allocative efficiency it is X-efficiency that needs to be pursued. But, that will not banish the problem of hard choice in investment allocation because better management of past investments does not mean no new investment is going to be necessary. There are many issues at stake in respect of investment allocation. Only a few assertions are made here.

It is increasingly becoming clear that spread of industrialization is closely linked with agricultural prosperity. Therefore, the pattern of investment allocation that favours agricultural growth will also favour deepening of the industrialization process. Yet, it is doubtful whether heavy subsidization of agriculture over the long haul could be justified. For, in agriculture as much as in industry the long-term aim has to be that of making business units fend for themselves.

One shift in policy desired for several reasons is federalizing of the economy as well as policy. India at the dawn of the twenty-first century will be either the United States of India (Samyukta Bharat) or only the name of a sub-continent. Federalism in its fossilized meaning so far has meant devolution of resources and powers from the Centre to the provinces (euphemistically called states in India's Constitution). Real federalism involves what may be called a spectrum approach to policy making—it permits a federating unit to be on its own and distinct from the other units and yet be in constant interaction with them. More concretely, the pumping in of resources for agricultural growth from the Central pool, as justified in the preceding paragraph, needs to be accompanied by a rigorous fiscal management at the province (state) level. A similar logic in fact will apply to fiscal management within a province (state).

In this connection, a very strong case exists for decentralizing, even dispersing, the pattern of expenditure on social welfare programmes including those meant for poverty alleviation. By dispersion is meant a process whereby not only the lower levels within the framework of government are induced to mobilize resources locally, the idea itself is spread effectively to institutions outside the government. This is one area in which to inculcate community sense will be neither retrograde nor anti-national. If this were to be done, urban poverty as against rural poverty will receive the attention it deserves.

That this sort of dispersion is essential can be seen from another angle. The hardest of choices to be made in the foreseeable future will be between defence and development—

why in future, the hard choice is already there. It is a right perception that nationalism has been and continues to be the only operative ideology, an easy inference is to say that in the limit, defence will tend to dominate. This is consistent with the accent on capital utilization and the need for minimizing fresh public investment including financial assistance to non-government sectors. If development expenditure is receding from the top to a lower position, commitment to social welfare programmes—hesitant, shaky and contrived that it generally is—will naturally tend to be underplayed.

That, incidentally, is also a pointer that in the sphere of labour relations the need of the hour is to move away from the 'adjudication' syndrome to collective bargaining approach within the organized sector and to work for a viable organizational frame for the informal sector. Strategy for growth with justice means something substantially more than a general approach to government expenditure and pattern of public investment.

# Some Premises of India's Development Strategy: 1950–90

KAMAL NAYAN KABRA

This paper attempts to analyse some premises underlying the strategy of economic growth (*ersatz* for development) which was evolved in India for the period 1950–90. As we see below, it is no accident that growth was treated as practically the same thing as development. It is not a matter of semantics alone, but affects substantive issues of policy goals, instruments, agencies and sharing of responsibilities, costs and benefits of 'growth'. It also affected in a decisive way the actual course of economic change in India since 1950. It may be clarified at the outset that by 'strategy' is understood an exercise to synthesize and harmonize various elements of a multipronged endeavour for attaining some large, long-term objective. The political, economic and social dimensions of a strategy would remain loosely linked, in the absence of their integration, with technological, financial and international factors.

### CONCEPT OF GROWTH

Basic to any strategy of development is the concept of development. Naturally, the concept of development is related to an understanding of the nature of underdevelopment, which was treated as absence of growth. The policy makers in India viewed underdevelopment (or inability to grow economically) as related to low per capita income, which came to prevail mainly as a result of stagnation of the economy over a long period, particularly in comparison with the rate of growth of population and technological possibilities. There was a certain degree of axiomatic and implicit identification of low per capita income with widespread poverty of an overwhelming majority of Indians, without regard to extreme inequalities of income, wealth, skills, cultural levels, and level and terms of participation in socio-political processes.

Our underdevelopment was also viewed in a certain international comparative context. As compared to the countries of Europe and North America, ours is a low income, poverty-stricken country. Little, if any, comparative attention was given to socialist countries. It was thought that we could not participate in the Industrial Revolution which occurred in the Western countries and as a result of lack of industrialization, our productive forces have remained underdeveloped and the potential resources of the country, particularly manpower and natural resources, are under-utilized. It was further thought that both the absolute and relative position of India worsened because of foreign rule as the colonial masters further accentuated India's underdevelopment by imposing unilaterally beneficial, parasitic colonial relations. Thus, it was inherent in our understanding of underdevelopment that it is very intimately connected with lack of industrialization, over-population, backward agriculture and a stagnant economy. The underdevelopment was considered a structural problem, which could be addressed only over a relatively long period of time. Low average per capita income limited the availability of surplus (ignoring potential surplus) and severely constrained extended reproduction which could have made use of known technological advances.

### AGGREGATIVE, NON-DIFFERENTIATED APPROACH
### SEPARATION OF GROWTH OF OUTPUT FROM DISTRIBUTION

In this aggregative approach, the nation was taken as the primary unit and poverty of the large majority of Indians was viewed as a reflection of low average productivity, without much occupational, sectoral, inter-class and inter-regional differentiation. Thus the approach was primarily to concentrate on increasing the level of per capita income in the country by increasing the rate of savings and capital formation, specifically in the form of provision of socio-economic infrastructure and investment in industries. The argument was that if distribution is given priority over accelerating the rate of growth of national income, it will mean distribution of poverty.

## NATURE OF THE STATE

The economic, political and ideological basis of according primacy to economic growth ought to be understood because, notwithstanding powerful critiques of these bases, this position is still powerful at the operational level. For one thing, the conflict between growth and development appeared to be a short-run affair, capable of being taken care of by addressing national energies to growth. Second, the state, as the main instrument for organizing the national endeavour of overcoming backwardness, was assumed to be a supra-class neutral state with a very high degree of autonomy, if not total autonomy. Hence, supremacy and independence of political power was viewed as capable of taking care of the secondary round of corrections, since the technical and physical pre-conditions for the task were presumed to be created by sustained growth of GNP.

By adopting a dirigiste role, the state was considered capable not only of creating conditions for self-sustained growth, but also, at the same time, of determining the pattern and content of the growth. The assumption was that those forces and classes whose energies and resources are catalyzed by the state for higher levels of production, introduction of advanced technologies and introduction of new products can always be controlled and subdued by the state, for furthering the interests of the weak, the poor and the deprived as required by general social or national interests.

A 'neutral' state was stipulated with a very high degree of objectivity and autonomy (both of internal and external economic forces) forming a part of the 'solution set' acting on the 'problem set'. To this was added another ideological stance: fear of totalitarianism and assumption of a certain degree of irreconciliability between political democracy and concentration of economic resources and power in the hands of the state. This view was based on the possibility of creating a competitive capitalism by restraining forces of monopolization and concentration through state policies.

## RECONCILING GROWTH WITH SOCIAL JUSTICE

In order to reconcile the immediate pursuit of growth of per capita income with a more equitable pattern of distribution in the future, a three-pronged approach emerged over time. First, the historical experience of 'developed' countries of the West where Industrial Revolution initially worsened distribution to increase the rate of accumulation and later on, through high wages, economic expansion, social security, increased prosperity and Welfare State, bettered the general standard of living, was cited as indicative of an emerging future. Second, it was hypothesized, though more as an after-thought, that there is a 'trickle-down' process inherent in faster growth, which carried the benefits of growth to the peripheral, marginal masses. Third, given our democratic constitution and legacy of the freedom movement, a number of social welfare programmes to finance social consumption for the poor were initiated under the Plans way ahead of our 'economic' capabilities and resources, something which did not happen in the West. Thus, it was thought that growth will be no mere *ersatz* for development but will really tend to approximate the latter. In a word, we devised a strategy of growth, shunning the excesses of primitive accumulation and early capitalism.

## INTERNATIONAL CONTEXT AND MIMETIC NATIONALISM

It was also realized that being a leader in the process of decolonization and being a country with its own distinct cultural heritage, India has to devise a concept and process of development according to its national genius. A nationalistic dimension, which is considered mimetic by many, was also attached to our concept and understanding of growth.

In any case, in terms of its complexity and size, the problem of underdevelopment of the Indian society can be considered as the crux of the global problem of underdevelopment. Any breakthrough in the pursuit of development in India would mean a major change in the nature and complexion of the global problem of underdevelopment. This becomes all the more significant as there is hardly any aspect of underdevelopment which cannot be found in Indian society. However, owing to the general conformity of the Indian concept and strategy with the

Western view and the modernizing Indian elite's strong intellectual, emotional and material links with it, the generalities of the phenomenon of underdevelopment, so to say, pushed into the background the specificities and differentiations characterizing Indian underdevelopment. This also served the interest of those who were in commanding positions in the modern segments of the economy like industry, trade and modern services.

ENSURING GROWTH: ACCUMULATION PROCESS

This concept of growth was sought to be operationalized by instituting national planning for development so that multi-dimensional interventions in many spheres of both promotional and regulatory nature could consistently and simultaneously be made. The state was to take positive steps to increase the rate of savings and capital accumulation, in particular, by pushing up the marginal rate of savings, providing infrastructural facilities both for agriculture and industry and regulating the working of the existing institutions. It was very clear that the rate of savings and investment had to be pushed up very significantly. This was so for many reasons. The size of the labour force itself required high rate of accumulation for providing effective employment. Lots of infrastructural facilities were required. Need for increasing both the means of labour and instruments of labour in agriculture was large. Then, industrialization required installation of modern machinery and factories many times larger than was the case for the countries which industrialized early. Given low levels of per capita income, a vicious circle was presumed to put brakes on the accumulation process, while the minimum need was to raise the rate of savings from under 10 per cent to over 20 per cent.

The task of the accumulation process increased, because there was little primary or primitive accumulation of capital, which is a pre-condition for sustaining modern capitalist accumulation. On the contrary, there was a drain of investible resources from the country by the British. Given a democratic framework, a number of social services and social consumption facilities had to be provided to the poor labouring classes, while abjuring methods of primitive accumulation.

This required that the market accumulation process had to be supplemented by a state accumulation process. The methods of capital accumulation available to the state were to be used in such a manner that, on the one hand, re-investible resources increase over time and, second, it does not become a zero-sum game in the sense that the increased state accumulation is offset by a fall in private market accumulation. These difficult choices were further reinforced by the fact that, given the nature of Indian industrial and rich agricultural classes, they expected high, quick and safe rates of return on their investments. Further, given the presently limited size of the home market, the most important pre-condition for encouraging investment was expansion of the home market, for then only the investment opportunities would become profitable. Here, there was a dilemma. The rate of relative and absolute surplus extraction could not have been increased very much because exploitation of labour beyond a point was not possible owing to our democratic polity. Then, given our low rate of savings, abundant supply of labour and low level of technological development, the scope for real subsumption of labour by capital-deepening was rather limited. Rates of return too could not, at least in theory, be permitted to go beyond a certain level because of the concern for balancing efficiency and equity.

In this situation, when profitable investment opportunities were increased by planning, public investment, availability of external finance and technology, the private sector decided to reconcile the conflict between the available high levels and low, permitted rates of return by resorting to regular and systematic avoidance and evasion of tax on a large scale. Thus along with the growth of private investment, there emerged a large and growing black economy, giving very high and quick rates of return to private investors. Of course, it was growth of investment according to the logic of the market and was not consistent with Plan priorities and social objectives. It also limited the possibilities of further state capital accumulation and 'open' private capital accumulation. This was among the factors which gave rise to the phenomenon of growing reliance on internal and external public borrowing for financing public spending both on current and capital account.

## AGRARIAN REFORMS

To some extent, it was thought essential to modify the existing institutions in so far as these were anti-growth, and also in some cases where institutions were so thoroughly anti-equity as to adversely affect growth. Among the latter, belonged a series of land reform measures for establishing peasant proprietorship, for removing intermediaries, for making tenancies secure and for making the ownership of land a little more equitable.

In addition to ideology, more mundane considerations of improving farm productivity by encouraging small farmers who were considered more efficient and motivated in relation to output and investment than large farmers and absentee landlords, provided the material basis for agrarian restructuring. This was also expected to widen the market for the expanding industry.

It goes without saying that the implications of the dichotomy between small commodity peasant agrarian relations, on the one hand, and capitalist and state capitalist production relations, on the other, was not even recognized, quite apart from the question of working out its implications. Thus the emerging pattern of industrialization, growth of tertiary sector, swelling of the unorganized sector and urbanization without urbanism could not be anticipated, let alone the question of their implications being incorporated as components of the growth strategy.

## STRENGTHENING OF PRIVATE PROPERTY RELATIONS IN THE NON-AGRICULTURAL SECTOR

However, concentration in the industrial and trading sector was accepted as this was not only *not* considered anti-growth but was considered essential both as a condition and a consequence of industrialization. This was particularly so in view of managerial constraints in the public sector and fears of state power likely to result from concentration of economic resources in the hands of the state. However, unbridled nineteenth-century industrial capitalism was considered neither feasible nor desirable. Hence, a major limitation on the possibilities of further concentration of industrial output and capital in private hands arose through the entry of public sector in some of the important branches of industrial production. This also helped in preventing the entry of MNCs in some critical areas. But, in general, property relations in the non-agricultural sector were taken as given and no change in this respect was consciously planned. Let alone confiscation, even nationalization with compensation did not emerge as an instrument of development policy.

### ROLE OF PUBLIC SECTOR

Many new industries in capital and intermediate goods sectors were required for filling in the gaps left by the lopsided pattern of colonial industrial growth and for providing the sinews of sustained industrialization. Diversification of the industrial structure was an essential consequence of import-substituting, imitative industrialization. Many of the new industrial thrust areas required huge financial resources and required a long gestation period. For starting their production import of foreign technology and capital goods through a protracted process of international negotiations were required. These products also lacked ready demand and hence were regarded by private entrepreneurs as risky, having low expected profitability. Hence, it was unlikely that Indian capitalists would have come forward to invest in these industries. Both political leadership and business classes were reluctant to permit foreign companies to take exclusive responsibility of setting up these industries. Hence the public sector had to assume this responsibility. This *functional* role of public sector also tended to fulfil the role of being a countervailing force and also an ideological, political mobilization role reflected in the proclaimed goal of 'socialistic pattern of society'. The institution of rural moneylending was also sought to be eventually eliminated, so that institutional financial intermediation could start operating in the rural and agricultural sectors as well. Except for these and other measures like land reform and introduction of state capital in key industries, the existing institutional framework of the economy was taken almost as given and was made the basis for development.

## EQUITY FACTOR

Operationally, this process of pursuing growth, with the non-agricultural institutional framework taken as given, would have fostered a great deal of social and economic inequities. The authors of the strategy of growth were not unaware of these implications. Some of them have been very sharp critics of capitalism and imperialism and have openly expressed their sympathies for a socialist order. However, they also had strong reservations regarding excessive centralization of economic resources and power in the hands of the state. Hence, they thought of various regulatory measures for redistributive purposes, largely in the footsteps of Fabian socialists. Thus, on the one hand, they thought of various programmes for the welfare of the weaker and poorer sections of society, i.e. for a policy of increasing public spending for social welfare, and, on the other hand, they thought of an *ex post* redistributive scheme of taxation which covered income, wealth, gifts, inheritance and expenditure in line with the Kaldorian thinking on taxation. These considerations played a large part in the fiscal policy for resource mobilization. Equity and full employment were part of the stated objectives of planning.

## EMPLOYMENT, INDUSTRIALIZATION, SMALL INDUSTRIES

Industrialization was to be the main instrument for creating additional employment opportunities. Given high capital-intensity of modern import-substituting industries, their locational concentration, high import-content and long maturation period, a deliberate choice for modernizing cottage artisan industries and setting up of small industrial enterprises was made. Various promotional and preferentially discriminatory measures were evolved for the purpose. These small industries were an important second string to the bow of the strategy of giving relatively greater priority to capital and intermediate goods industries.

Thus it was expected that new industrial employment will be able, over a reasonably long period of time, to introduce structural improvement in the occupational distribution of labour and by reducing the pressure on land improve the land-man ratio. This change in the occupational structure would contribute to higher agricultural productivity, increase reinvestible surplus and reduce disguised unemployment (a confused term for ineffective employment). Thus industrial growth, by taking people off the land, would create conditions for a viable small farmers' economy, supported by service co-operatives for producing essential wage goods, industrial raw materials, export-surplus and hopefully even surplus for investment.

However, in the Plan strategy, employment generation was generally regarded as a by-product of planning for increased output, and there emerged an absence of active manpower planning. In the industrial sphere, employment implications of import-substituting industrialization (based on imported technology and machinery which provided answers to an altogether different factor-endowments, relative cost-structure and cultural needs) could not have brought about a structural correction, particularly in view of anticipated relatively modest levels of public and private investment, which was a corollary of what was called 'democratic planning'.

Small industries of both modern and traditional variety partly depended on a prior breakthrough in large-scale industry and agriculture generating massive employment for creating a rapidly growing market for small industry's products. Then, the strategy unrealistically required indigenous technological upgradation of conventional industries in an environment of technical collaborations with MNCs and big gap between government research laboratories and industrial needs. The policy of reservation for protecting small enterprises and preferential discrimination in their favour seemed to be impervious to the logic of competition between various highly unevenly placed strata of industrialists, for markets, resources and access to government support.

If wage-employment could not have been expected to increase according to the anticipations and tacit assumption of the Plan strategy, worse performance was in store for self-employment in lower forms of production, particularly agriculture, artisan production and traditional service occupations. The problem with self-employment is its level of productivity and availability of markets. If productivity of self-employment rises to make it effective employment and if their demands for consumption and investment goods can partly be met from within the sector (for producing mutual propagation effect) and if their sphere is not encroached upon by larger entrepreneurs, self-employment may gradually move into higher forms of production necessitating wage-labour. Owing to our institutional framework in the industrial corporate sector, structure of national income and employment worsening land-man ratio, abolition of zamindari with right or resumption for self-cultivation and liberal compensation (which weakened the prospects for a small farm, peasant proprietorship economy with increased labour absorption in agriculture), import of capital intensive technology, emphasis on capital intensive products, stimulation of private capital investment without regard to employment generation, and limited size and weak implementation of government programmes for employment generation, the indirect approach of obtaining additional employment opportunities by stimulating production was unlikely to prevent disturbingly large increase in unemployment.

As a result, a large number of people would be forced into make-do, ineffective employment of various kinds simply on the basis of over-extension of human ingenuity in a vast and growing 'informal' sector, mainly in urban areas (involving activities ranging from rag-picking and street-peddling to boot-legging). This would become a vast receptacle of the reserve army of labour which our capitalist growth under national planning did not attempt to employ effectively, so much so that even the natural additions to labour force from the non-agricultural sector were unlikely to find jobs in the secondary and organized tertiary sector and would swell the size of the 'informal' sector. This situation, too, in the ultimate analysis, may be regarded as an outcome of the growth-centred concept of development and its pursuit largely on the basis of existing institutional set-up, marginally modified by planning, public sector and a mild dose of unsuccessful agrarian restructuring.

### GROWTH AND EMPLOYMENT: TRADE-OFF AND FEEDBACK

Given the trade-off between employment growth and output growth, we seemed to have cast the dice in favour of the latter.

However, there exists a certain inevitable feedback between employment growth and output growth and as a result of slow growth of one, the other would come in for adverse performance. While employment growth resulting from output growth is a function of labour-intensity (where a wide range of choices exist), employment growth can also give varying rates of output growth depending on the product-mix and levels of productivity chosen. However, the feedback does not operate with equal strength both ways.

In so far as employment targets are kept high, the choice of capital-intensive techniques with very high 'productivity' does not become available. On the contrary, working primarily with output targets, in a framework where it happens to be the main indicator of development, there would be a tardy pace of employment generation which restrains market-widening. Market-widening stimulates all-round growth of productivity. At the same time, increasing concentration of income and wealth, i.e. market-deepening may not give rise to a comparable growth of home market as both the quantum and pattern of effective demand resulting from market-widening and market-deepening are different. This would be so because output growth working through market-deepening and weak employment stimulus may taper off the positive feedback on employment generation, particularly as compared to direct employment and man-power planning which addresses itself to the task of taking care of the backlog of ineffective employment and annual additions to work force.

The resources diverted to deal with rising unemployment by various schemes of public works and schemes for containing social tensions (food subsidies, direct policing, etc.) would reduce the surplus available for further output growth. Then, having built heavily capital-intensive industries (which could be under the control of a narrow entrepreneurial base further accentuate market-deepening) their backward and forward linkages would produce heavy demands for further investment in similar industries. This snowballing process would worsen capital-output ratio to yield a slow rate of growth of output, which worsen the position of employment growth. If the new capital-intensive products are able to divert demand away from conventional goods and services produced by small and artisan enterprises, pursuit of output growth may produce negative net employment effect. Thus the primacy to output growth path may become its own undoing, producing serious jamming of the output growth process. It is not implied that poor employment effects and crises of markets (under-consumption) will by themselves lead to a breakdown of the system. However in an economy prone to weather-induced fluctuations in the availability of wage-goods, dwindling work-opportunities and inflationary pressures, these contradictions may pull down growth rates to levels which even private capital may find troublesome. Thus indirect stimulation of employment and primacy to output growth in resolving the trade-off between output and employment may ultimately bring down output growth to near stagnation levels, deprived of its social relevance.

### EXTERNAL ECONOMIC RELATIONS AND SELF-RELIANCE

The growth strategy we are examining cannot be adequately and correctly understood unless it is recognized that it was an attempt by post-colonial society. The nature of the world economy, the complexity of diverse linkages between India and the rest of the world, particularly with the ex-colonial powers, exercised a considerable influence on our growth strategy. Since our underdevelopment and the colonial nexus were closely interrelated, our growth concept had to incorporate the objective of self-reliance but not autarky. Given the size of the country, magnitude of underdevelopment and constraints on inter-national resource transfers to meet our savings, foreign exchange and technological gaps without compromising national economic independence, there was a recognition of the primacy of internal factors. It is this which lead to policy guidelines such as developing the capacity to pay our way in international markets, import-substitution in key production spheres, diversification of trade and financial partners, etc. It was also based on a recognition, derived, in part, from the Prebisch thesis, of limited possibilities of expanding our exports, particularly through conventional exports.

Given the strategic long-term perspective of self-reliance, a short-run tactical perspective of inter-national resource transfer (capital and technology) was adopted. The guiding principle was that we would resort to foreign 'aid' only in order to do away with the need for foreign 'aid'. The short-run tactical perspective of encouraging the flow of official development assistance and foreign private capital, in the form of both loan and equity, even by jumping tariff walls, was adopted. If such a tactical perspective were to succeed it was essential that (a) international concessional or commercial borrowing should be made self-liquidating, (b) that import-substitution should reduce our net demand for all imports, including for maintenance imports and for upgradation of technology (i.e. by buying and absorbing total technology packages, including R and D capabilities, prevention of repetitive and imitative import of technology by individual firms) and (c) export capacity should be developed on the basis of long-term, dynamic comparative advantage linked to domestic demand and production pattern and for building balance of payment surpluses to liquidate outstanding external loans.

Whatever direct investments were to be made by MNCs should pass the tests of positive net foreign exchange contribution and genuine transfer of relevant technology and be made to follow their business interests within the framework of national control. It is doubtful if the 'donor' creditor and investing countries would have found these terms of new non-colonial (as opposed to neo-colonial) linkages profitable and acceptable. The pursuit of GNP growth, in any case, tended to ignore whether tactical external linkages contributed to the long-term strategic perspective of self-reliant development.

### ASSUMPTIONS REGARDING THE STATE'S CAPACITY

The entire strategy of growth was based on the capacity of the state:

i. to raise the rate of savings and capital accumulation, particularly for financing planned investment projects;
ii. to restructure agrarian relations and make farmers improve yields;
iii. to induce large private investments in a regulated way according to Plan priorities, mainly in the industrial sector, in order to ensure fast growth, growing employment and create a basis for self-sustained growth;

*iv.* to borrow from the world economy and obtain modern technology from its proprietory owners in former colonial countries at economic prices without getting into a debt-trap and dependency syndrome; and

*v.* to prepare and administer Plans and programmes for the public sector and policies for the regulated behaviour of the private entrepreneurs which would require a new administrative system.

It goes without saying that the strategy stipulated reciprocal response patterns from various classes and groups. It also assumed a world environment in which the ex-colonial powers would be more or less 'partners in progress' on the basis of mutually beneficial relationship. In any case, the availability of an option in the socialist world for finance, capital goods, technology and export markets implied not only direct benefits offered by them, but also improved our bargaining position vis-à-vis the West.

The strategy involved transfer of savings from the household sector to the government and the corporate sector. The corporate sector was also to be made to provide resources to the government as part of the decision to increase the marginal rate of savings. Various methods were to be devised to increase the propensity to save and invest, both in financial and physical assets. Partly as a means of forcing a cut in incremental consumption, particularly in the unorganized and rural sectors, indirect taxes were to be supplemented by deficit financing. A mild dose of inflation was considered an inescapable feature of a developing economy, conducive to a soaring of business sentiment.

Steep increase in the marginal rates of direct taxes were considered necessary for introducing equity without weakening incentives for the supply of savings, effort and entrepreneurial initiative. This was needed particularly because the state was doing so much for encouraging the growth of private industrial capital, especially by means of maintenance of a seller's market and direct creation of market by a high and rising level of public spending. In this situation the genesis of tax avoidance, tax-evasion, black-marketing and profiteering was inherent in so far as the actual realized rates of profit were considered inadequate by the general run of entrepreneurs, with their mercantile and usurious background. The fact that there were ample opportunities to violate various economic laws was not considered as a real danger to and a limitation of the strategy of growth. How would the unleashing of such tendencies distort and derail the growth strategy was not examined, particularly owing to a rather weak link between Plan formulation and Plan implementation.

## DID THE GREEN REVOLUTION REDEFINE THE GROWTH STRATEGY?

For operationalizing the growth strategy, we have with us now the experience of almost four decades of planning. Many things appear to have changed concerning the concept, strategy, technical perspective and design of development planning. Yet it can be said with some finality that none of the changes are of a fundamental nature as such. Probably, at one level of interpretation, the year 1965–6 can be regarded as a point of significant departure as an important change was made in relation to the strategy of agricultural growth as well as its relative place in the overall strategy of planning. The Green Revolution did mean a change in the strategy of achieving the accepted goal of growth and downgrading of various elements of the strategy which were to contribute to equity, particularly in the sphere of agrarian relations and yet it cannot be considered as a redefinition of the growth strategy.

This strong element of continuity in the concept and strategy of 'development', in our view, is based on the primacy of the pursuit, at the operational level in the Plans so far, of the objective of a sustained and sizeable growth of GNP, other goals being operationally secondary. The evidence provided by the experience of the period 1950–88 also indicates that no other objective has been achieved in a manner in which the objective of sustained economic growth has materialized.

No doubt, the idea was also to ensure that the growth of GNP is adequately reflected in the growth of per capita income. However, the growth of per capita income has not been commensurate with expectations, mainly on account of the population factor. The major factor of the orchestrated strategy seeking to achieve a simultaneous and organically interlinked pursuit of growth and equity, both as equally important objectives, could not become the operational guiding star. It was all along felt that growth would lead to the achievement of the other objectives, though some talk of growth with equity or basic needs was also occasionally heard.

In sum, it can be said that as far as the growth of GNP is concerned, the idea was to ensure that the built-in depressors operating in the Indian economy prior to 1947 be replaced through planning, by the introduction of some built-in propellors of growth like: public spending on current and capital account; public sector production of some important wherewithal of growth like basic capital and intermediate goods; import-substitution in a generally protectionist framework; continued though not too-strong inflation which provides rising rates of return on capital; extensive financial intermediation by the state in order to make household savings available to private corporate sector and government sector for investment, provision of an improved input package for raising agricultural production; raising public spending on social services for the twin goals of producing skilled and satisfied manpower, etc.

## GREATER OPENING UP AND LIBERALIZATION

Another element which seems to mark a reckonable departure from the earlier practice is concerning the relationship of the Indian economy with the rest of the world. Under the influence of the policy of import-substituting industrialization and the Mahalanobis model, India aspired to carve out a relatively independent place for herself in the world economy. Since foreign aid and private foreign capital were made important operational elements for attaining the goal of self-reliance by the early seventies there arose serious difficulties in continuing with import-substituting industrialization, particularly in view of rising debts and a burgeoning maintenance and energy import bill. Hence the pursuit of higher growth by further opening up of the economy to foreign capital, finance and technology with greater reliance on private initiative and increased recourse to the market instead of pursuing a path which emphasized planning, the public sector and greater use of domestic resources.

Such opening up of the economy and its concomitant

'liberalization' in the domestic economic policy, particularly concerning private industry, large industrial houses and foreign private capital and technology, do not amount to replacement or downgrading of the pursuit of GNP growth. These are attempts towards making private enterprise, both domestic and foreign, the prime engine of growth, with public sector remaining confined to public utilities and infrastructure. This is a significant change in growth strategy, though it does not compromise the primacy of growth of GNP. If anything, it brings about a relatively greater degree of rapport and integration between the concept and process of growth and the choice of the engine of growth. Earlier, growth of GNP concept was pursued through national planning, public sector, regulated growth of private industrial capital, agrarian restructuring, etc. **which in their totality and interlinkage** constituted a Statist, Welfarist perspective. The content, form and instrumentality of growth were somewhat ill-at-ease with each other, often leading to many tensions and distortions. Strong democratic pressure and movements were essential to resolve these tensions in favour of the stated social objectives. Since these pressures did not emerge, the inherent exercise of strengthend economic power created political clout which harmonized the growth concept, instruments and process towards relatively more privatized, non-Statist perspective. Growth was no longer to be seen as *ersatz* for development because growth had become acceptable by itself, fully and legitimately, without any operationally relevant concern for the stated social objectives.

We have discussed the growth concept and the strategy for its **achievement** without giving it an overall characterization by means of a single, comprehensive label. If we have to attempt such a thing, it is clear that we have been discussing the strategy of capitalist growth in post-colonial India, which had to be a Statist exercise, giving rise to a strong state capitalist sector. It appears that this model of growth may have a tendency under certain socio-political configurations to move towards a non-Statist, relatively more privatized, model. Whether it can be sustained for a reasonably long period of time may be in doubt, but it certainly does not automatically resolve itself into a more socially cohesive and humanized model.

# Growth Strategy: Past, Present and Future

AUROBINDO GHOSE

What strategy of growth will bring peace, progress and prosperity to the Indian economy and its 780 million inhabitants? This question is as relevant today as it was in the past.

The question is not simple. It involves both a theory of governance (which 'group' or 'class' interest does the state subserve?) as well as a distinction between the appearance and reality of state policy, between what the rulers declare they will do and what they actually do.

More than four years have passed since the air was rife with talk of a new strategy of growth, a take-off into the twenty-first century. We heard of wasteland development and district-wise industrialization, modernization and high-tech, export-led growth and import liberalization, of the competitive spirit and opening up to multinationals, privatization and economy in public expenditure. There were great expectations. The stock markets witnessed an unparalleled boom.

Now the veil of illusion lies tattered. Exposures and hindsight reveal that the enthusiasm for indiscriminate and large purchases of imported equipment, particularly for defence, was but an excuse to make a fast buck in commissions and kickbacks. The shrill cry of 'export or perish' to ostensibly bolster the foreign-exchange crisis was, it now appears, a mere cover for flight of capital into secret Swiss accounts.

The expected trade-off between likely losses to domestic industrialists because of freer entry of foreign capital and technology, and their anticipated gains on account of the promised privatization of the public sector, has not been realized. The virtually unhindered advance of a multinationals' juggernaut into a market hitherto protected by high tariff walls and severely restricted to direct foreign investment has led to a demand recession in domestic industry. This is true of the public, private, organized, unorganized, large-scale and small-scale sectors, sizeable segments of each of which are threatened with imminent closure. Currently, more than 100,000 industrial units are lying idle or sick, involving a capital stock of about Rs 20,000 crores. Therefore, the much-touted New Economic Policy has turned out to be an orange without its juice, and holds little attraction for the Indian industrial houses. Indian business feels cheated by the 'new' strategy of growth. Their confidence having been shaken, share prices have also plummeted.

The 'old' strategy of growth of the Nehru-era, launched in 1956, was likewise deceptive. The difference was that it did not set out to deceive domestic capitalists. It was the cheerful economists and statisticians of the mid-fifties (apart from the middle classes) who were mostly carried away by the lure of rapid growth, heavy industrialization, self-reliance, the socialist pattern, the public sector and the control of monopolies. They provided the theoretical embellishment and academic legitimacy to what was essentially a strategy of development of capitalism, particularly of domestic monopolies, rich capitalist farmers and multinationals, under the aegis of the Indian State. Apparently, they were not bothered by the gap between theory and practice.

Businessmen were, however, quick to understand and anticipate this gap, it being in their interest. Their gut reaction to the post-Avadi Budget of 1955 was picturesquely summed up by the *Economic Weekly*'s stock exchange correspondent: 'Dalal Street Wants More of this Socialism'.

Could their reactions have been different, we may ask, once it is recalled that leading Indian industrialists were pleading, even before Independence, for the kind of planning and mixed economy they got from 1956 onwards. In the *Plan for Economic Development for India*, published in 1944 (popularly known as the Bombay Plan), eight leading Indian business tycoons—Purshotamdas Thakurdas, J. R. D. Tata, G. D. Birla, Ardeshir Dalal, Sri Ram, Kasturbhai Lalbhai, A. D. Shroff and John Mathai—argued for the development of basic and heavy industries, particularly power; active government intervention and a predominant role for the public sector; and State control over the private sector. Looking much beyond their noses, they even added two important reservations to their basic proposals. First, that government management of the public sector is not absolutely vital. Second, that once the initial phase of development is over, the government can hand over the public enterprises to private capitalists. This was in 1944, not 1985.

The difference between the statement and intent of economic policy in India is also tellingly brought out by the joint-sector experiment. The Industrial Licensing Policy Inquiry Committee (popularly known as the Dutt Committee) suggested in 1969 the apparently new idea of the joint sector to 'control' Indian monopoly. But the FICCI and the Tata Memorandum promptly welcomed this very instrument of their subjugation. The mystery was cleared when it was discovered that the joint sector was a device fashioned precisely to obtain more institutional finance and greater state patronage, with management and control secure in the hands of private promoters. It was also found that far from originating in the Dutt Committee, the joint sector concept was first developed in 1961 by a committee set up by the Maharashtra government to ameliorate the difficulties of the private sector. This committee was headed by R. G. Saraiya, who was once president of the FICCI, and included Naval Tata as one of its members.

On the strategy of growth, there are other problems we cannot neglect. The mid-fifties' economists focused only on 'growth'. The distinction between 'growth' and 'development' emerged later out of the review of the actual growth experience of the newly-independent economies. There is a basic distinction. 'Economic growth' means the sustained growth of real per capita output of an economy in the long run. 'Economic development' implies, in addition, a positive impact of growth of production on the lives of the people in underdeveloped countries through significant reductions in the levels of poverty, unemployment and income inequalities. Arising out of this distinction and based on an examination of the growth experience of several developing underdeveloped economies, a proposition that gained currency in the 1970s was: 'There can be growth without development, but no development without growth.' Our own stock-taking of the implementation of

India's strategy of growth leads us to question this proposition.

Is it at all possible to have *sustained growth* without development, without an expansion of the home market through substantial reduction in the numbers of people below the poverty line, the magnitude of the unemployed and the grossly underemployed, and the extreme inequalities in income? Put in another way, the question we are raising in the present debate is: Can a strategy of growth alone be adequate to achieve growth or do you need a strategy of development?

Another important distinction is between the 'forces of production' (or the physical–technological aspects of production) and the 'relations of production' (or the ownership-institutional aspects of economic decision-making). An analysis of the strategy of growth based on this distinction can give us vital insights into the connections, nay the nexus, between the technological and institutional aspects of the growth process. For instance, the issue of increasing effective demand and expanding the home market in a developing country is both a technological and an institutional issue. The technological choices relate to the choice of industries, location of units, the magnitude of output and employment, as also the choice of technique. The connection between technology and institutions is obvious because decisions concerning these variables are themselves a function of the nature and structure of ownership of the means of production, whether socially owned or privately owned, whether competitive or dominated by monopolies and multinationals. Nothing is gained by hiding the fact.

It is our contention that this all-sided approach gives a better insight into the working of growth strategies than do the existing critiques of India's strategy of growth after Independence. The two polarized viewpoints—what may be called the institutional neo-Marxist critique and the rural development-oriented neo-Populist critique—while uncovering part of the truth, suffer from exclusiveness of approach.

The institutional critique does not even think of questioning the relevance of the physical–technological strategy of emphasizing basic and heavy industries successfully implemented in a sparsely populated, labour-scarce economy, such as the Soviet Union after 1917, and its wholesale transfer to the relatively highly populated, labour-abundant, capital-scarce economy like

India with a tremendous backlog of unskilled and unemployed (or grossly underemployed) labour. This neo-Marxist critique is content with attributing the failure of India's strategy of heavy industrialization to the absence of institutional reform, of implementing a 'socialist' strategy in an economy (India) hitherto dominated by foreign companies, domestic monopolies and landlords without any meaningful changes in the socio-economic structure.

Likewise, the rural development-centred critique virtually turns a blind eye to questions regarding the ownership of the means of production. To them the problems of inadequate growth, its uneven distribution (geographically speaking), its impact on mounting unemployment, poverty and rapid migration from the villages to the cities, are ultimately attributable to the technological characteristics of the strategy of India's growth. They just blame the large-scale capital-intensive, import-intensive, urban-biased, geographically concentrated (rather than dispersed) and displacement-oriented character of India's model of growth. To them 'small is beautiful'—the regional or district approach to industrialization based on 'intermediate' or 'appropriate' technology is all. The small industrial units being set up in the districts may be owned or managed by ugly faces of multinationals, but these neo-populists would remain unruffled.

Applying the logic of our approach, we find that both the 'old' and the 'new' strategies are formulated to focus on growth, rather than development. Likewise, they exhibit a contemptuous disregard of the appropriate technological and institutional requirements and their respective mutual consistencies.

The 'old' strategy of growth, implemented in the main between 1956 and 1966, put emphasis on industry as compared to agriculture. Within industry, the emphasis was on investment going to basic and heavy industries like steel, aluminium, machine tools, heavy engineering and electricals, rather than consumer goods and machinery for consumer goods industries like textile and sugar machinery. The declared aim was to lay the economic foundations for future growth at a relatively faster rate, and to promote economic independence and self-reliance through a strategy of indigenous substitution of imports of commodities, capital as well as technology.

The focus was on GNP growth. Problems of poverty and unemployment were to be indirectly and residually treated, through the 'trickle-down' effects of growth.

It was indeed an ambitious project. For its success, it required an extremely high rate of domestic saving and capital formation (25–30 per cent of national income to be saved and invested annually). A balanced and corresponding growth of agriculture, industry and services, and also of consumer's and producer's goods industries, was also a requirement. The self-reliance objective necessitated a well-thought-out R and D programme and policy of indigenous development of technology. Additionally, and crucially, a wider market for mass consumer goods was needed to demand the intermediate products and basic inputs invested in. In the absence of a responsive external export market, this could come about only through a wider and more equal generation and dispersal of employment and income opportunities domestically.

All this implied certain institutional requirements: completion of land reforms in agriculture; the control, if not the doing away, of domestic monopolies and multinational corporations in industry; a political will to tax the rich both in agriculture and industry; equal relations with trade partners and foreign aid donors; a strong state within a federal structure; genuine planning; and the actual participation of the people in the process of development.

How far were these fulfilled? Because practically none of these technological and institutional requirements were met in the Indian context, the strategy of growth failed, predictably. While the rate of growth of national income and per capita income was positive and substantially larger than before Independence, it started faltering from the mid-sixties. While new industries came up in a big way, excess capacity soon emerged particularly in the public sector, transforming them into white elephants. Regional and sectoral disparities widened. Industrial concentration became conspicuous. Technological dependence increased, as revealed by growing numbers of multiplicative and repetitive foreign collaborations, even in such simple items as dry battery, sewing needle and common medicines. An unplanned flourishing market for luxury consumer goods emerged, as did a resurgent parallel black economy. There was a rapid growth of the landless labour force. Unemployment, poverty and income inequality increased by leaps and bounds. After 1966, with the onset of industrial recession and problems of availability of resources, long-term planning itself was abandoned. The strategy of heavy industrialization and the phenomenal emphasis on the public sector was given up in practice.

Let us explore some of the reasons for the above failure. Resources have never been lacking in India, but they are not being mobilized. According to Charles Bettelheim, India has enough natural and human resources to emerge as the fourth strongest industrial power in the world. Its current ranking in the world in terms of real per capita income is, however, around 120th. While agriculture is still the single most important economic sector, there is no income tax on agriculture. Instead of mobilizing the resources where it existed in the upper income groups of the rural and urban sectors, indirect taxes on mass consumer goods, deficit financing and foreign aid were increasingly relied upon to resolve the 'financial crisis'. These methods turned out to be both inequitious and inflationary.

How the public sector came to serve the monopolies and multinationals can be illustrated by the case of the aluminium industry. In the Industrial Policy Resolution (IPR) of 1956, aluminium was put in schedule B, implying that it would mainly be the preserve of the public sector. When the large electricity project was started under the UP Electricity Board in 1955, the idea was that it would service the sister aluminium concern in the public sector. According to the Dutt Committee Report, the IPR of 1956 was violated at the instance of the then Prime Minister (Jawaharlal Nehru), and the aluminium licence was given to G. D. Birla. Thus emerged the Hindustan Aluminium Corporation, a collaboration concern of the Birlas and the Kaiser Aluminium of the USA. The Birlas entered into a 20-year contract in 1957 with the UP Electricity Board to get electricity at a subsidized, less than cost, rate. The argument was that aluminium, an electricity-intensive intermediate product, would generate waves of growth elsewhere. However, no corresponding distribution quota on aluminium or price control was imposed. The Birlas could freely indulge in monopolistic practices such as restriction of output and price escalation. While the UP Electricity Board went red and ran into hundreds of crores of losses, the Hindustan Aluminium Corporation declared dividends of 40 per cent, repeat 40 per cent. The price of Hindalco shares shot up in the share market. This is how the public sector became the handmaiden of the private monopolies, to be used as also to be abused.

The distortions of the strategy of heavy industrialization are no less evident from what has happened to the steel industry. Steel was the centrepiece, so to say, of the entire strategy of self-reliance. The steel industry has been built at very heavy public cost. Steel, like electricity, has been priced low to benefit private industry. However, the appropriate steel technology has not been developed. The result is that thousands of tonnes of steel are being imported every year, even while the public-sector steel plants are running at about 70 per cent capacity utilization. This is not because of the lack of domestic availability of the basic raw material, iron ore. The tragedy is that iron ore itself is being exported, contrary to the original objective. Even some steel produced by the Steel Authority of India Limited (Sail) is diverted to the production of 'Classic (stainless) Steel' crockery and cutlery for the super rich, and being marketed through, of all places, the Super Bazar.

The 'new' strategy is no different from the 'old'. The 'new' strategy has not infused much growth in the real sense. It generated speculative expectations, but now, as we have already demonstrated, the honeymoon is over. On the other hand, this strategy, if pursued further, will lead to greater subordination of the economy as well as the Indian capitalists to multinationals, will accentuate the inequalities within the Indian economy also between India and the advanced economies, and finally restrict the rate of economic growth. This is the inevitable logic of global profit maximization, illusory transfer of technology, transfer pricing and exorbitant capital intensity that the Multi-National Corporations (MNCs) imply.

We must not, also, forget the social and political dimensions of the current crisis.

India and the Indian people are passing through an extremely difficult period. The problems posed by terrorists, state terror, communalism, increasing repression of the working people, minorities and *dalits*, and the systematic encroachments on the rights of the people in general, are escalating everyday.

People's rights—the very right to life, livelihood, housing, freedom of faith, expression, association and organization, the equality of women, etc.—are under severe attack by the state, as well as different interest groups and fundamentalists of all kinds.

There is considerable division and fragmentation in society on the basis of caste, creed, language, region and religion. A clever state manipulates and attacks the different societies of India in such a way that each attack divides them further. Carnages and riots pit one community against another, diverting them from their basic economic and political struggles, and obfuscating the real oppressors. Mutual fear and suspicion are emerging as the hallmarks of present-day Indian society.

We clearly visualize an imminent threat of Fascism—one more Emergency—more ruthless and oppressive than the previous one in its attack on the working people of the country and their institutions and organizations. This will depend not on any one individual's predilection for such things but is likely to follow from the needs and requirements of the present socio-economic system.

What is the alternative? India seems today at crossroads. One path, the capitalist, leads towards the authoritarian state. The other, the path of socialism, can much more probably take the country out of its morass of economic stagnation, social division, political instability and human degradation.

This brief survey is not negative. It suggests an alternative strategy of growth for the Indian economy at the present stage—a strategy of growth plus development. The problems of poverty and unemployment must be attacked directly. While the existing basic and heavy industries have to be utilized to their full capacity, and a balance maintained between large-scale and small-scale units as also between labour-using and capital-intensive technology, the stress has to be on nurturing thousands of district- and village-based growth points meeting basic human needs, incorporating the indigenous technology, utilizing local resources and employing surplus labour in the immediate vicinity. As our analysis has shown, this approach cannot be given effect to within the present capitalist framework. The alternative institutional framework is, therefore, of socialist ownership of the means of production in the main, both in agriculture and industry. This has of course to be combined with the completion of land reforms and a 'land-to-the-tiller' policy in the most backward semi-feudal rural pockets.

This is not the time nor the place to spell out the entire blueprint of the kind of socialism we need. It is sufficient to say that state ownership of the means of production is but the means and not the end of socialism. Socialism cannot be contemplated without socialist democracy. The socialism envisaged here would not be a one-party dictatorship. It would be based on adult franchise, on an opposition, newspapers and freedom of the press, fundamental civil liberties and democratic rights, particularly the right of workers to organize themselves.

It should be obvious that a socialism such as envisaged here cannot be built on the basis of terrorist violence. All democratic and legitimate methods should be adopted in order to unite different sections of the Indian working people, only such a united force can resist the incoming authoritarianism and build the massive peoples' movement which alone can end the tyranny of capitalist class rule.

# Resource Mobilization, Resource Allocation and the Economic Strategy

SANJAYA BARU

Reports in the press suggest that the Planning Commission is hard put to find the resources for the proposed public sector. By contrast sections of the private corporate sector appear to be flushed with funds. A resource crunch for the public sector and a resource boom for the private corporate sector are not incongruities but manifestations of a singular process of income generation and distribution that has unfolded in this country resulting in the 'fiscal crisis of the state', and the decline of state capitalism in India.

## I. STATE CAPITALISM AND THE MOBILIZATION OF RESOURCES

An important feature of post-colonial economic development in India has been the central role assigned to the state and to planning. This of course is not a typical characteristic of Indian economic development alone but is a phenomenon common to several post-colonial societies. As Kalecki remarked, 'We are all "planners" today, although very different in character.'[1]

Planning and state intervention and participation in economic development have been seen in India as instruments of capitalist development, particularly relevant in the context of its colonial

---

[1] M. Kalecki, 'Economic and Social Aspects of Intermediate Regimes' in *Selected Essays on the Economic Growth of the Socialist and the Mixed Economy*, Cambridge University Press, 1972, p. 163.

past. State capitalism was viewed as a vehicle of transition to 'full-blooded' capitalism by some while others viewed it as an instrument for the establishment of a 'socialistic pattern of society'.

Whatever the validity of these alternative perceptions it is perhaps safe to suggest that 'underdeveloped countries, striving to expand their economic potential as fast as possible . . . tend to draw up plans of economic development. The next step is to provide for a large volume of investment in the public sector, since, as shown by experience, the private initiative cannot be relied upon to undertake an adequate volume of investment of appropriate structure. Thus state capitalism is closely connected with planning of one form or another which underdeveloped countries can hardly avoid today.'[2]

In other words, for the Indian business class, state capitalism essentially appeared as an inevitable 'transitionary phase' (though some like Kalecki viewed it as an 'intermediate regime' while yet others like the 'Nehruites' viewed it as a transition to socialism) in the general direction of capitalist development. Irrespective of the variations in these perceptions all of them recognized one important aspect of state capitalism, namely, the task of resource mobilization assigned to the state. This important task must be viewed in the context of the narrow resource base for industrialization that had been built up through the colonial period. Another important source of capital mobilization was the process of 'primitive accumulation' which was also left incomplete as a result of the operation of colonial rule and the state was now assigned the responsibility of pushing through this process.

In what follows we shall briefly examine some of the more important sources of resource mobilization in India and the role of state capitalism, before we proceed to examine the implications of recent trends both for resource mobilization and allocation in India.

II. RESOURCE MOBILIZATION FOR THE PRIVATE CORPORATE SECTOR

i. *The Primitive Accumulation of Capital.* Clearly one of the

---

[2] Ibid., p. 163.

important implications of colonial rule in India was to restrict the resource base for indigenous capitalism. Despite the fact that the 'tribute' extracted from the Indian countryside was of a sizeable magnitude this went largely into European coffers. On the other hand, other routes for primitive accumulation like trade were also limited in scope as far as the indigenous business class was concerned. The systematic outflow of the 'tribute' extracted by the colonial state, the deindustrialization of traditional manufacturing activity, the pauperization of the peasantry, and so on had all resulted in constraining the growth of the home market for capitalism even as this resulted in the 'primitive accumulation of capital'. In other words, colonial rule imposed certain fetters on the process of 'primitive accumulation of capital' translating itself into a process of development of the home market for indigenous capitalism. It was this disjunction which state capitalism was required to bridge. The state was called upon in the early post-colonial period to reorient the on-going process of 'primitive accumulation of capital' into becoming a basis for indigenous capitalist development.

It was in this context that the business classes viewed the role of land reform and public investment in agriculture. It was precisely within this perspective again that Kalecki emphasized the importance of the 'antifeudal' policies of state capitalism and argued that 'the key to "financing" a more rapid growth is the removal of obstacles to the expansion of agriculture, such as feudal land-ownership and domination of peasants by moneylenders and merchants.'[3] However, for a variety of reasons, which are well recognized in the literature on the subject, agrarian reforms in post-colonial India did not effectively remove the barriers to rapid development of capitalism. On the other hand, the persistence of certain pre-capitalist forms of surplus appropriation imposed constraints on this process resulting in the emergence of what Utsa Patnaik has characterized as 'the Junker-style landlord capitalism' which has preserved effective land monopoly.[4] An important consequence of

---

[3] M. Kalecki, 'Problems of Financing Economic Development in a Mixed Economy', op. cit., p. 152.

[4] Utsa Patnaik, 'Reflections on the Agrarian Question and the Develop-

this inability to break land monopoly and unleash productive forces in the countryside was that it restricted the ability of the state and of the business class to 'tap the agricultural surplus for its own industrialisation effort'.[5]

Thus, state intervention in the Indian economy was constrained by the *extant* relations of production in agriculture and the inability of state capitalism to alter these in any fundamental way through agrarian reform. As a result, an important source of surplus (resource) mobilization, namely, the primitive accumulation of capital was limited in its scope. Not only were rural surpluses inadequately mobilized for industrialization, the policies pursued by the state with respect to agricultural development, pricing, and so on resulted in a transfer of rural surpluses into the hands of the rural oligarchy. On the other hand, it is true that the continued pauperization of the rural poor, their increasing market-dependency in a regime of rising prices and the displacement of rural artisans by modern industry resulted in a constrained process of 'primitive accumulation' appropriating the incomes of the poor.

The net effect of all this has been to place an unequal burden on the rural poor, even as the rural oligarchy is left relatively untouched, in the mobilization of resources for capitalist industrialization. This is our first proposition.

ii. *Deficit Financing as Resource Mobilization*. It is here that the role of the state is most important and explicit. The private corporate sector viewed deficit financing as an important source of finance for industry. Deficit financing is a process by which real incomes are transferred from the wage and salary earning classes to the property-owing classes through the intermediation of the state. Indeed, one could in fact argue that deficit financing is essentially a form of primitive capital accumulation especially in a transitory economy in which a vast mass of poor people are increasingly being drawn into the cash nexus.

In India, typically, deficit financing implies credit creation. The public financial institutions, banks and the central bank are all involved in the process of credit expansion which is typically

---

ment of Capitalism in India', *First Daniel Thorner Memorial Lecture* (mimeo), Delhi, 1985.

[5] Ibid., p. 17.

a form of deficit financing. As one analyst noted, 'credit expansion has played an increasingly important role in financing capital formation during the first three plan periods in India'.[6] What is important to note is that a bulk of this credit was made available through the banking sector and through the non-banking financial intermediaries (NBFIs). The latter are an important instrument of state capitalist development in India. The banks and the NBFIs channellize household savings and create credit for the private and state capitalist sector. In the three Plan periods put together, households contributed nearly 84 per cent of the total source of financial saving available to the banking and non-banking financial institutions, while foreign savings accounted for only 16 per cent.

S. K. Rao[7] makes two important points regarding the availability and utilization of credit as a channel of resource mobilization for the private sector in India. Firstly, that much of this credit was made available not because upper income group savings had in fact increased but because the forced savings of the poor had been pushed up through a decline in their real consumption levels. Secondly, that the utilization of this credit was such as to generate inflationary pressures in the economy so that through profit inflation, luxury consumption had actually increased while that of necessaries had not.

Rao's empirical exercise on the impact of the pattern of credit creation attempted by the government and the trends in savings recalls to our mind the theoretical discussions of Kalecki on the question of financing economic development in mixed underdeveloped economies. Kalecki had warned against the inflationary consequences of credit financed development which did not simultaneously make available an adequate flow of necessaries. In such an event credit financed investment would fuel an inflation in the prices of necessaries thereby passing on the burden of deficit financing to the poor. This could be prevented if the excess liquidity in the system were mopped up through

---

[6] S. K. Rao, 'Constraints on Credit Expansion in Three South Asian Countries' in W. T. Newlyn (ed.), *The Financing of Economic Development*, Clarendon Press, Oxford, 1977, p. 222.

See Table VI.6, p. 220: Proximate Sources of Finance for Net Investment.

[7] Ibid., p. 234.

direct taxes on the rich or through the public distribution of necessities.[8]

In short, inflationary credit financing, which has been an important source of funds for the private corporate sector and the state capitalist sector, has meant a fall in the real consumption levels of the poor and middle income groups who are either not protected or are inadequately protected from inflation. This implies that there has been a real transfer of income from the poor to the rich property and asset owning classes who have either directly, or indirectly, through the state capitalist sector, been the beneficiaries of this income transfer. As we shall argue below, the absence of adequate direct taxation has only added to the inequitous nature of this process. Hence, our second proposition would be that deficit financing, which has been an important source of funds for industrialization in India, has been yet another process of transferring real incomes from the poor and middle income groups to the upper income groups and has thereby been an inequitious form of resource mobilization.

iii. *Taxation.* The only way the state can extract a share of the economic surplus accruing to the private sector, household and corporate, given its own resource requirements, would be through taxation, preferably direct taxation since indirect taxes are easily passed on to the poor and middle income (wage and salary earning) classes.

However, in actual practice the importance of direct taxes has been dwindling in India from one Plan period to another so much so that demands are now being made in favour of a total abolition of direct taxes. Direct taxes as a percentage of GNP are a lowly 2.5 per cent and as a percentage of total tax revenues have come down from being over 50 per cent to about 13 per cent, and, at present rates of taxation, cover hardly 4 per cent of the total population. What is worse is that not only are direct taxes being evaded with impunity but indirect taxes are being stepped up from budget to budget adding to the potential

---

[8] For an elaboration of Kalecki's arguments in the Indian context, see his 'The Problem of Financing Economic Development', *Indian Economic Review*, 1955; and Prabhat Patnaik, 'Some Macro-Economic Propositions around the Current Budgetary Policy', *Economic and Political Weekly*, 19 March 1984.

burden on the poor. According to one estimate, for 1973–4 as much as 55 per cent of all indirect taxes came from households with a monthly per capita expenditure of less than Rs 100.[9]

Hence, while the upper income groups do not bear a heavy burden of direct taxes they do not even bear a larger share of the burden of indirect taxes. This only strengthens our earlier propositions that the burden of resource mobilization in India has fallen unevenly on the poor and the middle income groups.

iv. *Foreign Aid*. For India this has not been as important a source of investible funds as it has been for most other post-colonial economies. Nevertheless, the importance of foreign aid and capital has in fact increased over the successive Plan periods. Despite the protestations regarding self-reliance, Indian industry, especially the private corporate sector, has been unable to reduce its external dependence, both in terms of capital requirements and technology and technical know-how, all of which have only increased in importance.

The most important sources of foreign aid and capital for India have been the advanced capitalist nations and the multilateral institutions that they dominate like the IBRD and IMF and their concessional aid windows like IDA, IFC, and so on. However, these are all not 'neutral' sources of funds in that they are instruments of neo-colonial domination by the imperialist nations in post-colonial societies. External aid dependence has always run the risk of pushing the debtor nation into a relationship of dependence with respect to the advanced capitalist countries as a whole and the United States of America in particular. Liberal aid has almost always been a means of securing from the debtor nation an assurance of liberal trade policies. Hence aid has been a vehicle of neo-colonial trade domination. Further, multilateral aid agencies like the World Bank have also imposed an economic policy regime conducive to the interests of foreign capital and multinational corporations. The policy conditionalities that go with such aid programmes have in fact imposed additional burdens on the debtor nations which in turn are unequally borne by the poor and middle income groups in these countries. Not only do such 'conditionality' policies of 'structural adjustment' and 'stabiliza-

[9] *Indirect Taxation Enquiry Committee*, Government of India.

tion' imply a weakening of state capitalism and the penetration of imperialism into debtor nations but they also imply a further distortion of Plan priorities and a worsening of income distribution in these countries. Such a distortion of priorities inevitably results in a more capital-intensive, import-intensive and externally-dependent industrialization strategy.

It is true that foreign aid can in fact be used merely for the import of food and necessities in a poor nation in order to dampen inflationary pressures generated in the course of credit-financed investment. However, this is unlikely to be an important component of aid-financed imports. Further, it is the activities related to the repayment of the debt, the pressure for stepping up exports, and so on which may then have an inflationary impact on the economy if such activities are subsidized through deficit financing or if they imply import-intensive investment. Devaluation of the local currency in the context of import-intensive investment and a liberal trade regime can only increase the costs of production and exert further inflationary pressures in the domestic economy. While all this is not a necessary consequence of 'aid-financed' investment it is an aspect of neo-colonialism that a debtor nation can ill afford to neglect. Its implications for the poor in the debtor nations are indeed dubious and dangerous.

### III. RESOURCE MOBILIZATION PATTERNS AND INCOME DISTRIBUTION

In the foregoing we have identified four important forms of resource mobilization in India. Given these various forms of resource mobilization, all of which have implicitly inequitous implications, it would defy logic if in fact the distribution of income between social classes has not worsened over the planning period in India. One can hazard the conclusion that the structure of resource mobilization in India has implied a further worsening of income distribution and has involved a process by which the property-owning classes have gained considerably more than what they have contributed to the process of economic development in India. While the rural oligarchy has hardly contributed a fraction of its economic surplus to the state, it has in turn derived significant benefits from state-sponsored investment in agriculture and agriculture-oriented industries like fertilizers. Similarly, while the capitalist class, particularly the monopoly capitalist class has benefited from the process of capital accumulation under state capitalist development they have hardly contributed to state revenues through direct taxation of their incomes. On the other hand, the inflationary pressures generated by the above forms of resource mobilization, the general tendency to rely on indirect taxes, and so on have in fact imposed the real burden of resource mobilization on the poor and middle income groups.

An important implication of this process has been to curtail the resources available with the state resulting in the fiscal crisis of the state.

### IV. 'FISCAL CRISIS OF THE STATE' AND RESOURCES FOR THE STATE SECTOR

The inability of the state to tax the rich, to appropriate a share of the surplus generated in the private sector through state-sponsored, state-subsidized and credit-financed capital accumulation is at the root of the 'fiscal crisis of the state'.[10] While the ensuring resource constraint has emerged as a major barrier to the further growth of public investment and expenditure, the decline of the latter has become an important determinant of industrial stagnation in India. The resources shortage is doubly debilitating for the state capitalist sector. Firstly, it curtails state investment and thereby acts as a direct constraint on the expansion of that sector. Secondly, and equally importantly, it retards the 'efficiency' of that sector by imposing financial limitations on state enterprises which prevent them from investing in modernization of plant and machinery by forcing them to abandon projects midway, and, thereby making these projects uneconomical and so on.

In short, while the overall resource crisis of the state imposes a constraint on the growth of state enterprises, such a shortage

---

[10] See Prabhat Patnaik, ibid. and Prabhat Patnaik and S. K. Rao, 'Towards an Explanation of Crisis in a Mixed Underdeveloped Economy', *Economic and Political Weekly*, Annual Number, 1977. For an analysis of recent policy changes within this perspective, see Sanjaya Baru, 'State in Retreat?', *Economic and Political Weekly*, 20 April 1985.

makes state enterprises even more resource deficient by denying them the possibility of generating internal revenues through modernization and technical upgradation. In such a situation to ask the public sector to find resources for its growth through greater 'efficiency' would appear to be begging the question. It is the paucity of resources which often is the cause of 'inefficiency'. Of course this is not to deny that the public sector has within it several units which are badly managed, where labour productivity is low, and so on, and that a wide margin for increasing labour productivity and capital efficiency is available. However, to us it would appear that the 'inefficiency' of the public sector is primarily a reflection of the role assigned to it under state capitalism in which the private sector has systematically drained it of its surpluses and has made it incapable of operating 'efficiently' in a purely financial sense.

### V. PUBLIC RESOURCES AND PRIVATE INVESTMENT

From the foregoing the question that would follow would be this: how have these resources which have been mobilized through the expropriation of the poor and middle income classes been utilized? Here one may mention that a bulk of the so-called private sector investment is financed by public funds which have been provided to the former through a variety of public financing institutions. However, since these public financial institutions have rarely followed the principle of actually specifying what kind of investment they are willing to finance, the effective principle has remained one of 'project viability'. Product selection has never been a concern of the public financial institutions. As a result, the funds of these institutions have often gone into 'socially wasteful' areas. The public sector itself has often gone in for wasteful investment sometimes involving foreign collaborations and exchange outflows. In the private sector examples of socially wasteful collaborations abound, involving large magnitudes of foreign investment and royalty repatriation. The recent boom in foreign collaboration agreements within the automobile industry is an example of unplanned and indiscriminate import of technology and capital which entails uneconomic utilization of investible resources.

In theory the state was supposed to closely monitor the utilization of investible resources, particularly public resources, in the private sector, and this may still have happened in certain brief periods or in certain sectors, but in practice private investment has by and large followed only private economic calculus often in conflict with social benefit.

Not only has this process generated the growth of luxury goods industries but it has also resulted in a greater centralization and concentration of capital in industry given that a large part of the investment in the luxury goods sector has been undertaken by the monopoly houses and multinational corporations involving sizeable foreign collaboration component.

For a variety of reasons which are now well documented and discussed in existing literature, this entire pattern of industrialization has been limited and norrowly based. The stimulus that state capitalism had provided to industrial growth in the early planning period began to get exhausted both on account of the exhaustion and on account of the deceleration in public investment and expenditure.[11] The deceleration of the home market for mass consumption goods which followed from the decline in public investment and expenditure (and the fact that higher proportions of the real incomes of the poor and the middle income groups were being devoted to food consumption as a result of rising food prices during this period) reflected itself in the private corporate sector trying to alter its production structure in favour of elite consumption demand. The case of the cotton textile industry is illustrative of this general trend in the economy as a whole where the decline of the cotton-cloth producing mills was accompanied by the growth of mills catering to the upper end of the market producing superfine varieties of rayon and polyester yarn cloth.

Private corporate investment has, therefore, increasingly gone into elite consumption goods industries.[12] It is not,

---

[11] For a review of literature on the problem of industrial stagnation, see Deepak Nayyar, 'Industrial Stagnation in India' in A. K. Bagchi and N. Banerjee, *Change and Choice in Indian Industry*.

[12] For empirical support to this argument, see S. L. Shetty, 'Structural Retrogression in Indian Industry since the Mid-Sixties', *Economic and Political Weekly*, Annual Number, 1978.

therefore, surprising that such a restructuring of the production structure in favour of elite consumption goods industries should be accompanied by further demands for a liberalization of fiscal policies aimed at expanding the market for such goods. In other words, while the growth of elite consumption goods industries was in the first place encouraged by the changing pattern of income distribution in India, which put more money in the hands of the rich than in the hands of the poor and middle classes, the emergence of such industries only put further pressure on the state to further distort the income structure in the country in order to widen the market for elite consumption goods.

The upshot of it all has been to generate pressures on the state from the upper income groups in favour of 'liberalization', freer imports, reduced direct taxation (the economic advisor to the Tata Industries has in fact recommended complete abolition of direct taxes), and so on, all policies oriented towards putting more money in the hands of the rich so that they can buy more of the luxury goods that they in turn manufacture. The incestuous nexus of elitist indulgence is to be the basis of a new spurt of industrialization whose 'trickle-down effects', it is hoped, will generate employment and stimulate incomes of the poor.

### VI. PRIVATE RESOURCES FOR PRIVATE INVESTMENT

The above pattern of industrialization has largely been based on the flow of funds from the state and the poor and middle classes as we have already stated above. However, this entire process has left the rich with a larger volume of real income which is now finding its way into the capital market. The capital market in India has been slow in developing and traditionally it is the credit provided by the banks and the NBFs which has sustained private investment. Over the last few years, however, the capital market has begun to spread into various urban centres in India bringing into its fold the vast accumulated surpluses of the rich. For example, while the capital raised annually by companies through issue of shares and debentures through the capital market was around Rs 100 crores per annum through most of the 1960s and 1970s, it shot up three-fold to an average of over Rs 300 crores during the early 1980s.[13]

The share market now shows a definite tendency signalling a new phase in the evolution of the Indian capital market and the corporate sector. The stock market boom in 1985 and 1986 is a manifestation of this tendency. It is now clear that upper middle class and upper class households and the rural rich have entered the capital market, given the relatively high rates of return for certain companies *vis-á-vis* the prevailing interest rates. Company deposits, shares and debentures in select areas of investment yield far more than long-term bank deposits. The phenomenon of 'over-subscription' came to be noticed first in the late 1970s when several companies found to their surprise an enthusiastic response to public issue. Since then the process of widening and deepening of the capital market has gathered momentum. The banks find that the rate of growth of term-deposits has declined as a result of this diversion of 'savings' directly into the private sector.

It is too premature to speculate on the long-term implications of this phenomenon or even on its significance to resource mobilization for the corporate sector in India. However, it is time we took notice of this trend and examined its implications for planning and for planned industrial investment in India. Theoretically it may be argued that the capital market is the most efficient allocator of resources and that the share market is extremely sensitive to profit signals and it would never allow a suboptimal utilization of resources. However, in this context, the recent policy thrust reducing the fiscal levies on luxury consumption goods becomes relevant. It must be noted that in a developing economy with limited financial resources at its disposal, with the requirements of planned industrialization being often at variance with the private profit calculus of investors, the tendency towards a capital-marked-dictated industrialization is something one should be wary of. For 'efficiency' in this case would really have a restricted meaning and a privately 'efficient' allocation of resources, judged in terms of return on investment, may be socially 'inefficient' in terms of the kind of industries that are in fact promoted.

[13] T. K. Velayudhan, 'Debt-Equity Ratio', *RBI Occasional Papers*, vol. 5, no. 2, December 1984.

It is obviously not a coincidence that the recent stock market boom began in November 1984. The coming to power of Rajiv Gandhi and policy signals he sent through the New Computer Policy found favourable response in the stock market. As one observer of the stock market commented: 'The stock market's unbounded optimism reflects essentially its firm conviction about the dawn of a new era for the private sector. The policies initiated and implemented by the government headed by Rajiv Gandhi have infused a lot of confidence among the investing classes'.[14]

Can one interpret this boom as the beginning of a new phase of industrial growth? Clearly one can make no such inference on the basis of available evidence and on the basis of a purely stock market boom. What we can easily assert however is this, that the current stock market boom and the growth of the capital market in India which this boom in fact symbolizes signifies two things. Firstly, that fairly sizeable amounts of investible resources are in fact available with a certain special class that now feels confident enough to invest in certain types of industries rather than hold it in the form of assets like real estate, gold, commodity stocks, and so on. Secondly, one can assert that the dependence of the private corporate sector on the public financial institutions may decrease as a result of the growth of a capital market on a long-term basis.

Together, these two tendencies have one implication. They would facilitate the 'unplanned' growth of certain types of industries for which the market exhibits a 'pent-up' demand. The funds for such investment would be garnered from the capital market, both national and international, and the output sold within a particular class of consumers. It is, as we have termed it, an 'incestuous nexus'. The rich providing funds for the production of commodities which they in turn shall

[14] 'Stock Markets Running Wild', *Economic and Political Weekly*, 22–9 June 1985, p. 1064. 'The stock markets in India are making history. Never before in living memory have they been known to have moved so fast in a bull or bear campaign. The rise in quite a large number of scrips in the "specified" as well as "other securities" list could well be described as spectacular and staggering. The current upswing started about the middle of November (1984)'. Also see 'In Search of Quick Fortunes', *Economic and Political Weekly*, 17 August 1985, p. 1372.

consume. Such a pattern of investment would remain largely outside the ambit of planning and therefore would disturb 'national' or 'social' priorities as laid down by the Plan. In order to sustain this blossoming of the capital market, in order to sustain the demand for the goods that will be produced and finally in order to sustain the enterprises that will come up to cater to this demand, the government would be pressurized to further 'liberalize' its fiscal, industrial and trade policies. To the extent that 'conspicuous consumption' in third world societies is shaped by the international 'demonstration effect' such a 'elite-consumption-led-growth' will inevitably be both import-intensive and capital-intensive. The employment and foreign exchange implications of an import- and capital-intensive industrialization strategy are bound to be disastrous for a labour-surplus and foreign-exchange-deficient economy like ours.

Such a pattern of industrialization would not only entail a narrowing of the social basis of indigenous capitalism but would also mean a strengthening of imperialist intervention in the Indian economy through increased dependence on foreign capital and technology, and would also be implicitly more authoritarian given the fact that it would generate serious social conflict.

# Agricultural Development in India Since Independence

G. S. BHALLA

This paper briefly examines the performance of Indian agriculture since Independence and also brings out some of the main challenges facing Indian agriculture.

## Performance of Indian Agriculture

That the post-Independence period marks a turning point in the history of Indian agriculture is clear from the fact that the agricultural sector recorded a growth rate of about 2.7 per cent during 1950–1 to 1983–4 compared with a meagre rate of less than 1 per cent during 1904–5 to 1944–5. The rapid growth of agriculture in the post-Independence period has been achieved because of very high priority given to this sector by the Indian Government. The policy makers adopted a two-fold strategy with a view to regenerating agriculture. The first element of the strategy was to execute land reforms in order to eliminate the institutional bottlenecks. The second part was to undertake massive investment in irrigation and other infrastructure in order to update agricultural technology.

The main reasons for the stagnation of Indian agriculture during the colonial period were the existence and perpetuation of outmoded land relations, deliberate integration of the Indian economy into the colonial economy and lack of adequate investment in irrigation and other infrastructure. The Indian Government was committed to land reforms and consequently land reform legislations were passed by all the state Governments during the fifties with the avowed aim of abolishing landlordism, distributing land through imposition of ceilings, protection of tenants and consolidation of landholdings. One of the significant achievements of these acts was the abolition of absentee landlordism in large parts of India. However, land reforms were half-hearted with regard to the imposition of ceilings and security of tenure. Consequently, the skewness in land distribution was not reduced in any significant manner. Further, very large number of tenants were actually evicted all over India in the name of self-cultivation. Despite these limitations, land reforms brought about a significant change in land relations in so far as self-cultivation rather than absentee landlordism became a predominant mode of production in Indian agriculture.

Simultaneously with land reforms, agricultural technology was sought to be updated through huge investment in irrigation and other infrastructure as a part of overall planned development in India. The immediate pay-off of these policies was extremely high, this is clear from the fact that agricultural output registered a growth rate of 3.3 per cent during the fifties compared with a paltry rate of less than 1 per cent in the first half of the century. It is however important to note that during this period about 70 per cent of the total growth of output was accounted for by area increases and only 30 per cent through increases in yields. However, the acceleration in agricultural output achieved during the fifties could not be sustained beyond a decade. By the beginning of the sixties domestic output of foodgrains had started stagnating and large recourse had to be made to food imports.

This prompted the policy makers to make significant changes in their plan strategy. Their main concern was to find methods of increasing land yields through the use of modern inputs and improved methods of production. The new approach entailed a concentration of efforts on selected irrigated regions through intensive agricultural development programmes.

To begin with, the new strategy failed to make much impact, its culmination came about in the mid-sixties when the programmes for using high-yielding varieties and multiple cropping were successfully introduced in some regions of India. The new technology often known as the green revolution has had a profound impact on raising agricultural yields and increasing the income of cultivators in the irrigated regions of India. By increasing yields in a significant manner, the new technology was also able to alleviate the growing land constraint faced by Indian agriculture. In this context it may be mentioned that as a result of new technology, unlike the earlier period, yield rather than area increases have become the predominant source of growth of agriculture. Table 1 below gives some details about the spread and achievements of new technology. That the new technology has proved successful is obvious from the fact that during 1966-7 to 1979-80, as against a population growth rate of 2.1 per cent, agricultural output has been growing at a compound rate of 2.7 per cent per annum. The new technology has in no small measure contributed to India becoming almost self-sufficient in foodgrains production.

### Problems of Indian Agriculture and Tasks Ahead

Despite a very remarkable growth of agricultural output since Independence, it would be wrong to underestimate the various problems faced by this sector. The first problem is that notwithstanding all progress, India has only become marginally self-sufficient in foodgrains and continues to be a major importer in oilseed. With the envisaged increase in population, agricultural growth will have to be significantly accelerated in order to meet the demands of an increasing population. It is notable in this context that during the post-Independence period, population recorded a growth rate of 2.5 per cent per annum compared with a growth rate of only 0.83 per cent in the first half of the twentieth century. Taking the most optimistic estimates about decline in population growth during the current and the next decade, India will still end up with a population of about 1 billion by the year 2001. With this order of population, the demand for foodgrains along with seed and feed requirements is envisaged to be of the order of about 240 million tonnes, i.e. about 90 million tonnes higher than the current output. The enormity of the challenge can be brought out by the fact that whereas India was able to achieve an incremental output of 100 million tonnes in thirty five years from 50 million tonnes in 1950-1 to about 150 million tonnes in 1984-5 it will need to increase its output by 90 million tonnes over a period of fifteen years only. This is indeed a Herculian task and will necessitate further extension and deepening of the green revolution.

In this context, it may also be pointed out that the real cost of raising additional agricultural output is becoming increasingly greater because of several emerging constraints. The severest of these is the land constraint. Thus, the area under crops, which during the period 1952–3 to 1964–5 had grown at a rate of 1.28 per cent per annum, recorded a growth rate of merely 0.31 per cent during 1967–8 to 1979–80. This slow down has occurred even though irrigation, hitherto a major source of increasing intensity, has expanded at a faster rate during the latter period.

Furthermore, the new seed-fertilizer technology has so far been concentrated in irrigated areas only. Some notable developments are now taking place in dry-land agriculture. In rainfed areas, substantial resources constituted nearly 40 per cent of total net sown area, in order to increase their productivity in a significant manner.

The other set of problems in Indian agriculture are due to distortions introduced by both technological and institutional factors. For example, the green revolution technology has by and large been concentrated in irrigated areas and had led to widespread inter-regional disparities. Table 2 gives some details.

It is clear from the table that both during 1962–5 to 1970–3 and during 1969–72 to 1981–4, the highest rate of growth in agriculture has been achieved by the north-western regions of Haryana, Punjab and Uttar Pradesh. Interestingly, next to these areas it is the central dry region comprising Gujarat, Maharashtra, Rajasthan and Madhya Pradesh that has shown a remarkable growth rate during 1969–72 to 1981–4. (The growth rate of this region was dismal during the earlier period.)

On the other hand, except for Andhra Pradesh, the performance of the other southern states, Tamil Nadu, Karnataka and Kerala, has been rather disappointing. It is the eastern states— Assam, Bihar, West Bengal and Orissa—which have had the most dismal performance and continue to be the Achilles' heel of Indian agriculture.

The data on the levels and growth rate of foodgrains, given in Table 3, also brings out that it is the eastern sector that has

TABLE 1

Some Indicators of Agricultural Development of India, 1950–1 to 1983–4

| Year | Net Sown Area (m.h.) | Gross Cropped Area (m.h.) | Cropping Intensity | Net Irrigated Area (m.h.) | Gross Irrigated Area (m.h.) | Fertilizer Consumption (m. tonnes) | Area under H.Y.V. (m.h.) | Indices of agricultural production (Base: Triennium ending 1969–70 = 100) | Per capita availability Pulses (a) | Per capita availability Total food grains (b) |
|---|---|---|---|---|---|---|---|---|---|---|
| 1 | 2 | 3 | 4 | 5 | 6 | 7 | 8 | 9 | 10 | 11 |
| 1950–1 | 118.8 | 131.89 | 1.110 | 20.85 | 22.56 | 0.07 | — | 58.46* | 60.8 | 394.9 |
| 1955–6 | 129.2 | 147.31 | 1.140 | 22.76 | 25.64 | 0.16 | — | 71.62* | 70.5 | 430.6 |
| 1960–1 | 133.2 | 152.77 | 1.147 | 24.66 | 27.98 | 0.56 | — | 87.15* | 69.1 | 467.8 |
| 1965–6 | 136.2 | 155.28 | 1.140 | 26.34 | 30.90 | 0.78 | — | 81.29* | 47.8 | 403.7 |
| 1970–1 | 140.8 | 165.79 | 1.177 | 31.10 | 38.19 | 2.26 | 15.38 | 110.30 | 51.9 | 455.0 |
| 1971–2 | 140.0 | 165.19 | 1.180 | 31.55 | 38.43 | 2.66 | 18.17 | 111.20 | 51.3 | 468.8 |
| 1972–3 | 137.6 | 162.15 | 1.178 | 31.83 | 39.06 | 2.77 | 22.32 | 102.20 | 47.0 | 466.5 |
| 1973–4 | 143.1 | 169.87 | 1.187 | 32.55 | 40.28 | 2.84 | 26.04 | 112.40 | 41.2 | 422.4 |

| | | | | | | | | |
|---|---|---|---|---|---|---|---|---|
| 1974–5 | 137.7 | 164.19 | 1.192 | 33.71 | 41.74 | 2.58 | 27.33 | 108.80 | 40.7 | 450.8 |
| 1975–6 | 141.6 | 171.30 | 1.210 | 34.59 | 43.36 | 2.90 | 41.89 | 124.80 | 39.9 | 406.7 |
| 1976–7 | 139.5 | 167.34 | 1.200 | 33.75 | 43.55 | 3.43 | 33.56 | 116.40 | 50.8 | 453.3 |
| 1977–8 | 141.9 | 172.26 | 1.214 | 36.55 | 46.03 | 4.29 | 38.93 | 132.70 | 43.5 | 435.4 |
| 1978–9 | 143.0 | 174.76 | 1.222 | 38.06 | 48.31 | 5.12 | 41.10 | 137.80 | 45.1 | 472.2 |
| 1979–80 | 139.0 | 169.66 | 1.221 | 38.48 | 49.18 | 5.26 | 38.38 | 116.90 | 37.9 | 443.5 |
| 1980–1 | 140.3 | 173.32 | 1.235 | 38.80 | 49.58 | 5.52 | 43.05 | 135.20 | 34.1 | 431.9 |
| 1981–2 | | | | | | 6.06 | 46.50 | 142.70 | 38.2 | 453.7 |
| 1982–3 | | | | | | 6.39 | 47.68 | 137.00 | 38.9 | 442.2 |
| 1983–4 | | | | | | 7.20** | 52.00** | | | |

\* Indices have been calculated arithmetically shifting the base from 1961–2 to 1969–70.
\*\* Target
(a) Consultative utilization
(b) Average for two calendar years
Source: Economic Survey, Directorate of Economics and Statistics, Ministry of Agriculture.

### TABLE 2
### Regional Patterns of Growth of Production of Principal Crops in India during 1962–5 to 1970–3 and 1969–72 to 1981–4

|  | *(Per cent per annum)* Growth of Total Agricultural production | |
|---|---|---|
| States | I (a) 1962–5 to 1970–3 | II* 1969–72 to 1981–4 |
| 1 | 2 | 3 |
| **A. SOUTHERN STATES** | | |
| ANDHRA PRADESH | (−) 0.60 | 3.31 |
| TAMIL NADU | 2.47 | 1.12 |
| KARNATAKA | 3.66 | 2.44 |
| KERALA | 2.02 | 0.23 |
| **B. EASTERN STATES** | | |
| ASSAM | 2.54 | 1.96 |
| BIHAR | 0.54 | 0.49 |
| WEST BENGAL | 2.42 | 0.91 |
| ORISSA | (−) 0.30 | 2.28 |
| **C. CENTRAL STATES** | | |
| GUJARAT | 1.95 | 3.92 |
| MAHARASHTRA | (−) 3.77 | 5.59 |
| RAJASTHAN | 5.10 | 2.47 |
| MADHYA PRADESH | 1.39 | 1.65 |
| **D. NORTH WESTERN STATES** | | |
| HARYANA | 5.73 | 3.31 |
| PUNJAB | 7.91 | 3.92 |
| UTTAR PRADESH | 2.94 | 3.10 |
| ALL INDIA | 1.95 | 2.37 |

(a) Growth rates are taken from Bhalla-Alagh study, *Performance of Indian Agriculture—A District-wise Study*, Sterling, 1976.

* Growth rates have been worked out by fitting a trend line on indices of agricultural output constructed for each state based on production of 49 commodities. The indices have been prepared by the Commission for Agricultural Costs and Prices.

lagged far behind the rest of the country. That inter-regional variations have become quite pronounced is also clear from the fact that out of an incremental foodgrains output of 27.77 million tonnes as during 1973–4 to 1983–4, more than half was contributed by the three states of Haryana, Punjab and Uttar Pradesh. Another 30 per cent of incremental output came from the central region. On the other hand, Tamil Nadu and Karnataka accounted for only 1.57 per cent and the entire eastern region for only 3.7 per cent of the incremental output. Area specific policy measures will have to be taken to augment growth in the lagging eastern and southern regions.

The differential growth rates of agricultural output have increased the disparities in the living conditions of the peasantry in the different regions of India. Thus, in the fast growing regions of western Uttar Pradesh, Punjab and Haryana, not only has output increased but labour productivity has also recorded a rapid growth, despite a very rapid increase in agricultural work force. In the Gangetic areas of eastern Bihar, Orissa and West Bengal the growth of output has lagged far behind the growth of population, therefore the per capita productivity and incomes have tended to decline. Since in these areas the population pressure is very high, lack of adequate growth has led to the perpetuation of large scale poverty and destitution. The same is true about the slow-growing states of Tamil Nadu, Karnataka and Kerala. It is in these areas that a process of involution has taken place and prima-facie there are reasons to believe that the extent of poverty and destitution has tended to increase significantly.

Finally, institutional factors, primarily skewed distribution in ownership and operation of land, has led to large scale inter-personal inequalities. Table 4 gives details about the distribution of operational holdings. It is obvious from this table that whereas 68 per cent of cultivators tilling less than 5-acre plots account for only 24 per cent of the cultivated area, 8 per cent of the cultivators tilling more than 15-acre plots are able to claim about 40 per cent of the area. As the gains of the green revolution are more or less distributed according to land distribution, the income distribution has also tended to remain extremely skewed. In this situation, despite some increases in income, the economic condition of millions of small and

TABLE 3

*Regional Pattern of Incremental Output of Foodgrains in India, 1969–70 to 1973–4 and 1979–80 to 1983–4*

(Output '000 tonnes)

| States | 1969–70 to 1973–4 Output | % Share Output | 1979–80 to 1983–4 Output | % Share Output | Incremental output 1969–70/73–4, 1979–80/83–4 Output | % Share Output | Growth of Output |
|---|---|---|---|---|---|---|---|
| 1 | 2 | 3 | 4 | 5 | 6 | 7 | 8 |
| ANDHRA PRADESH | 7,495 | 7.28 | 10,725 | 8.20 | 3,230 | 11.63 | 3.65 |
| TAMIL NADU | 6,930 | 6.73 | 6,320 | 4.83 | −610 | −2.00 | −0.92 |
| KARNATAKA | 5,811 | 5.64 | 6,791 | 5.19 | 980 | 3.53 | 1.57 |
| KERALA | 1,303 | 1.27 | 1,314 | 1.01 | 11 | 0.04 | 0.08 |
| SOUTHERN STATES | 21,539 | 20.92 | 25,150 | 19.23 | 3,611 | 13.20 | 1.53 |
| ASSAM | 2,143 | 2.08 | 2,531 | 1.94 | 388 | 1.40 | 1.08 |
| BIHAR | 8,316 | 8.08 | 8,449 | 6.46 | 133 | 0.48 | 0.16 |
| WEST BENGAL | 7,274 | 7.07 | 7,380 | 5.64 | 106 | 0.38 | 0.14 |
| ORISSA | 4,925 | 4.78 | 5,339 | 4.08 | 414 | 1.49 | 0.81 |

| | | | | | | | |
|---|---|---|---|---|---|---|---|
| EASTERN STATES | 22,658 | 22.01 | 23,699 | 18.12 | 1,041 | 3.75 | 0.45 |
| GUJARAT | 3,596 | 3.49 | 4,742 | 3.63 | 1,146 | 4.13 | 2.80 |
| MAHARASHTRA | 5,526 | 5.37 | 10,171 | 7.78 | 4,645 | 16.72 | 6.29 |
| RAJASTHAN | 6,307 | 6.18 | 7,457 | 5.70 | 1,097 | 3.95 | 1.60 |
| MADHYA PRADESH | 10,720 | 10.41 | 12,135 | 9.28 | 1,415 | 5.09 | 1.25 |
| CENTRAL STATES | 26,202 | 25.45 | 34,505 | 26.39 | 8,303 | 29.89 | 2.79 |
| HARYANA | 4,355 | 4.23 | 6,133 | 4.69 | 1,778 | 6.40 | 3.48 |
| PUNJAB | 7,518 | 7.30 | 13,217 | 10.11 | 5,699 | 20.52 | 3.80 |
| UTTAR PRADESH | 17,714 | 17.21 | 24,289 | 18.58 | 6,575 | 23.67 | 3.21 |
| NORTH-WESTERN STATES | 29,587 | 28.74 | 43,639 | 33.38 | 14,052 | 50.59 | 3.96 |
| REST OF INDIA | 2,970 | 2.88 | 3,736 | 2.88 | 766 | 3.11 | 2.32 |
| ALL INDIA | 102,956 | 100.00 | 130,729 | 100.00 | 27,773 | 100.00 | 2.42 |

* Prepared by APC (Agricultural Prices Commission).

## TABLE 4

*Percentage Distribution of Households and of Area Operated by Size Class of Households Operational Holding*

|  | All-India<br>Number of sample<br>blocks and villages: 9,379 |  | Urban and Rural<br>Number of sample<br>household: 55,767 |
|---|---|---|---|
| Size class of household operational holdings (hectares) | Average area operated by household (hectares) | Percentage of Household | Percentage of Area operated |
| 1 | 2 | 3 | 4 |
| 0.00–0.002* | – | 41.30 | — |
| 0.002–0.20 | 0.09 | 11.69 | 0.48 |
| 0.21–0.40 | 0.28 | 9.52 | 1.23 |
| 0.41–0.50 | 0.44 | 5.71 | 1.13 |
| 0.51–1.00 | 0.75 | 18.86 | 6.40 |
| 1.01–2.02 | 1.45 | 22.35 | 14.76 |
| 2.03–3.03 | 2.46 | 11.84 | 13.24 |
| 3.04–4.04 | 3.48 | 5.86 | 9.26 |
| 4.05–5.05 | 4.47 | 4.19 | 8.53 |
| 5.06–6.07 | 5.51 | 2.23 | 5.60 |
| 6.08–8.09 | 6.93 | 2.95 | 9.30 |
| 8.10–10.12 | 8.97 | 1.70 | 6.91 |
| 10.13–12.14 | 10.99 | 0.97 | 4.83 |
| 12.15–20.24 | 14.95 | 1.55 | 10.49 |
| 20.25 and above | 29.91 | 0.58 | 7.84 |
| All sizes | 1.29 | 100.00 | 100.00 |

* This represents the category of landless labourers.
Source: National Sample Survey, Twenty-sixth Round 1971–72, No. 215 (All-India).

marginal farmers remains quite unenviable even in the green revolution areas. In other slow-growing regions, their conditions have deteriorated. It is quite understandable, therefore, that the extent of rural poverty is as high as 40 per cent. It is also important to note that poverty is more pronounced in areas where agricultural growth has been low.

In the green revolution belt, on the other hand, high growth of agricultural output has also made a visible dent on poverty.

To sum up, Indian agriculture has been successful in the historic challenge of feeding its increasing population in the post-Independence period. This has been possible because of both institutional changes brought about through the implementation of land reforms and technological changes brought about by increased investment in irrigation, credit and other infrastructure.

However, the pattern of development has led to increased interregional variations. Simultaneously, because of very large inequalities in land distribution, inter-personal inequalites have also tended to remain very wide. Thus, in spite of growth, the economic condition of landless labour and the marginal small farmer has not improved to any appreciable degree and they continue to suffer from large scale poverty and destitution, more so in areas where agricultural growth has been tardy. It would be necessary not only to accelerate growth in the lagging regions, but also to take specific measures for increasing the assets of the rural poor with a view to providing them with productive employment.

# India's Agricultural Performance: Growth amidst Neglect

B. M. BHATIA

I have just a few things to say about the agricultural policy. But before I do that, I would say a few words about the performance of the agricultural economy in India and the pattern of agricultural development in recent years.

The first thing that strikes me is that there has been a sea change in the Indian agricultural scene over the last thirty years. Up to 1965, India was considered to be a basket case which deserved to be dumped into the sea to save others in the boat from sinking. Several American experts were talking about India as almost a lost case and it was recommended that the little amount of food available by way of international help should be given to those countries which had some chance of survival. India did not appear to have much chance of survival. This was the situation in 1965. Then came the turn around for which we have to thank President Johnson of the United States, on the one hand, and serious drought for two consecutive years, on the other. Famine conditions prevailed in Bihar and Orissa which were worst affected by drought. Then there was the war with Pakistan in September 1965, which added to our troubles at that time. India, however, did not bend or break down in the face of the daunting challenge to her self-respect and survival. In terms of food assistance we got just 10 million tonnes of wheat one year and 14 million tonnes the next year from the USA under PL 480 to tide over the crisis. We then decided to get rid of this abject dependence on foreign aid in such a vital matter as food supply and that is the genesis of our Green Revolution. C. Subramanium, Sivaraman and M. S. Swaminathan were the architects of the Green Revolution which started in 1967. By 1979, the results were evident and India was being quoted in the US official documents (*Report of the Presidential Commission on World Hunger*, 1980) as, 'the only developing country in the world which has built a solid system of food security'.

Now this is what Indian agriculture has done over the last twenty years to our food situation. From the sinking boat analogy, India has come to a stage where it is being held up as a model of development on the food security front which other developing countries would do well to emulate. We now have a large buffer stock and a well-established public distribution system. India is one of the few countries in the world, with a sound base in food security and it is a matter of national pride that this is so. We can even export some quantity of food.

In the last thirty years food surpluses have been used as an instrument of foreign policy and for exercising power by the food surplus countries. Food is a very important weapon against a hungry nation and the Americans have used it to promote their foreign policy interests. Therefore, the fact that we have got out of this dependence and got freedom so to say from international food imperialism, is something we can feel proud of. We are in a position today to help some of the third world countries in distress. We have given some amount of food to relieve distress in Etheopia and a wheat loan to Vietnam.

Some idea of the progress made may be seen from the following figures. If you take 1951–2 food grain production at 54 million tonnes, this increased to 108 million tonnes in 1970–1, 131.8 million tonnes in 1978–9 and 152.4 million tonnes in 1983–4. The growth rate of foodgrain comes to 2.7 per cent per annum compared to the population growth of 2.2 per cent per annum. The latest figure for per capita availability is 483 gms (1984–5) as compared to 365 gms in 1950–1. The 1950–1 figure includes imports which have subsequently been eliminated and the 1984–5 availability figure is based on domestic production.

One the other side, there are some negative aspects of performance. The first is that foodgrain production is concentrated in certain areas. For example, in 1984–5 out of a total procurement of all foodgrains of 18.2 million tonnes, Punjab accounted for 9.2 million tonnes, Haryana 3.8 million tonnes, Uttar Pradesh 3.2 million tonnes and Andhra 1.1 million tonnes, making a total of 16.3 million tonnes, or roughly 90 per cent of the total procurement. Three states—Punjab, Haryana and U.P.—accounted for 83 per cent of the total procurement.

It has been suggested that paddy production should be increased, by an extension of the Green Revolution to the eastern and central states. I think this is going to be an extremely important contribution, among other things, to the solution of the Punjab problem. The situation in which one state becomes the bread basket for the whole nation is bad for national unity and integrity. Spatial diversification of agriculture is, therefore, very important, for apart from giving push to agricultural production it is going to be a solution of the Punjab problem.

Another problem is that the Green Revolution has mostly benefited wheat. Rice production is looking up, giving a boost to *kharif* production which was lagging behind *rabi* production. As a result *kharif* is again becoming important in total grain production: a new development that is important for reducing instability of output.

Pulses pose another problem. The per capita availability of pulses was 75 gms per day per capita in 1950. It fell to 37 gms and the latest figure is 42 gms. Given the vegetarian dietary habits of the people in this country, pulses are important as they are the only inexpensive source of protein in the diet other than milk, which is also becoming expensive. Another food item in which we have been left behind is oilseeds. We are spending about Rs 1000 crores annually on import of oilseeds and that is a very big drain on our limited foreign exchange resources. This is another gap in our agricultural development.

This was in brief an account of the performance of agriculture. Coming now to policy, there are three points I would like to make. First, that since 1954–5 or since 1967–8 whether you take the government pronouncements, or you take the recommendations of working groups, or of the National Commission on Agriculture or any other body of the above kind, the emphasis is on HYV-fertilizer technology for delivering the goods so far as agricultural growth is concerned. This technology, it is believed, will do everything, but experience has shown that reliance on technology alone would not do. Take the case of foodgrains production in 1983-4. There was a boost of 20 million tonnes that year over the previous year. An important contributory factor to the welcome increase in production was the 7.5 per cent reduction in the price of fertilizers followed by a further discount of 10 per cent on the old stock of fertilizers decreed by the Food Corporation of India. This had an immediate effect on the use of fertilizers and through that on the size of crop production. A side effect of that policy measure was the sharp increase in the subsidy amount. This went up to Rs 2000 crores from Rs 1300 crores. Now, this Rs 2000 crores subsidy and Rs 1250 crores on food subsidies equal the deficit financing of the Union Government. How long can you go on bearing such a burden? And over and above that, bonus prices have been given, which raise the subsidy amount still further.

Therefore, the Green Revolution was not triggered by HYV technology alone. The policy factor played its part. It was because of a crucial decision taken by the Lal Bahadur Shastri Cabinet at that time. A strong Cabinet Minister, T. T. Krishnamachari, opposed tooth and nail the proposal to give a 15 per cent price rise for wheat immediately. But G. Subramaniam insisted that only when this rise is given will this technology be taken up by the farmers, otherwise not. This change in price policy in 1965 was one of the most important factors, to my mind, that triggered the Green Revolution. This factor is often forgotten. If technology is not supported by appropriate policy on price, appropriate policy on land reforms, appropriate policy on several other matters that are there, technology would not work. This is one lesson in agricultural development that one has to remember.

Secondly, we followed in planning the Mahalanobis model and gave the highest priority to industrialization in our bid for development. We have shown residual consideration for agriculture. The problem is that even now our way of thinking is that industrialization and infrastructure are necessary for development. This remains the sheet-anchor of our planning. Instead, the whole approach should have been employment-oriented from the beginning and agriculture should have been given the highest priority. Then we would not have come up against high capital output ratios nor would we have required all these resources, all these sophistications and development models borrowed from the West for our planning. Plan priorities would have been different and the poverty problem and the problem of rural unemployment would have been solved long back. These two problems could be tackled if labour were absorbed in agriculture, and agricultural productivity of small and marginal farmers raised.

I think there is need for change not only in the strategy of economic development as a whole but a new agricultural development strategy is also required. This strategy should not be based on the recommendations of working groups which call for spreading the technology responsible for Green Revolution to the north-east and central India. Instead a strategy should be devised in which agriculture could become the centre point of all planning. Labour absorptions will be the most important element and objective in that and the growth strategy of the whole economy will be built around a 5 per cent growth in agriculture. I repeat my writings from the *Yojana* Annual Number, January 1984, 'Put agriculture in the lead, let industry follow'. Beginning with the Seventh Five Year Plan, if you adopt this model then within the next fifteen years I forsee a very bright future for India and the Indian economy and the future will be much brighter than the past thirty-five years' planning record.

Finally, the programme that was started three years ago of giving 20 kgs in kits, of fertilizers and seeds to small farmers to grow more oilseeds under the 20-point programme is commendable. This programme should be extended to all crops.

# Performance of Indian Agriculture and the Rural Sector in the Post-Green Revolution Period

### H. LAXMINARAYAN

The Green Revolution gave a big push to the production of wheat in the country largely due to its success in north-western India. This success achieved by Punjab, Haryana and western Uttar Pradesh in particular was commendable. Area under high yielding wheat increased from 7.86 million hectares in 1971–2 to 17.80 million hectares in 1981–2. Details relating to area under high yielding varieties are given in the following table:

TABLE 1

*High Yielding Varieties Programme—Area Sown*

(Million hectares)

| Year | Paddy | Wheat | Maize | Jowar | Bajra | Total HYV |
|---|---|---|---|---|---|---|
| 1 | 2 | 3 | 4 | 5 | 6 | 7 |
| 1971–2 | 7.41 | 7.86 | 0.44 | 0.69 | 1.77 | 18.17 |
| 1972–3 | 8.17 | 10.18 | 0.60 | 0.87 | 2.50 | 22.32 |
| 1973–4 | 9.98 | 11.03 | 0.87 | 1.16 | 3.00 | 26.04 |
| 1974–5 | 11.21 | 11.19 | 1.00 | 1.31 | 2.53 | 27.33 |
| 1975–6 | 12.44 | 13.46 | 1.13 | 1.96 | 2.90 | 31.89 |
| 1976–7 | 13.34 | 14.52 | 1.06 | 2.37 | 2.27 | 33.56 |
| 1977–8 | 16.12 | 15.80 | 1.24 | 3.14 | 2.63 | 38.93 |
| 1978–9 | 16.88 | 15.89 | 1.35 | 3.07 | 2.94 | 40.13 |
| 1979–80 | 15.99 | 15.03 | 1.35 | 3.05 | 2.96 | 38.38 |

TABLE 1 (Contd.)

| Year | Paddy | Wheat | Maize | Jowar | Bajra | Total HYV |
|---|---|---|---|---|---|---|
| 1 | 2 | 3 | 4 | 5 | 6 | 7 |
| 1980–1 | 18.49 | 17.39 | 1.39 | 4.18 | 3.80 | 45.25 |
| 1981–2 | 20.70 | 17.80 | 2.00 | 4.30 | 3.70 | 48.50 |
| (Target) | | | | | | |
| (Actual) | 19.33 | 17.66 | 1.51 | 4.11 | 4.07 | 46.68 |

Source: 1. Economic Survey, 1981–82.
2. Report 1981–82, Department of Agriculture and Cooperation, Ministry of Agriculture.

In the case of paddy it increased from 7.41 million hectares to 19.33 million hectares. Out of a total area of 46.50 million hectares, paddy and wheat accounted for 38.5 million hectares. Maize, jowar and bajra occupied about 10 million hectares in 1981–2 as against 2.90 million hectares in 1971–2. It is obvious that the Green Revolution in terms of use of high yielding varieties of seeds affected only wheat and paddy, particularly wheat in north-western India. In the case of dry land cereals the increase was very limited and the success was confined to maize, bajra and oilseeds only with jowar and pulses being almost untouched by the Green Revolution. Apart from the use of high yielding seeds other factors which contributed to the increase in agricultural production were irrigation and fertilizers. The contribution of minor irrigation in particular to the success of the Green Revolution was considerable. The number of energized pumpsets/tubewells increased from 27.9 lakhs in 1976 to 46.6 lakhs in 1982.[1] Details relating to energization of tubewells/pumpsets are given in Table 2.

The table indicates that there has been 67 per cent increase in energized tubewells. While tubewells have been energized what is lacking is the timely supply of power to tubewells.

[1] *Indian Agriculture in Brief*, 18th and 19th edn., Directorate of Economics and Statistics, Department of Agriculture and Co-operation, Government of India.

## TABLE 2
### Irrigation Pumpsets/Tubewells Energized

| States | Year ending March 1976 | Year ending March 1982 | % increased in 6 years | Annual increased in % |
|---|---|---|---|---|
| ALL INDIA | 27,92,339 | 46,55,161 | 66.77 | 11.13 |
| ANDHRA PRADESH | 2,94,017 | 4,96,675 | 68.95 | 11.49 |
| BIHAR | 1,18,055 | 1,51,985 | 28.74 | 4.79 |
| HARYANA | 1,41,885 | 2,37,036 | 67.06 | 11.18 |
| KARNATAKA | 2,24,910 | 3,32,416 | 47.80 | 7.97 |
| MADHYA PRADESH | 1,46,739 | 3,54,645 | 141.69 | 23.61 |
| MAHARASHTRA | 4,12,068 | 7,19,283 | 74.55 | 12.42 |
| PUNJAB | 1,46,475 | 3,07,392 | 109.86 | 18.31 |
| RAJASTHAN | 93,826 | 2,33,578 | 148.95 | 24.82 |
| TAMIL NADU | 7,49,880 | 9,45,520 | 26.09 | 4.35 |

Total irrigated area in the country increased from 5.3 million hectares in 1967–8 to 47.6 million hectares in 1978–9 giving an annual growth rate of 72.4 per cent. Haryana and Punjab show high percentage of irrigated area to total area under all crops. In Punjab the percentage of irrigated area increased from 63.7 per cent in 1967–8 to 83 per cent in 1978–9 and in Haryana from 34.6 per cent to 53.9 per cent. Andhra Pradesh (35.8 per cent), Bihar (32.6 per cent), Jammu and Kashmir (40.9 per cent), Tamil Nadu (49.7 per cent) and Uttar Pradesh (43.5 per cent) also show reasonably high percentage of irrigated area. Irrigated area was particularly low in Kerala (12.3 per cent), Madhya Pradesh (11.4 per cent), Maharashtra (11.6 per cent), Rajasthan (19.7 per cent), Himachal Pradesh (16.7 per cent), and Gujarat (18.6 per cent). These are the states which grow unirrigated crops and which depend almost entirely on rainfed irrigation. Production of course cereals and pulses is largely concentrated in these states.

Increased consumption of fertilizers was another important factor which contributed to the success of the Green Revolution. The all-India consumption of fertilizers per hectare (NPK) increased from 16.09 kgs. in 1971–2 to 32 kgs. in 1980–1. There was almost a doubling of fertilizer consumption. States applying a relatively higher dose of fertilizers are Punjab (117.9), Tamil Nadu (63.2), Uttar Pradesh (49.3), Andhra Pradesh (45.9) and Haryana (42.5). Fertilizers consumption is very low in Assam (2.8), Madhya Pradesh (9.2), Orissa (9.6), and Rajasthan (8.0). States showing relatively higher level of fertilizer consumption are the states where the Green Revolution achieved substantial success as in the case of wheat and paddy.

In the case of rice, yield per hectare increased from 1422 kgs. in 1968–9 to 2106 kgs. in 1983–4 in Andhra Pradesh, from 1188 kgs. to 2406 kgs. in Haryana, from 2037 kgs. to 2066 in Jammu and Kashmir, and from 1361 kgs. to 3063 kgs. in Punjab. In the case of wheat, the yield increased from 1701 kgs. to 2499 kgs. in Haryana, from 2167 kgs. to 3015 kgs. in Punjab and from 2000 kgs. to 2596 kgs. in West Bengal. In the case of jowar, pulses and other coarse cereals, the increase in yield was much less. In the case of pulses, the all-India yield increased from 499 kgs. to 541 kgs. while in the case of wheat it increased from 1169 kgs. to 1851 kgs. It appears that the Green Revolution is continuing in the case of rice and wheat in Punjab, Haryana, Andhra and Tamil Nadu, etc. and if this growth rate is maintained the Green Revolution may continue further in these states. However, what should bother us is the limited success obtained by the Green Revolution in a large number of states particularly in the case of pulses and jowar. In the case of these crops it may safely be said that there has hardly been any success. Due to suitable high yielding varieties, bajra, oilseeds and maize have shown considerable increase in yield in some states, though the success is much less than in the case of wheat and rice. States where yield increased have been limited as mentioned above, largely depend upon rainfall and do not have a high percentage of irrigated area. In Gujarat out of 19 districts, 11 districts fall in the category of low rainfall area. In Rajasthan out of 26 districts, 20 districts belong to the category of low rainfall area. In Punjab, 9 out of 12 districts and in Haryana 10 out of 11 districts belong to the low rainfall category. However, these states depend upon assured irrigation because of the growth of tubewell irrigation and canal irrigation which have given them a high percentage of irrigated area. Details relating to factors responsible for failure of technology are given in the section on dry land agriculture.

Details relating to growth rates in area, production and yield of important crops in the period 1968–9 to 1983–4 are given in the following table:

TABLE 3

*Percentage Annual Increase in Area, Production and Yield of Important Crops*

| Crops | Area 1968–9 to 1980–1 | Area 1980–1 to 1983–4 | Production 1968–9 to 1980–1 | Production 1980–1 to 1983–4 | Yield 1968–9 to 1980–1 | Yield 1980–1 to 1983–4 |
|---|---|---|---|---|---|---|
| RICE | 0.63 | 1.02 | 2.84 | 4.09 | 2.03 | 3.59 |
| WHEAT | 3.21 | 3.13 | 7.95 | 7.94 | 3.42 | 4.08 |
| SUGARCANE | 0.63 | 6.53 | 2.35 | 5.86 | 1.58 | −0.55 |
| JOWAR | −1.39 | 1.62 | 0.59 | 4.53 | 2.39 | 3.02 |
| BAJRA | 3.99 | 12.83 | 3.99 | 12.88 | 3.99 | 12.88 |
| MAIZE | 0.39 | −0.60 | 1.61 | 5.48 | 1.17 | 6.13 |
| BARLEY | 3.33 | 1.84 | −0.52 | −0.75 | 3.33 | 1.84 |
| PULSES | 0.54 | 1.45 | 0.59 | −15.09 | 0.50 | 3.24 |
| OILSEEDS | 0.15 | 8.64 | 1.60 | 18.39 | 1.42 | 7.73 |

In the case of wheat, the annual growth rate of yield has increased from 3.42 per cent in the period 1968–9 to 1980–1 to 4.08 per cent per annum in the period 1980–1 to 1983–4. In the case of rice, the yield rate has increased from 2.03 per cent per annum to 3.59 per cent per annum. In the case of bajra, it has increased from 3.99 to 12.88 per cent per annum and in the case of maize from 1.17 to 6.13 per cent per annum. In the case of oilseeds, it has increased from 1.42 to 7.73 per cent per annum. As compared to these crops the annual growth rates (per cent) are low in the case of jowar (3.02), barley (1.84), and pulses (3.24).

In the case of rice, production growth rate has increased from 2.84 per cent per annum (1968–9 to 1980–1) to 4.09 per cent per annum (1980–1 to 1983–4) due to increase in the area from 0.63 per cent per annum to 1.02 per cent per annum and increase in yield. In the case of wheat, production in the period 1980–1 to 1983–4 maintained a constant growth rate (7.99 per cent per annum) as in the earlier period (1968–9 to 1980–1). Similarly in spite of negative growth rate in yield (−0.5 per cent per annum), sugarcane showed an increase in growth rate of production for the above mentioned period from 2.35 per cent per annum to 5.85 per cent per annum, mainly because of increase in area.

Coming to dry crop performance during the period 1968–9 to 1980–1 and 1980–1 to 1983–4, in the case of pulses, in spite of substantial increase in yield, production has gone down from 0.53 per cent per annum to a negative growth rate of 15.09 per cent per annum. In the case of jowar, both yield and production have increased because of the success of high yielding varieties and good rainfall in some of the jowar growing areas in the country. The same is true of oil seeds, production of which has increased from 1.42 per cent per annum to 7.73 per cent per annum. Area increase has played a significant role in increasing production in the case of sugarcane (from 0.63 per cent per annum to 6.53 per cent per annum). Production of both bajra (from 3.39 per cent to 12.83 per cent) and oilseeds (from 1.6 per cent to 18.39 per cent) increased considerably. Thus overall both the increase in area and yield have played an important role in contributing to increase in production in the case of some crops.

Coming to interstate variations, in the case of rice, on the one hand, Assam, Haryana and Karnataka show negative growth rates in yield and, on the other, Rajasthan, Uttar Pradesh, Bihar and Gujarat show high growth rates. In the case of wheat, increases in yield have been high in Maharashtra (7.22 per cent per annum), West Bengal (18.42 per cent per annum) and Uttar Pradesh (5.16 per cent per annum). In the case of wheat, growth rate has been moderate except in Jammu and Kashmir, Rajasthan, West Bengal and Gujarat. This indicates that wheat revolution has spread to these states. In the case of rice, production growth rate is high in Gujarat, Punjab and Rajasthan. In the case of wheat, Madhya Pradesh also shows a high growth rate in production.

Coming to dry land crops, in the case of bajra, the yield increase is higher in Rajasthan (37.52), Tamil Nadu (10.27) and Gujarat (8.81). In the case of bajra, except for Jammu and Kashmir and West Bengal, all other states show positive growth rate in production, particularly Gujarat, Karnataka, Orissa, Punjab, Rajasthan and Tamil Nadu. In the case of maize, Rajasthan, Uttar Pradesh, Madhya Pradesh and West Bengal show high growth rates in yield while Andhra Pradesh, Jammu and Kashmir and Maharashtra show negative growth rates. In the case of maize, a large number of states show moderate increase in area. However, Assam, Bihar, Kerala, Punjab and Uttar Pradesh show negative growth rates. In the case of jowar, Gujarat, Haryana and Tamil Nadu show negative growth rate while Uttar Pradesh, Rajasthan and Kerala show high growth rate in yield. In the case of pulses, Jammu and Kashmir, Punjab, Tamil Nadu, Uttar Pradesh and Himachal Pradesh show negative growth rate while Gujarat, Maharashtra and West Bengal show high growth rate in yield. In respect of area except for Gujarat, Tamil Nadu and Rajasthan which show high growth rate, most of the other states have shown negative growth rates. In the case of oilseeds, Assam, Madhya Pradesh, Gujarat and Haryana show high growth rate in yield. Except in Punjab, Haryana and Uttar Pradesh most of the other states have high growth rates particularly Andhra Pradesh, Assam, Bihar, Gujarat, Jammu and Kashmir and Madhya Pradesh.

*Interstate Variations in the Share of Different States in Production of Important Crops*

Production of rice is concentrated in the states of Andhra Pradesh, Uttar Pradesh, West Bengal, Bihar and Orissa. These states accounted for 55.75 per cent of the country's production of rice in 1983–4, though their share has gone down from 58.84 per cent in 1968–9 to 55.75 per cent in 1983–4. Amongst the states recording increases in their share of rice production the most significant increase has taken place in Punjab whose share has increased from 1.15 per cent to 7.58 per cent. The share of Uttar Pradesh has increased from 7.34 per cent to 11.36 per cent. Bihar's share has declined from 13.7 to 8.34 per cent. In the case of wheat, Uttar Pradesh (36 per cent) and Punjab (20.86

per cent) account for nearly 57 per cent of country's output of wheat. Haryana (9.91 per cent) is another important state for wheat. In the case of sugarcane Uttar Pradesh and Maharashtra account for nearly 59 per cent of production.

In the case of dry land crops, Madhya Pradesh, Rajasthan and Uttar Pradesh account for nearly 54 per cent of the production of pulses. In the case of jowar, 72 per cent of the output is concentrated in Maharashtra, Madhya Pradesh and Karnataka. In the case of bajra, nearly 76 per cent of production is concentrated in Gujarat, Maharashtra, Rajasthan and Uttar Pradesh. Nearly 56 per cent of the production of maize is concentrated in Bihar, Karnataka, Rajasthan and Uttar Pradesh. Though Gujarat and Maharashtra account for nearly 31 per cent of the production of oilseeds the production of the remaining 69 per cent is widely spread over the country. Tamil Nadu and Uttar Pradesh account for nearly 34 per cent of the output. The pattern of output of dry land crop shows that they are largely concentrated in Madhya Pradesh, Rajasthan, Gujarat, Maharashtra and Uttar Pradesh. Concentration of area also largely follows the same pattern not only in the case of dry land crops but also in the case of irrigated rice and wheat. States accounting for the bulk of production are also accounting for the bulk of area.

### Dry Farming Technology

At the early stages dry farming technology laid emphasis on conservation of soil and moisture particularly through contour bunding. This did not have much impact on productivity in the absence of improved varieties of seeds. High yielding varieties programme introduced in the mid-sixties supplied the missing biological components, namely, hybrid for a few coarse varieties of foodgrains like jowar, bajra and maize.[2] It was not possible to introduce dry farming technology in the case of other dry farming crops like pulses, oilseeds and coarse cereals other than those mentioned above.

The all-India coordinated research project for dry lands started in 24 centres in the Fourth Plan period, it developed HYV based packages of practices, for cultivation of bajra, jowar

[2] P. Rangaswamy, 'Dry Farming: Potential and Constraints.'

and maize. These HYV varieties had some impact on productivity. The major handicap of this programme was that the hybrid varieties were confined to these 24 centres only and there was hardly any diffusion of this technology. The major handicap was the absence of extension agencies outside these 24 centres. The following important elements of the dry farming technology developed in these centres have been competently pointed out by Dr Rangaswamy:[3] (*a*) Off season tillage to increase infiltration of rain water and reduced run off, (*b*) early maturing hybrids which make efficient use of available rainfall and are able to store moisture, (*c*) early sowing of kharif crops to avoid incidence of pests and diseases, and (*d*) balanced use of NPK. According to Dr Rangaswamy, a judicious combination of these practices, if adopted on a wider scale, can possibly provide a breakthrough in dry farming.[4]

There are no studies throwing light on the extent to which these practices have been adopted. Experiments conducted in 15 of these 24 centres cover only four practices of which the important ones are fertilizer application, use of pesticides and weeding. These studies show that the adoption in the case of improved seeds is fairly high for several crops because of low input costs. The adoption of fertilizers and plant protection measures are relatively lower. These inputs are profitable in normal years but they require high investment which is risky under uncertain weather conditions.

HYV is the basic input and once it is available and adopted, other complementary practices follow. Such HYV are available for crops like rabi-jowar, ragi, bajra, wheat, paddy and groundnut. Adoption rates for rabi crops are above 50 per cent. With regard to crops like kharif-jowar, maize and gram there are some other problems with the HYV and hence adoption rates are low. In the case of gram the main constraint is low moisture availability, since it is risky to store moisture in kharif fallow land during rabi season. Different crops have attained different degrees of success in different areas. For example, HYV jowar had 100 per cent adoption in Kovilpatti while its adoption rate was nearly zero in Anantpur and Rajkot and only

[3] Ibid.
[4] Ibid.

11 per cent in Hyderabad. Adoption of HYV bajra was 85 per cent in Sholapur and less than 20 per cent in Nagpur. Adoption of gram was high in Varanasi and low in Hissar district.

Generally, improved dry farming technology is widely adopted in heavy black soil area rather than in red soil area. This is because of high fertility and moisture retention of black soil. HYV and fertilizers normally require more moisture than traditional inputs. Even improved cultural practices require better moisture conservation. They are profitable only when a minimum level of moisture is available for conservation.

Deficiency and uncertainty in the availability of moisture is the basic reason for the adoption of dry farming technology. This fact is responsible for lower success of HYV technology. Similarly, there are constraints in respect of soil. The main problem is one of surface crushing affecting red soil and soil erosion caused by run off water.

In respect of fertilizer use the basic handicap is that the current level of fertilizer use is very low, often less than 10 kgs. per hectare even in good rainfall years. This may be due to *low return and high risk and the resource constraint of majority of dry land farmers who have little access to institutional credit.* Available fertilizer is diverted to irrigated crops where there is very little risk. Hence, there is under-investment in fertilizers in dry land agriculture.

By and large, production of coarse cereals, pulses and oilseeds in dry areas is lagging behind the growth of superior cereals. Even rice (58 per cent) and wheat (35 per cent) are rainfed. In dry land areas their yields are much lower than in the case of irrigated areas.[5] All the same it is necessary to increase the yield of dry land crops as they are not only the staple diet of the rural poor, but their poor yield performance has also led to regional imbalances. Production of coarse gram has not increased due to loss of area to competing crops. The competing crops are grown under irrigation conditions and have adopted technological improvements. They also offer higher price. The extension of input supply has also lagged behind in the case of dry HYV crops.

[5] P. Rangaswamy, 'Production Constraints and Prospects of Dry Land Crops'.

## Implementation of Dry Land Projects

Apart from technological handicaps there are also other problems such as slackness in implementation of dry farming project. For example, in Mahendergarh district of Haryana, there is very little progress in projects for propagation of water conservation, harvesting technology and popularization of seed-cum-fertilizer drill, improved varieties of seeds, fertilizers, etc. Out of the sanctioned grant of Rs 8.42 lakhs in 1983-4, only Rs 36,000 have been spent and another Rs 1.5 lakhs were spent up to October 1984 out of the sanctioned grant of Rs 10.1 lakhs. Ambala district shows better progress. Nearly Rs 11.3 lakhs were spent from April 1984 to October 1984 on water harvesting technology. However, this district is not a typical dry farming area. Working of dry farming projects in Tamil Nadu and Rajasthan are no better than in Mahendergarh in respect of implementation.

While both area and yield have contributed to increased production in the case of wheat and rice, it was largely yield increase that increased the production of jowar, bajra and ragi. Pulses have lost both in area and yield. Only maize and ragi have gained in area.

## Inequalities and Diversification in Agricultural Activities in India and China

Both in India and China nearly 80 per cent of the population lives in rural areas. Between 1971 and 1981 the percentage of rural population in India has come down from 80.09 to 76.69. Of the important states, Gujarat, Maharashtra and Tamil Nadu have only two-thirds of the population living in rural areas. So far as the Chinese data is concerned, we have depended on a paper by Griffin and Ashwani Saith.[6] The concept of income adopted by Griffin and Saith covers net output from crop production and forestry, animal husbandry and fishing, and other side-line activities like rural industry, construction and handicrafts.

---

[6] Keith Griffin and Ashwani Saith, 'The Pattern of Inequalities in Rural China', *Oxford Economic Papers*, vol. 34, 1982.

In the case of India we have taken comparative data for village Walidpur and Meerut district of Western Uttar Pradesh. Walidpur data relates to the year 1983-4 while Meerut district data relates to the year 1971–2. In the case of Walidpur we have taken details relating to ten biggest farmers and ten smallest farmers of the village. The data has been compared with information for Hebel Province in China for the year 1978. I have given below data for China and India:

*Comparison of China and India in Respect of Income and Other Details*

I.  China
   1. Average size of households — 4.31
   2. Number of workers per household — 1.64
   3. Dependency ratio — 1.63
   4. Per capita collective income (Chinese Currency: Yuan) — 75.74
   5. Ratio of highest to lowest per capita country income — 4.78

II. India (Walidpur)

| | Big Farmers | Small Farmers |
|---|---|---|
| 1. Average size of families | 7.4 | 5.4 |
| 2. Number of workers per household | 2.1 | 2.4 |
| 3. Dependency per household | 5.3 | 3.00 |
| 4. Dependency ratio | 1.39 | 1.80 |
| 5. Per capita income (Rs) | 4,306.14 | 921.60 |
| 6. Per capita income ratio | 4.67 | 1.00 |
| 7. Per household income (Rs) | 31,865.40 | 4,976.63 |
| 8. Per household income ratio | 6.40 | 1.00 |

A comparison of size of household indicates that the average size of families in China is considerably smaller than that of families in the case of both small and big farmers in Walidpur. However, the number of workers per household is more in India than in China. Because the number of workers is more, dependency ratio is in favour of China. It appears that the income inequalities' are more in India than in China.

Comparison of collective rural income in China indicates that crop production contributes to 64.7 per cent of rural income, side-line occupation for 26.4 per cent, forestry for 2.3 per cent, animal husbandry for 1.5 per cent, fishing for 0.4 per cent and miscellaneous sources for 4.8 per cent. In the case of marginal and small farmers of Walidpur crop production contributes to 23.92 per cent of net income. Out of the total income, income from hiring themselves out accounts for 3.41 per cent, income from services to 72.76 per cent. Thus in India unlike in China crop production accounts for nearly 1/4 of the income while almost the entire balance is accounted by services. In the case of big farmers net income from agriculture accounts for 91.68 per cent and other occupations for the balance. Thus big farmers are almost entirely dependent upon crop production while small farmers are dependent upon services. This was the situation in 1983–4 in village Walidpur which is situated in Western Uttar Pradesh. In 1971–2, information available for Meerut district indicates that the percentage of income from crop production increased with the increase in size of holding.[7] In the higher size level almost the entire income is earned from crop production. These trends indicate that while the Chinese economy has attained certain diversification by developing ancillary activities, the Indian rural economy has not attained the necessary diversification in spite of the fact that the average size of the holding is small. The only diversification which small and marginal farmers have attained is moving out of land and taking up service occupations in urban areas while the Chinese farmers have developed diversification within agriculture so that there is no need for them to move out of agriculture. *Perhaps there is something which India can learn from China in this respect.* The need for diversification is particularly necessary for dry farming areas where technological breakthrough has made uncertain progress except in the case of maize, oilseeds and bajra. Other dry crops have not been able to attain the necessary breakthrough. In this respect the position of pulses is most unsatisfactory. A study

[7] R. R. Vaish, 'Income, Savings and Investment: Meerut District', Agricultural Economics Research Centre.

done in Karnal district of Haryana by the Agricultural Economics Research Centre indicates that in the period 1969–70 to 1971–2 income from crop production increased with the increase in the size of the holding.[8] I give in Table 4 the percentage share of income from various sources.

Both Karnal and Meerut districts, particularly Karnal district, were affected by the Green Revolution. In this district there is considerable diversification of income from agriculture.

### Integrated Rural Development Programme (IRDP)

Since 1970 a number of Rural Development Programmes have been started with a view to increasing employment opportunities. The following are a few of such programmes:

1. Drought Prone Area Programme.
2. Small Farmers Development Agency and Programmes for marginal farmers and agricultural labourers started in 1970.
3. Food for Work Programme, now called National Rural Employment Programme, started in 1977.
4. Minimum Needs Programme to secure basic amenities in the

TABLE 4

## I. Percentage Share of Income from Various Sources

| Size of farms | Cultivation | Other Agricultural activities | Total |
|---|---|---|---|
| I Below 2 hectares | 68.5 | 30.7 | 99.2 |
| II 2–4 hectares | 79.7 | 19.0 | 98.7 |
| III 4–7.5 hectares | 85.7 | 13.3 | 99.0 |
| IV 7.51 and above | 90.3 | 9.5 | 99.8 |
| All Size Groups | 86.7 | 12.7 | 99.4 |

[8] Veena Nabar, 'Income Savings and Investment of Farmers in an Agriculturally Prosperous Area: A Case Study of Karnal District, Haryana,'

TABLE 4 (Contd.)

## II. Income of Sample Farmers from Various Sources in Karnal District

| Size of farm | Cultivation | Dairy | Poultry | Family labour hired out | Bullock labour hired out | Tractor, tubewells, and pumpsets hired out | Other receipts | Total |
|---|---|---|---|---|---|---|---|---|
| I | 45,697 (85.29) | 1,140 (2.13) | — | 5,200 (9.71) | — | 1,540 (2.87) | — | 53,577 (100.00) |
| II | 1,19,664 (85.66) | 19,570 (14.01) | — | 200 (2.14) | — | 266 (0.19) | — | 1,39,700 (100.00) |
| III | 3,32,404 (88.36) | 39,735 (10.56) | — | — | — | 4,070 (1.08) | — | 3,76,209 (100.00) |
| IV | 6,82,401 (92.23) | 59,919 (8.00) | — | — | — | 6,490 (0.87) | — | 7,49,045 (100.00) |
| All Groups | 1,80,401 (89.52) | 1,20,364 (9.13) | — | 5,400 (0.41) | — | 12,366 (0.94) | — | 13,18,531 (100.00) |

field of education, health, drinking water, electrification, roads, etc.
5. Command Area Development Programme.

None of these programmes covers the whole country. In spite of these programmes in the first half of 1970s only 40 per cent of the rural households were covered.[9] In this background, *the objective of the Integrated Rural Development Programme was that of concentrating on the removal of poverty by selecting the poorest of the poor households.* They generally belong to the category of small and marginal farmers, agricultural and non-agricultural labourers, rural artisans and craftsmen, scheduled castes and scheduled tribes. The objective was to cover all persons who were living below the poverty line. Only those families of five persons with an annual income of Rs 3500 were considered as poor people. Of the 32 crores people below the poverty line, 26 crores are in rural areas.

The Sixth Plan used IRDP as a method for replacing multiple agencies by a single integrated programme for each district by developing agriculture and allied sectors. Initially the programme was taken up in 2,300 blocks and extended every year at the rate of 300 new blocks. It is only in 1980 with the revised Sixth Plan that the decision was taken to extend the benefits of the programme to target group families in 5011 development blocks.[10] In the same year NREP was merged with the IRDP. All the blocks were provided with an allocation of Rs 35 crores per block during the Sixth Plan period. The allocation was to be shared between the Centre and the states on a fifty–fifty basis. At least 3,000 families were expected to be directly assisted under the Programme in each block over the five-year period. During the Sixth Plan, assistance was to be provided to 150 lakhs families.

This beneficiary-oriented Plan (integration of sectoral programme, special integration, integration of social and economic prosperity for removal of poverty and employment generation) aimed at providing assets to rural poor. During the Sixth Plan period (1980–5) assistance was given for minor irrigation

---

[9] Nilkantha Rath, 'Garibi Hatao', *Economic and Political Weekly*, February 1985.

[10] *India 1982*, Pubications Division, Government of India, p. 254.

programmes, acquiring milk cattle, sheep, goat, etc.

The name IRDP was a misnomer.[11] All that happened under this programme (a substitute to multiple agency approach) was preparation of an inventory of physical resources in the district. The basic strategy was to promote self-employment for the poor by providing assets to small and marginal farmers. This plan was to be supplemented by the National Rural Employment Programme.

According to the Sixth Plan, on an average 10 to 12 thousand households in a block were considered poor, of whom 3,000 households per block were to be covered in the Plan period. Asset receivers were to be helped with the requisite asset and training through bank loans and Government subsidies to carry out additional economic activities which would help them to rise above the poverty line. Two thousands of these beneficiary farmers were to be included under animal husbandry, 500 in village and cottage industries and 500 in services.

Since the objective was to select the poorest of the poor, poor households were to be identified and ranked and the poorest were first to be chosen as beneficiary. The subsidy amount ranged from one-fourth to small farmers, to one-third to marginal farmers and landless labourers and in any case it was not to exceed Rs 3,000 for any household, except in the case of those belonging to schedule tribes, for whom the subsidy was 50 per cent of the assets and even in their case the subsidy was not to exceed Rs 5,000. The Plan provision was for a subsidy of Rs 15,00 crores and bank loan of Rs 3,000 crores giving a total investment of Rs 45,00 crores to cover 15 million beneficiary households spread over nearly 5,000 blocks.

According to the latest information, subsidy under the Integrated Rural Development Programme during the Seventh Plan period may be raised from Rs 1,000 to Rs 2,000 per beneficiary household which will entitle them to a credit of Rs 4,000 from financial institutions.[12] This is being considered with a view to increasing the level of investment per household in the Seventh Plan and to compensate for price escalation. It is

---

[11] Nilkantha Rath, 'Garibi Hatao', *Economic and Political Weekly*, February 1985.

[12] 'IRDP Subsidy to Double', *Economic Times*, 28 March 1985.

also reported that the Planning Commission holds the view that subsidized assets will have to be given to 60 per cent of the previous recipients at an average rate of Rs 500 per household. An amount equivalent to 25 per cent of this amount may be provided for establishing infrastructure, training and stipends in order to avoid any erosion of subsidy.

The total number of beneficiary households during the Sixth Plan was projected to be 12.58 million assuming that every beneficiary belongs to a separate household and that no beneficiary received benefits twice under different heads. During the Sixth Plan period the IRDP would have actually touched 16 million households out of 90.87 million rural households (1981) in the country. According to the National Sample Survey, nearly 50 per cent of the people lived below the poverty line in 1977–8. At this rate 46.12 per cent of the households in rural India were poor. The IRDP programme covers 34 per cent of these households. If we add to this, the 2 million covered by IRDP during 1970–80, the percentage of poor rural households covered by IRDP comes to 38.[13] The total loan to be advanced would be Rs 3,000 crores and subsidies of Rs 15,00 crores.

In trying to find a solution to the shortcomings of the multiple agency approach of the earlier Plan, the present IRDP programme has developed its own handicaps. Firstly, while the Plan target for loans and subsidies were at 1979–80 level prices, the actuals are at current prices thereby reducing the real value of investment. Secondly, though 12.58 million households had been identified as poor, in practice a large number of these households had many times more income then Rs 700 per capita a year laid down by the Government of India.[14]

According to a survey conducted by the Kerala Planning Board in 1980–1 on the basis of annual income, about 23 per cent of the beneficiary households had been misclassified as poor.[15] According to the survey done by Kanta Ahuja and Bhargava in 1984 in Rajasthan, 14.7 per cent of the beneficiaries in Jaipur district were misclassified as poor while the Evaluation

---

[13] Ibid.
[14] Ibid.
[15] Ibid., p. 241.

Report prepared by the NABARD places misclassification at 21.4 per cent.

The NABARD study shows that in two districts of Gujarat, 47 per cent of the sample beneficiaries were misclassified as poor. This percentage comes to 42 per cent in Assam, 17.6 per cent in Haryana, 35 per cent in Punjab, 13 per cent in Maharashtra, 19 per cent in Madhya Pradesh, 11 per cent in Tamil Nadu and Karnataka, 7 per cent in Andhra Pradesh and 1 per cent in Orissa.[16] *It is obvious that the Antyodaya approach is not being followed in the selection of poor households.* The NABARD study shows that the major type of assets created by loan and subsidy were livestock, including goats and sheep. *According to the NABARD study the extent of leakage of the money advanced was 26 per cent.* Moreover the animals selected were of poor quality.

Thus a number of evaluation studies done so far indicate that beneficiary oriented approach of the IRDP has not served the purpose as the benefits are going to wrong type of households like in the case of multiple agency programme. It appears that the programme like NREP in spite of many leakages is superior to IRDP programme.

### A Resume

In the post Green Revolution period, paddy and wheat production continued to reach new heights in Punjab, Haryana, Tamil Nadu and Andhra Pradesh. In the case of wheat the capital-output ratio increased between 1960s and 1980s, from 0.44 to 0.61 in Haryana, from 0.40 to 0.51 in Punjab and from 0.39 to 0.54 in Uttar Pradesh.[17] In the case of rice, capital-output ratio increased from 0.39 to 0.46 in Andhra Pradesh, from 0.23 to 0.36 in Bihar, and from 0.27 to 0.31 in Orissa. Wheat-growing states showed a positive relationship between capital–labour ratio and crop yield.[18] Punjab had the highest capital–labour ratio as well as the highest yield. In the case of wheat,

---

[16] Ibid.
[17] M. S. Bhatia, V. K. Sharma and T. K. Haque, 'Changes in Factor Relations and Productivity in Indian Agriculture', *Agricultural Situation in India*, January 1984, p. 630.
[18] Ibid., p. 630.

the capital–labour ratio increased from 2.47 to 2.92 in Haryana, from 2.58 to 3.69 in Punjab, and from 2.65 to 3.42 in Uttar Pradesh. This trend was only partially true in the case of rice. Capital-labour ratio in the case of paddy declined from 2.17 to 1.99 in Andhra Pradesh, from 1.45 to 1.07 in Bihar and from 1.23 to 1.19 in Orissa. West Bengal and Tamil Nadu showed marginal increase. Thus in the case of rice the inter-regional perspective remained more or less unaltered. High capital output ratios show a declining trend in production. The high capital–output ratio was partly due to improved varieties of seeds and partly due to bringing more area under high yielding varieties. Increase in irrigated area, particularly in assured irrigation areas, and increased use of fertilizers (from 16.09 kgs to 32.0 kgs per hectares) gave a push to this trend.

However, in dry areas where the supply of assured irrigation is extremely limited and where crops are dependent upon rainfall the success was of a mixed nature. There have been some breakthrough in the cases of bajra, oilseeds and maize due mainly to success of hybrid varieties in some areas. The same is not true of hybrid varieties of jowar and pulses, as they have not been able to develop suitable hybrid varieties. Slow growth of output of coarse grains which is the staple food of poor farmers and rural labour force is rather a discouraging trend. The coarse grains are generally concentrated in Gujarat, Maharashtra, Karnataka, Madhya Pradesh, Rajasthan and parts of Andhra Pradesh and Tamil Nadu.

In the case of wheat, the most encouraging trend has been the spread of the Green Revolution to states outside the northwestern parts of India. These states are West Bengal, Rajasthan, Gujarat, and Jammu and Kashmir. While both yield and area have contributed to increase in productivity of paddy and wheat, it is not true of all dry crops to the same extent, except in the case of maize, bajra and oilseeds. In the case of sugarcane increase in production has been largely due to area effect.

Increase in foodgrains production, particularly in the case of pulses, was not adequate to overtake the population growth rate in the period 1973–4 to 1982–3. In six out of ten years population growth rate overtook increase in growth rate of foodgrains production. This is not a happy situation. In fact in 1983 India imported 3.73 million tonnes (net) of cereals. This only shows that given the current level of consumption we are not able to attain the requisite breakthrough in production to keep the population at least at a reasonable poverty line level. While we have been able to make some breakthrough in developing hybrid seeds in the case of bajra and maize the position is not satisfactory in the case of other crops.

In order to make the population of dry areas attain subsistence level it is necessary to achieve a breakthrough. At the same time, it appears that the technological changes which have taken place in the case of many dry crops are not encouraging and we may not come out of the vicious circle. *Perhaps at least a partial solution seems to lie in developing non-cultivation activities within the agricultural sector.* China has attained considerable success in developing ancilliary agricultural activities like pig raising, poultry keeping, handicrafts, etc. Income inequalities in Chinese agriculture are lower than in India. India can benefit by the example of Chinese agriculture in terms of diversification of agricultural activities. It is necessary for the Indian farmer also to move in this direction. While non-cultivation activities contribute to one-third of income of small and marginal farmers, their income levels are rather low. It is necessary for the Government to think more in terms of developing non-cultivation activities for raising the income of small and marginal farmers, particularly of those in dry land areas, instead of solely depending upon crop research in experimental stations as crop production is very much subject to vagaries of rainfall. In most of these areas it is not possible to develop assured irrigation through canals and tubewells as in Punjab and Haryana. It is because energized tubewells are not working to full capacity due to power shortage.

The Integrated Rural Development Programme has not served the purpose for which it was established as people look to it as a subsidy programme. So long as subsidies are given people take it. The assets and subsidies given are to be linked to vital economic activities outside cultivation. The present machinery for implementation of even the existing programmes is most inefficient. They are not only selecting wrong type of beneficiaries (those who do not need subsidy) but are also slow in implementing the programme. It is essential to gear up efficiency at all levels including administrative level. All said and done there is scope for concentrating on activities like **National Rural Employment Programme** where in spite of leakages some benefits reach those who need them.

As mentioned earlier, subsidies given under the IRDP programme are reaching the wrong people due, in many cases, to wrong selection of beneficiaries. In fact, the IRDP programme is meant for the poorest of the poor. Even in the case of other activities like agricultural production, reports are coming that the enormous subsidy given is reaching the wrong type of people. In 1984-5 the total amount of subsidy given was more than Rs 3000 crores out of which nearly two-thirds was fertilizer subsidy. Fertilizer subsidy which was introduced in 1976-7 has increased from Rs 60 crores to Rs 1932 crores. During the same period food subsidy increased from Rs 506 crores to Rs 1100 crores. It is the urban population which has taken advantage of the food subsidy. In rural areas adequate arrangements are not there to distribute subsidized food to the rural poor. The spread of the public distribution system has not kept pace with the increase in population. As a result, the average number of people covered by each Fair Price Shop / Ration Shop has gone down from 4510 in 1970 to 2430 in 1984.[19] The coverage has gone down particularly in Gujarat, Bihar, Haryana, Madhya Pradesh, Jammu and Kashmir, Tamil Nadu and Uttar Pradesh. The coverage has increased in West Bengal and Maharashtra which have considerable urban population. Fertilizer subsidy is being taken advantage of by the affluent farmer. While the tax payer is bearing the burden of fertilizer subsidy there is an idle capacity of 30 per cent in the fertilizer industry. A better alternative would be to lower fertilizer prices by making use of idle capacity.

In Western Uttar Pradesh where nearly 40 per cent of the livestock population (cattle, buffalow, sheep, goat, pig and poultry) is concentrated the condition of activities ancillary to cultivation is extremely inadequate. It needs better attention as income from cultivation is very small for those whose size of

---

[19] *Bulletin of Food Statistics, 1982-84*, Directorate of Economics and Statistics, Department of Agriculture and Cooperation, Government of India, p. 8.

holdings is tiny The average size of holdings in Eastern Uttar Pradesh is 1.10 hectares as against 2.65 for Uttar Pradesh as a whole. In Eastern Uttar Pradesh 75.4 per cent of holdings are less than 1 hectare in size.

# Some Observations on the Rate and Pattern of Industrial Growth

R. K. ROY

I have to confess to one disadvantage: I am a journalist used to spot reactions rather than theoretical analysis. I find myself in an uncomfortable situation amongst really top theoreticians.

There are some facts which bother us journalists. We take the index of industrial production with the 1970 base. The growth rate for 1980–1 was 4 per cent, for 1981–2, 8.6 per cent, for 1982–3, 3.9 per cent, for 1983–4, 5.5 per cent and the estimated growth rate for 1984–5 is 7 per cent.

I want to draw attention to something which the *Economic Survey* of 1981–2 mentioned. According to it, it was a matter of concern that in five out of ten years in the seventies, the growth rate of industrial production was less than 3.5 per cent. Furthermore, the Survey notes that a year of reasonable growth and recovery has been inevitably followed by one or even two years of stagnation in industrial production.

This is one puzzling factor which continues to bother people who have to write on economic problems. The *Economic Surveys* have over the years analysed the factors underlying this kind of development—the fluctuation in the growth rate and the inadequacy of the growth rate. First, they point out the infrastructural constraint. Second, tardy implementation of new industrial projects. Third, high cost of production.

Reasons No. 1 and 2—infrastructure constraints and tardy implementation of industrial projects—assume additional output would have been possible, but for the retarding factors. Demand constraint is not brought explicitly into the picture. It is true that in reason 3—high cost of production—there is an implicit suggestion of demand constraint. The high cost is associated with lags and the fruition of development projects, of various investment delays.

The thrust of the diagnosis of the *Economic Surveys*, it should be noted, is similar to that of the *Report on Currency and Finance* published by the Reserve Bank of India. Commenting on the rise in industrial production by 5.5 per cent in 1983-4, against 3.9 per cent in 1982-3, the *Currency and Finance Report* states that the performance would have been still better but for the operation of certain factors which impeded industrial production. The impeding factors are identified as shortfall in supply of electricity, coal, steel; port and dock workers' strike; slow pace of modernization; outdated machinery and technology in textiles, steel and power, and sluggishness of demand for certain products at home and abroad.

Now though the demand factor is mentioned, the emphasis is on inadequacy of supply—of inputs and of investment.

Now the reference to sluggish demand, let us take that on. The reference here is to weak demand for domestic steel following imports of steel. I do not want to go into the reasons why we imported steel. That is a political matter. But we imported steel and as a result domestic demand for steel declined and following lower steel production, there was an adverse impact on railway traffic, on the growth of railway goods traffic and on the demand for coal, and coal stocks increased.

Summing up, the reasons underlying the slow and uneven growth of industrial production as given by these two *Reports* are: inadequate investment and growth of infrastructure; slow pace of modernization in the public and private sectors, labour relations; port and dock workers' strike, strikes in jute and textile industry, etc.

However, there is a reference to export demand. Barring gem and jewellery and marine products, export dependence is hardly significant in any industry other than in the traditional ones like tea, etc. By and large, the issue has been of depriving the domestic market for squeezing out an export surplus. So export demand is not really the key to fluctuations in the industrial growth rate.

We find that the index of industrial production fluctuates very sharply and it has tended to be below a certain minimum level in a large number of years. Also we find that a rise in a particular year is inevitably, to quote the *Economic Survey*, followed by a decline in the growth rate. However, paradoxically, we simultaneously find that the value of industrial production in the small scale sector (at 1979–80 prices) has shown a sustained annual increase of 8 to 10 per cent during the period from 1980–1 to 1983–4.

I did not have enough time to go into data for earlier years. I am taking this as more or less representative. We find fluctuations in the growth rate in the large industrial sector. Now the factors that retard production, the factors that contribute to the fluctuation in production in the large sector or the organized sector should surely have contributed to fluctuation in the output growth rate of the small-scale sector? But we find a reasonably stable growth rate of 8 to 10 per cent per year in the small-scale sector.

The factors retarding growth of industry in the large sector had obviously not had the same adverse impact on production in the small-scale sector. Production in the small-scale industry is generally believed to be in ancillary relationship with the large sector. The segment which is in ancillary relationship is obviously becoming small. This is a purely inferential statement. I have no data to support it. It is the other (non-ancillary) segment which is presumably dynamic and which is resulting in a sustained increase in the overall growth rate of the small-scale sector.

Now, faced with this kind of result, let us look at what the Raj Working Group on Savings had to say in their *Report* in 1982. The Raj Committee noted that while the overall savings of the corporate sector had not shown a sustained rise, the savings rate of the household sector had increased. A segment of the household savings was going into real estate, transport and small industries. This was pointed out by the *Raj Committee Report*.

It would seem that there has been a change in the pattern of investment. There has been an inadequate growth of investment in steel, power, coal, railways. But there has been investment in other sectors. Overall these other investments should have raised the rate of industrial production but available data do not show this.

I go back again to the *Currency and Finance Report* published by the Reserve Bank of India. The explanation offered by the *Currency and Finance Report: 1983–84* is as follows. The current official index of industrial production with the base period of 1970 does not fully reflect the performance of some of the rapidly growing industries such as petroleum, petro-chemicals, electronics, polyester filament yarn, nylon tyre cord, etc., which are either not covered or have low weights in the index.

The *Currency and Finance Report* adds that the index is based largely on data furnished by registered manufacturers and organized units which report to CSO. Data relating to the unregistered manufacturing sector is a point highlighted by the *Raj Committee Report* as it does not get fully reflected in the index. So we seem to be arriving at a situation, where the growth rate of industrial production as measured by the index, seems to be distorted by under-reporting and the growth rate of industrial production, therefore, taking all factors into account, is higher than what is being reported.

How much higher, we do not know. But it does definitely follow that there has been diversification of investment and production. The question is whether diversification of investment and production represent a countertrend, that is, whether it (diversification) is taking place at the expense of (or neglect of) investment in basic and capital goods industry, in infrastructure, in social investment like health and education, or whether this diversification represents additional investment.

If the answer is that diversification of the pattern of production that is on, is at the cost of investment and production in basic industry and infrastructure, then the question that will have to be posed is whether the growth rate of industrial production, after you have corrected for under-reporting, is sustainable. It is easy to see that in the scenario given here there is an imbalance in investment.

The shift in the pattern of investment imparted by supply side policies initiated in the latest Budget will further skew the imbalance.

Finally, a related point that needs to be made. The latest *Economic Survey* notes that there is no reason why Indian industry should not be able to grow by 8 to 9 per cent a year and that domestic demand should not always be the basis for determining the scale of production. In this context the *Economic Survey* notes that a disturbing feature of our development has been the slow pace of growth in employment in manufacturing and services.

If the achieved growth rate of industrial production is 8 to 9 per cent, corrected for all the under-reporting, and if we boost it to 9 to 10 or 11 per cent, what will it mean in terms of withdrawal of the pressure of population on land?

The *Economic Survey* just makes the assumption that if there is improvement in growth rate in industry, and employment in the manufacturing sector increases, there will be a decline in the pressure on land. But will the decline be of a significant nature?

Furthermore, is the required order of investment (for significantly withdrawing pressure on land) in manufacturing feasible? The cost of job creation in industry, in textiles, electronics, etc., is of the order of Rs 33,000 per job at 1983–4 prices. (I have taken this figure from ICICI and the Electronics Industry.)

One cannot go by this low figure alone. Investment in non-tradables, power, transport, etc., is expensive and this is what pushes up the average cost of new jobs in industry. This is what makes overly simplistic the assumption that growth in manufacturing industry can be taken to a point where pressure on land can be significantly reduced.

I am only giving a spot reaction to the data I have gone through. Industrialization in terms of the achievable rate will, given the prevailing investment–employment relationship, not make a significant impact on employment. That is to say, even if we upgrade our technology and industrial growth rate, we will still have this problem of two societies, one very poor and one living relatively well off in an enclave.

# Industrial Development: Issues and Policy Options

N. S. SIDDHARTHAN

One set of economists attribute the low growth rates of South Asia, and India in particular, to the strategy of import substitution that these economies followed in contrast to what these economists call the export-led growth strategy that the East Asian countries have followed. Thus countries like Japan and South Korea are supposed to have followed export-led growth while India followed an import substitution policy. While the former regimes liberalized externally, the Indian regime was very restrictive in the domestic as well as in the foreign sectors.

Facts do not, however, support these assumptions about Japan and South Korea. To start with, both these countries followed import substitution policies till recently, which enabled them to develop a strong industrial base and which later on enabled them to expand their exports. The rapid growth of their exports was the result of their development and not the other way round.

In recent months there have been signs of change in the economic policy of the Government of India. It is important, however, that the contemplated change should not aim at taking the economy even closer to the neoclassical ideal of free trade, liberalization, free operation of market mechanism and price variables. Development consists in the production of new goods, introduction of new methods of production, creation of new markets and materials, all of which depend on non-price and non-free market variables like technological change, R and D and innovations.

## General Economic Indicators

In the last twenty-five years India has made tremendous progress in mobilizing the savings of its population, increasing the gross domestic investment rate of the economy and in diversifying the industrial production structure. The Indian gross domestic saving rate which was only 14 per cent in 1960 increased to 20 per cent in 1981 and is about 22 per cent at present. This rate compares very favourably with the rate enjoyed by the advanced industrialized countries. In fact with the exception of China, no other country in the world with a per capita income comparable to that of India has succeeded in achieving this rate. The Indian gross domestic investment as a percentage of national income increased from 17 per cent in 1960 to 23 per cent in 1981 and is likely to touch 25 per cent this year. The Indian mobilization of tax revenue had also been very impressive. What is more, the high investment rate was mainly a domestic effort. Thus during 1981, the gross domestic savings excluding the net current transfers from abroad as a percentage of gross domestic investment was as high as 93.2 and including net current transfers from abroad was 99.0. Despite this impressive mobilization effort, the share of the manufacturing sector in GDP increased from 14 per cent in 1960 to only 18 per cent in 1981. Despite thirty years of effort, around 70 per cent of the Indian labour force still remains in agriculture. Therefore, in terms of increasing the share of the manufacturing sector in the GDP the Indian performance has not been impressive. In this context, it would be worth examining the Indian performance in relation to the performance of other major Asian countries in similar fields.

Basic socio-economic indicators of eleven major Asian countries are given in Table 1. These eleven countries are grouped under three heads: South Asia, East Asia and China. As seen from the table, in addition to the geographical distance many socio-economic indicators also seperate the South Asian countries from the East Asian. The Chinese performance by and large is somewhere in between these two groups. The major South Asian countries like Bangladesh, Burma, India, Sri Lanka and Pakistan are by and large much poorer than the East Asian ones like Thailand, Philippines, South Korea, Malaysia and

Japan, if one goes by per capita income. The East Asian per capita income is more than double the South Asian per capita income. In addition, the annual average growth rate of the per capita income of the South Asian countries has been very poor compared to that of the major East Asian countries during the last twenty years. The growth rate of per capita GDP of the South Asians in general, and Indians in particular, has been less than half that of the major East Asian countries and China. The growth rates for South Korea and Japan have been more than three times that of the South Asian countries and almost five times that of India. If the past trend continues, then the gap between India and its South Asian neighbours on the one hand and the East Asians and the Chinese on the other is likely to widen, and widen substantially, in the years to come. Already the differences in per capita income between India and the East Asian countries like South Korea, Malaysia and Japan is more than six times.

It is at times rightly argued that per capita GDP between countries is not strictly comparable for various valid reasons and hence it is desirable to look into certain other indicators before drawing conclusions. Cols. 9 and 10 of the table deal with adult literacy rates and life expectancy at birth, the two non-economic indicators that ought to be taken into account in inter-country comparisons. Life expectancy in particular could reflect the general well-being of the population much better than a variable like per capita income, as in addition to income it could also reflect certain other indicators like access to health services, water supply, nutrition and government welfare measures. Even in terms of these indicators, the East Asians appear to be definitely better off than the South Asians, with the exception of Sri Lanka. An average East Asian lives at least a decade more than a South Asian. Indian life expectancy is low compared to even Burma, let alone Sri Lanka. An average Burmese, despite being much poorer than an average Indian, enjoys a higher life expectancy. An average Sri Lankan lives seventeen years more than an Indian. When it comes to the literacy rate, most of the South Asians are illiterate unlike the East Asians, the exceptions being Burma and Sri Lanka. The Indian literacy rate of 36 per cent does compare very unfavourably with those of Burma (66 per cent), Sri Lanka (85 per cent), Thailand (86 per cent), Phillippines (75 per cent) and South Korea (93 per cent), not to

TABLE 1

Socio-Economic Indicators

| | GNP Per Capita | | Annual Average Growth Rate (Per Cent) | | | | Share of Manufacturing in GDP | | Adult Literacy 1980 | Life Expectancy at Birth 1981 |
|---|---|---|---|---|---|---|---|---|---|---|
| | Dollars 1981 | Annual Average Growth 1960–81 (per cent) | Agriculture | | Manufacturing | | 1960 | 1981 | | |
| | | | 1960–70 | 1970–81 | 1960–70 | 1970–81 | | | | |
| | 1 | 2 | 3 | 4 | 5 | 6 | 7 | 8 | 9 | 10 |
| SOUTH ASIA | | | | | | | | | | |
| BANGLADESH | 140 | 0.3 | 2.7 | 2.4 | 6.6 | 11.2 | 5 | 8 | 26 | 48 |
| BURMA | 190 | 1.4 | 4.1 | 4.7 | 3.4 | 4.6 | 8 | 10 | 66 | 54 |
| INDIA | 260 | 1.4 | 1.9 | 1.9 | 4.7 | 5.0 | 14 | 18 | 36 | 52 |
| SRI LANKA | 300 | 2.5 | 3.0 | 3.0 | 6.3 | 2.1 | 15 | 16 | 85 | 59 |
| PAKISTAN | 350 | 2.8 | 3.9 | 2.6 | 9.4 | 4.4 | 12 | 17 | 24 | 50 |

| | | | | | | | | |
|---|---|---|---|---|---|---|---|---|
| EAST ASIA | | | | | | | | |
| THAILAND | 770 | 2.6 | 5.6 | 4.5 | 11.4 | 10.3 | 13 | 20 | 86 | 63 |
| PHILIPPINES | 790 | 2.8 | 4.3 | 4.9 | 6.7 | 6.9 | 20 | 25 | 75 | 63 |
| SOUTH KOREA | 1700 | 6.9 | 4.4 | 3.0 | 17.6 | 15.6 | 14 | 28 | 93 | 66 |
| MALAYSIA | 1840 | 4.3 | – | 5.2 | – | 11.1 | 9 | 18 | 60 | 65 |
| JAPAN | 10080 | 6.3 | 2.1 | 0.2 | 11.6 | 6.5 | 34 | 30 | 99 | 77 |
| CHINA | 300 | 5.0 | 1.6 | 2.8 | 11.2 | 8.3 | – | – | 69 | 67 |

Source: World Bank, *World Development Report*. In the case of China, Cols 5 and 6 refer to industry.

speak of Japan (99 per cent). Thus, except in the case of Sri Lanka, differences in per capita income do seem to reflect fairly well the differences in the levels of development.[1]

### Manufacturing Sector

During 1960, the share of manufacturing in GDP in East Asian countries was more or less similar to that in India. It was 14 per cent for India, 13 per cent for Thailand, 14 per cent for South Korea and 9 per cent for Malaysia. However, in a span of twenty years, the East Asians were able to double this ratio: Thailand to 20 per cent, South Korea to 28 per cent and Malaysia to 18 per cent, while India could increase it by only 4 percentage points, namely to 18 per cent.

This is reflected much more sharply in the average annual growth rate of manufacturing in the last two decades. While the Indian growth rate has been 5 per cent, Thailand and Malaysia experienced double the Indian rate, while South Korea enjoyed more than three times the Indian rate. When it comes to growth rate of agriculture, the Indian performance is poor compared to both South Asian and East Asian countries. For the last two decades, the average annual growth rate of agricultural output was less than 2 per cent for India, while it was more than 4 per cent for Burma, 3 per cent for Sri Lanka, around 5 per cent for Thailand and more than double that of India for Philippines and South Korea. It is worth noting that most of these countries that experienced more than double the Indian growth rate in agriculture are rice-growing countries where technological change was low. The East Asian countries also experienced certain other interesting developments which the aggregate figures given in the table do not fully reflect. For instance, South Korea experienced no increase in inequality in income during the period of rapid growth.[2] Further, during the period 1965–75, the real wages in manufacturing and agriculture increased at annual average rates of 7.75 per cent and 4.8 per

---

[1] Some economists attribute these differences to religion and culture, namely, Hindu in the case of India and Buddhist in the case of Sri Lanka and Burma. For instance, see Sen (1982).

[2] Refer to Little (1981).

cent respectively in South Korea. Thus, in the last two decades, South Asia in general and India in particular have not done well compared to East Asia. The poor Indian performance is puzzling as India has done very well in the field of resource mobilization as seen from its high saving and investment rates.

## Import Substitution Strategy

One set of economists attribute the low growth rates of South Asia and, in particular, of India, to the strategy of import substitution that these economies followed in contrast to what these economists call the export-led growth strategy that the East Asian countries followed. A list of such economists would include such prominent names like Anne O. Krueger, at present Vice-President of the World Bank, and Jagdish N. Bhagwati.[3] To Bhagwati (1978) import substitution strategy could be growth reducing as the import substituting industries happen to be capital-intensive. Further, import substitution uses more of direct controls as distinct from price measures. While comparing India and South Korea, Bhagwati observes that while the Indian regime consisted mainly of dont's the Korean regime consisted mainly of do's.

To Krueger (1978), under import substitution, industry plans would be based mainly on the profitability of the sheltered domestic market and the monopoly power that accrues to those starting new production activities. Monopoly power, exercised by increasing the domestic price of the commodity above its international level, would only result in the reduction of the already small domestic market. Because of the protected environment, substandard quality and high costs would persist. All these affect growth adversely. The logical answer to the problem of a low growth rate would be to open the economy to foreign goods and investments. These authors argue that South Korea and Japan switched over to export-led growth strategy and achieved spectacular results.

The basic assumption behind these conclusions is that Japan and South Korea followed export-led growth while India followed an import substitution policy; while the former

[3] Refer to Bhagwati and Desai (1971), Bhagwati (1978), Krueger (1978).

regimes liberalized externally, the Indian regime was very restrictive in the domestic as well as in the foreign sector. However, facts do not support these assumptions about Japan and South Korea. To start with, both these countries followed import substitution policies till recently, Japan till 1962 and South Korea till 1967. It was the import substitution policy that enabled these countries to develop a strong industrial base which later on enabled them to expand their exports. Their rapid growth of exports was the result of their development and not the other way round.

In explaining the rapid development of Japan, Ishikawa (1981) emphasized the role of 'learning effects', which mainly consisted in promoting the domestic production of goods, which would be to start with of a lower quality and higher cost compared to the ones imported. Japan did follow this strategy. In later periods, however, the Japanese not only produced far superior quality goods compared to what was traded in the world market but also at a substantially lower cost. Ishikawa was also categorical in his conclusion that the competitiveness of the individual industries increased in the domestic and subsequently in the foreign markets. In this context Japan pursued protectionist policies with a relatively long gestation period.

As stated by Johnson (1982), during the 1950s the Japanese even realized the importance of large-scale production and the role of scale economies to help them make a dent in the world market. To exploit scale economies they needed more customers, but they sought these customers in the potential market of Japan itself. Their exports were the result of their rapid industrial development which was in turn due to their domestic policies which resulted in the creation of institutions of high speed growth. As early as 1953, the Industrial Rationalization Council called for the 'Keiretsu-ization' or cartelization of trading companies and manufacturers. This meant in practice that the Ministry of International Trade and Industry would assign an enterprise to a trading company. In this way around twenty big ones were created, each serving a bank, a cartel of small producers and a full complement of companies. Enterprises Rationalization Promotion Law (1952) provides direct governmental subsidies for experimental installation and trial operations of new machines and equipment, in addition to rapid amortization of exemption from local taxes of all investment in research and development. It also authorized industries to depreciate the cost of installing modern equipment by 50 per cent during the first year. Further it committed the government to provide the infrastructure facilities. Japan External Trading Organization, which is an international commercial intelligence service, was set up.

Despite its rapid industrial development and despite becoming one of the foremost leaders in technology, Japan continues to discourage imports and the entry of foreign multinational corporations. South Korea has also consistently followed a policy of discouraging multi-national direct investments and imports. In this context, the conclusion of a detailed study by Westphal, Rhee and Pursell (1981) is worth reporting, namely, that Korea clearly has not had to rely on foreign entrepreneurship to identify profitable ventures to manage their operations. This had made it possible for Korea to 'unbundle' the package of resources that typically is made available by foreign direct investments, and had thus permitted the selective use of individual foreign resources. And their final conclusion that Korea's industrial competence resulted primarily from indigenous effort is important.

Japan and South Korea are two examples of countries that achieved rapid economic development which did not follow the neoclassical paradigm that is strongly advocated by the set of scholars who favour export-led growth. On the other hand, the strategy of encouraging free market operations, liberalization, privatization and export-led growth strategy were mainly followed by the Latin American countries in general, and Chile in particular, with disastrous consequences. The Japanese development was an anti-thesis of the neoclassical paradigm.[4] The Japanese state took the role of the main promoter of industrial development. Free play of the market forces was not allowed and imports and foreign direct investment were restricted and regulated.

## The Schumpeterian Paradigm

For an explanation of the rapid industrial development of these countries, one may have to turn to the Schumpeterian para-

---

[4] Refer to Siddharthan (1984a).

digm, which emphasizes the role of non-price variables like skill, technology, innovation and market structures, as well as to certain non-economic variables like culture and ethos. In this paper I shall concentrate on the Schumpeterian variables rather than on the role of ethos.[5]

While the role of price variables and the importance of atomistic competition were emphasized by the neoclassicals, Schumpeter emphasized the role of non-price variables, large enterprises and quasi-monopolies in industrial development. Schumpeter not only considered the disappearance of atomistic competition as inevitable, a thought that he shared with Marx, he also considered perfect competition as inferior and not desirable.[6]

The policy implications of these two paradigms will differ substantially. If one went by the neoclassical paradigm, one would be advocating a policy aimed at breaking the formation of cartels, promoting atomistic competition, operating through price variables and avoiding state intervention and control. The Schumpeterian paradigm, on the other hand, would recognize size and scale advantages, will emphasize more expenditure on research and development and skill formation and will promote innovations. It will not expect the state to intervene in the market to promote a competitive structure.

Consciously or unconsciously, without being pure Schumpeterians, the Japanese seem to have followed more of the Schumpeterian principles than the neoclassical ones. They consciously followed a policy that actively encouraged the emergence of large conglomerates and forced the smaller units to join one of the large conglomerates. They tackled the problem of concentration of economic power through management reform, abolition of hereditary Zaibatsus and holding companies. They emphasized more on technology transfer, research and development and skill formation. Both Japan and South Korea aimed at and achieved very high literacy rates, 99 per cent and 93 per cent respectively. Both these countries spent a very large proportion of their national income on research and

---

[5] For works emphasizing the role of ethos, refer to Morishima (1982) and Siddharthan (1984a).

[6] See Schumpeter (1943), p. 106.

development. Their emphasis was more on a science and technology plan rather than on a plan that would fix firm targets for output of specific industrial products. They created a large number of institutions that would encourage introduction of new products, new methods, discover new sources of raw materials and markets, and they introduced changes in the market structures, all of which are considered as important constituents of economic development by Schumpeter.[7]

India, despite its policy of import substitution and planned economic development, has been much more neoclassical in actual practice than the Far East. Unlike the Far East, India did not introduce a comprehensive land reform which would genuinely give land to the tiller in agriculture, and correspondingly, hand over management of the industrial enterprises (both in the public and private sectors) to professional managers—two preconditions for rapid development. Our emphasis on price variables, namely, profit rates, tax concessions, subsidies, differential interest rates, saving rates, etc. has been excessive to the relative neglect of non-price variables. Our effort at improving the skill content of the population has been very meagre, and as a result of this neglect the adult literacy rate even now remains at a miserably low level of 36 per cent. Our expenditures on R and D is only 0.06 per cent of the national income. Most of the direct controls, as seen from the MRTP Act, etc. derive their inspiration from the neoclassical outlook that atomistic competition is the ideal situation and conglomeration and trustification is wrong. The alternative paradigm would recognize the role of minimum economies of size, exploit size advantages, promote massive investment in R and D and would tackle the evils of concentration of economic power through land and industrial management reforms. In India, such a reform is not difficult as most of the industrial corporations are minority share holders who control management mainly through government support. Even initial steps in these directions have not been taken. On the other hand, anti-trust laws on typical neoclassical lines have been enacted that are bound to fail in the modern corporate world.

[7] Schumpeter (1934: reprinted 1961), p. 66. For the role of Schumpeterian variables in Indian industrial performance, refer to Siddharthan (1984b).

## Importance of Managerial and Organizational Reform

Rapid development resulting from innovations, introduction of new products, new methods of production, expansion of the markets and changes in the structure, is not possible without giving the decision-making power to those who run the enterprises, either in agriculture or industry. In agriculture this is achieved through a comprehensive land reform that gives land to the tiller and in industry through organizational and managerial reform. In the case of the private sector, this would mean passing on the power from the hereditary owners to the professional managers and other staff; for the public sector this would involve the transfer of power from the ministry to the enterprises. In the case of Japan, the foundations of their rapid industrial development were laid soon after the war, with a comprehensive land reform that really gave land to the tillers and the abolition of the hereditary Zaibatsus which transferred the power to the professionals.

Some of the socialist countries like Hungary, Yugoslavia and Romania have also introduced managerial and organizational reforms in their state-owned organizations by transferring power from the ministries to the enterprises with very positive results. Through these managerial reforms they were able to substantially increase their productivity, make their industries competitive, successfully compete in the export markets and usher in rapid technological change, without resorting to de-nationalization. The basic principle involved in both these cases is: transfer of power to those who run the enterprise, be it a farm, corporate unit or a public-sector undertaking, from the non-cultivating landlord, non-professional hereditary owner and the ministry official respectively.

In India, little has been done to move towards this direction. The public sector is dominated by the ministry officials, both directly and indirectly; directly, as many of the officials in the ministry, who have very little experience in or aptitude for managing an enterprise, are put in charge of these organizations and later transferred back to the ministry; and the indirect control is exercised through a complex system of financial and physical regulations that virtually make it impossible for the enterprise even to take minor decisions without the consent of the ministry officials. In the case of the private sector, the power mainly rests with certain hereditary families, even though they hold only minority shares. Some of them could be professional managers, while others are not. In any case, the power they enjoy does not depend on their managerial ability but on their inheritance. The main casualties in this structure are enterprise, innovation and development.[8]

Of late there have been signs of change in the economic policy of the Government of India. The contemplated change should not aim at taking the economy even closer to the neoclassical ideal of free trade, liberalization, free operation of market mechanism, privatization of the public sector and increased emphasis on price mechanism and price variables. These were the very policies tried in the Latin American countries with disastrous consequences. As has been theoretically emphasized by Schumpeter, and demonstrated by the countries of the Far East and some of the socialist countries like Yugoslavia, Hungary and to a lesser extent by Romania, development consists in the production of new goods, introducing new methods of production, creation of new markets and materials, all of which depend on non-price and non-free market variables like technological change, R and D and innovations. The precondition for exploiting technology and to be innovative is an institutional reform: land reform in the case of agriculture and managerial reform in the case of industry. The way to development is to launch a bold institutional reform, a massive effort to substantially improve the skill content of the population by fixing and achieving physical targets for literacy, and increasing the proportion of the skilled population, and to substantially increase the expenditures on R and D. Liberalization and non-interference of the state cannot achieve any of these objectives. On the other hand, all these are possible within our resource constraint and their implementation depends on a clear perception of issues based on an understanding of the

---

[8] The managerial reform suggested here is not as difficult to implement as it appears at first sight. First, the hereditary owners, by and large, own only a minority of shares, and second, certain industrial houses like the Tatas have already elevated professional managers to the position of chairman and managing director.

theories of development (not the theories that help us manage existing structures, namely, neoclassical, but those that help to change the structures and create new ones), and an examination of the policies pursued by countries that have succeeded and those that have failed with disastrous consequences.

### REFERENCES

Bhagwati, Jagdish N. and Padma Desai (1970), *India: Planning for Industrialisation* (Oxford University Press).

Bhagwati, Jagdish N. (1978), *Anatomy and Consequences of Exchange Control Regimes*, NBER, New York.

Ishikawa, Shigeru (1981), *Essays on Technology, Employment and Institutions in Economic Development* (Tokyo: Kinokuniya Co.).

Johnson, Chalmers (1982), *MITI and the Japanese Miracle: Growth of Industrial Policy 1925–75* (California: Stanford University Press, Stanford).

Krueger, Anne O. (1978), *Liberalisation Attempts and Consequences*, NBER, New York.

Little, I.M.D. (1981), 'The Experience and Causes of Rapid Labour-Intensive Development in Korea, Taiwan Province, Hong Kong, and Singapore and the Possibilities of Emulation' in Eddy Lee (ed.), *Export-Led Industrialization and Development*, ILO.

Morishima, Michio (1982), *Why Has Japan Succeeded? Western Technology and Japanese Ethos* (Cambridge: Cambridge University Press).

Schumpeter, Joseph A. (1961), *The Theory of Economic Development* (1934) reprinted (New York: Oxford University Press).

Schumpeter, Joseph A. (1943), *Capitalism, Socialism and Democracy* (London: George Allen and Unwin).

Sen, Amartya (1982), 'How is India Doing?', *The New York Review*, 16 December.

Siddharthan, N. S. (1984a), 'The Non-Neoclassical Paradigm: Buddhism and Economic Development', *Japanese Journal of Religious Studies*, Vol. II, No. 4.

Siddharthan, N. S. (1984b), 'Industrial Structure, Non-Price Competition and Industrial Development', *Economic and Political Weekly*, Annual Number.

Westphal, Larry E., Yung W. Rhee and G. Pursell (1981), 'Korean Industrial Competence: Where it Came From?' *World Bank Staff Working Paper*, 469.

# Privatization of the Development Process

BALRAJ MEHTA

I am always very diffident in talking to academics because I have very inadequate academic training myself. But being a journalist, I might be able to contribute a few thoughts for your consideration and discussion.

Take the question of privatization of the development process. I think I was the first one to report the move in *Economic and Political Weekly*. But the idea of privatization should not be taken in a very simplistic fashion. The idea that large public sector enterprises can or will be just sold to the private business interests is nonsense for the simple reason that many of these enterprises are not making profit and no private party will be willing or able to buy them. The privatization moves are actually being conceived in two specific terms and levels which are important. Their significance and meaning should be evaluated by experts and specialists.

It is proposed that public sector enterprises which make cash losses over a period of time should be regarded as junk. Such units are proposed to be broken into relatively small bits and pieces for the purposes of selling these separate bits and pieces to private parties. Reports have appeared that the Haldia fertilizer plant is regarded as the most suitable for such treatment. The Haldia plant as a whole cannot be sold to any private party. This is obvious enough. Nobody is there to buy it. But if the plant can be broken into smaller segments, segments of the plant can be sold to private parties to their advantage. That is how the concept of privatization is being advanced in the case of large public sector plants which make losses.

Secondly, bugetary support to the public sector enterprise is proposed to be reduced so that public sector enterprises will have to depend more and more on the open market for funds—on debenture issues, deposits and bank finance. But it is realized that such devices cannot raise adequate resources for investment in public enterprises. Debenture is a commodity in the market and it is traded in the market. There is not going to be much appreciation of the value of debentures issued by public enterprises. Such appreciation takes place in the case of shares and stocks of large and profitable private companies. There is no question, therefore, of funds for investment in public sector being raised in a big way through deposits and debentures. If budgetary support for investment in public sector is to be reduced, if not withdrawn, further expansion of public sector on lines envisaged by the Industrial Policy Resolution of 1956 will thus not take place.

Thirdly, a special merit is being found in private sector management, its norms and practices. That is an essential part of the move for privatization of the public sector enterprise. Bright managers from private sector are proposed to be inducted as the panacea for the ills of public enterprise and its management deficiencies. This is something which is not a novel idea. This was mooted way back in the middle of the seventies. It was tried much earlier in the case of public sector steel. It was applied in the case of some other undertakings also. But experience soon showed that, by and large, the rejects among the private sector managers tended to be inducted into the public sector industrial enterprises. People who knew nothing of steel industry were placed as managers of public sector steel industry. Already, public sector industrial enterprises are required through prices and other mechanisms to extend infrastructural support to private sector industrial enterprise. With the large-scale placement of managers from private sector in public enterprises, coordination between the two sectors will become not only closer but investment in public sector will tend to be determined by the needs of private enterprise, especially of new industries that are coming up with foreign collaboration in the private sector. Activity in public sector will thus be more closely coordinated and geared to support and subserve private enterprise. This is the kind of privatization that is being talked about. It is not merely a plan to sell outright public sector units to private parties.

Now I move on to another point in regard to industrial policy. Attention has been drawn in the course of discussion to growth of competitiveness in the small sector and the medium sector. It is often contended that growth in the small and medium sector is not recorded in official statistics. It is true that there is a great deal of competition that big business and large industrial units are facing from medium and small-scale sectors even in segments of what may be called modern industry. There are also exemptions from taxes on the basis of the size of production units. This is supposed to give small-scale producers an edge in the market. Competition is said to have become intense, especially in manufacturing. Even in machine building, relatively simpler tools and things like that which are manufactured in small and medium sectors are creating problems for big industry. It was quite interesting, therefore, to find in the fiscal proposals in the Budget for 1985–6 that excise duty on what is called Item 68 was increased from 10 to 12 per cent. In other cases, excise duty was not increased. Item 68 is actually the most competitive to the established large industry. New industrial units which undertake new production or new lines of production are clubbed together under Item 68 for excise purposes. Those products which are exempt from excise levy come under Item 60. A large number of small and medium, mainly small units, in which modern technology too is being used have been set up largely as self-employment enterprises. A weeder comes up to set up a small engineering unit and so on. This is a fairly widespread enterprise. The Budget for 1985–6 reduced the exemption limit for the purpose of excise levy and many units were brought under the excise net under Item 68 to subject them to increase in excise levy. That was the only exemption limit which was brought down in the budget proposals when in the case of personal income tax, the exemption limit was raised and a large number of income tax payers were dramatically thrown out of the income tax net. The Finance Minister boasted that he had thrown a million persons from out of the income tax net. But in the case of small-scale sector, he did not say how many new units of production had been dragged into the excise net. If a survey is undertaken, it will be found that a very large number might have been brought into the excise net. In the case of small-scale industry it is not only the payment of excise but it is also the inspectors Raj which follows which is a big problem. The competitiveness of the small-scale sector versus the large-sector was admittedly blunted in 1985–6 by the fiscal instrument.

At the same time, in the case of project imports, customs levy was reduced in the budget for 1985–6 from 55 to 45 per cent. But in the case of components and parts, customs duty was increased from 61 per cent to 85 per cent. Why? What could be the rationale and philosophy behind this move? The All-India Manufacturing Organization (AIMO) rightly pinpointed the issue at stake when the move was proposed. According to the Chairman of the AIMO, the adjustment of duties in favour of project imports and against imports of parts and components meant that there would be no new investment by Indian entrepreneurs in high-tech areas. The point was rightly made that when an entrepreneur enters a high-tech area, he has, to begin with, to undertake a lot of import of components and parts as part of a plan to gradually indigenize his enterprise. Under the new fiscal dispensation, this would no longer be possible. Complete plants would tend to be imported because these imports would find a preferential basis. It would be more profitable to import complete plants instead of setting up production facilities within the country and gradually indigenize them. This problem will be faced, in particular, by entrepreneurs who set up new industries, especially in electronics and computers areas. Those who had set up production facilities on the basis of a phased indigenization programme were thus placed in a difficult position and felt the pinch of the new liberalized imports of ready-to-start complete machines, which were extended a preferential fiscal dispensation. Already there was strong competition in the areas of high technology. But once the complete machines could be imported at 45 per cent customs duty instead of 5 per cent earlier and parts and components had to be imported by paying a much higher duty which was increased to 85 per cent, indigenization of production was bound to suffer. This fiscal dispensation has thus its own implications in terms of indigenization as well of blunting the competition in the domestic market in favour both of foreign capital and Indian big business against small and medium enterprise.

Together with privatization of public sector and the encouragement that is being given to foreign capital and Indian big business, the scenario has tended in recent years to become more and more interesting. What appears to be in the offing is the drive of official policy in favour of concentration and compradore capital which are being relied upon as the prime factors of growth or as the main engine of economic growth.

# Economic Class and Economic Policy in India

B. B. BHATTACHARYA

In the traditional literature on political economy the households were divided into two economic classes: workers and capitalists. It became soon apparent that the peasant, who uses his own labour and land for production, is a distinct class of its own. As the economy and society developed many new socio-economic classes emerged, such as bureaucracy and urban professionals. A modern economy—whether capitalist, socialist or mixed economy—is therefore far more complex than classical political economy characterized by Marx and Ricardo.

The Indian nation in the post-Independence period consists of various heterogeneous socio-economic groups. It is also divided into racial, religious, caste and linguistic groups, which cut across all socio-economic classes. Further, there are geographical, regional and sub-national identities. All these factors influence both economic policies and political decisions in India and, consequently, it is not easy to characterize economic policies in India in terms of simple class interests. The class interests have however influenced economic policies pursued by both central and state governments during the planning era (Mitra, 1977 and Bardhan, 1984).

### Indian Class Structure

Ignoring religious, caste and linguistic differences, etc., households in India may be divided into ten broad socio-economic classes[1]: 1. agricultural labourers, 2. peasants, 3. capitalist far-

[1] Classification here more or less follows Bhattacharya and Dasgupta (1984).

mers, 4. non-agricultural rural households (artisans, blacksmiths, weavers, etc.), 5. private industrial workers, 6. public industrial workers, 7. capitalists, 8. bureaucrats (government, civil and defence employees), 9. urban self-employed professionals and 10. urban informal sector households (small shopkeepers, workers in small and unorganized industries and trading establishments, etc.). Agricultural labourers, who are mainly landless labourers, form numerically the biggest class in India. This is also perhaps the poorest economic class. Wages of agricultural labourers are neither indexed to the price level nor do they (with possible exception in Kerala and some parts of West Bengal and Jammu and Kashmir) enjoy the benefit of a public distribution system. Being heterogeneous and unorganized this class also has a very poor collective bargaining power. Except in Punjab and Haryana, real wages of agricultural labourers have remained the same, if not fallen, during the post-Independence period (Rao, 1975).

Peasants may be defined as subsistence farmers using mainly household labour. Peasants have very little market transactions. In contrast, capitalist farmers hire agricultural labourers and produce food and non-food agricultural crops for the market. Until recently Indian agriculture was pre-dominated by peasant farming. But in recent years, thanks to Green Revolution, capitalist farming has gained importance, and presently, this class, though numerically smaller than the peasant class, exercises far greater influence on state economic policy, particularly agricultural pricing policy, than peasant and other economic classes.

Rural non-agricultural households, along with urban informal sector households, are highly unorganized. Although numerically these two classes are quite big, being unorganized and poor, they perhaps do not influence economic policies very much. Fragmented evidence on their economic conditions suggest a stagnancy, if not deterioration, in their real income over time. Like agricultural labourers their incomes are not indexed, neither do they enjoy the benefit of the public distribution system.

Industrial workers in both public and private sectors are fairly well organized. When inflation occurs, wages in both public and private industries are adjusted almost proportionately. There are, however, some time lags, particularly in private industries. Industrial workers also enjoy social security benefits. Wages in public industries are also generally not constrained by productivity and profitability. The average standard of living of industrial workers is better than that of not only agricultural workers but also of rural non-agricultural and urban informal sector households. The incidence of poverty among rural landless households is far higher than amongst industrial workers and urban self-employed households.

The analysis of bureaucracy as a separate class is a relatively recent phenomenon. The early writings on bureaucracy, following Weber, regarded the bureaucrat as a mere agent of public policy implementation with no vested interest of his own. Modern writings on bureaucracy disregards this simplistic view and considers it as a separate economic class— Buchanan (1979) and Jackson (1983). Bureaucracy in India, as in other democracies, is highly organized with strong collective bargaining power. Modern governments also have a tendency to satisfy the interests of bureaucrats at the expense of other economic classes. The government, unlike capitalist farmers and industrialists, is not constrained by productivity and profitability in paying higher wages to bureaucrats. The government also enjoys a special power, i.e., capacity to pay wages through deficit financing. Nor is there any inverse relationship between employment and real wage in the public sector.[2]

## Democracy and Economic Decision-Making

Economic policies have generally three objectives: growth, stabilization and distribution. Some policies are primarily growth-oriented and some others are for stabilization of income, employment and price level. There are other policies where distribution objectives are more important than other objectives, for instance, generating tax resources for anti-poverty programmes. Ultimately, all economic policies, whether primarily aimed for growth or redistribution, have

---

[2] For an analytical model of consumption, saving and income of different economic classes in India, see Bhattacharya and Dasgupta (1984).

some implications for inter-class and inter-person income distribution. No policy in that respect is neutral with respect to distribution. In an authoritarian regime or in a military dictatorship, the class or group interest in economic policy may be easily identifiable. In a popular democracy, however, class or group interest in economic policy is often difficult to identify because the government's 'revealed preference' may be different from avowed policy objectives. Moreover, the political compulsions in a democracy may result in shifting class interest from time to time, so that no single group or class may dominate economic policy decisions for a long time.[3]

It is often held that democracy enables a majority decision on economic and political issues. Since majority of economic households are generally poor, democracy should enable the poor to dictate in economic policy decision. In that sense the economic policy of the government in a democracy should be oriented towards economic welfare of the poorer economic classes. This is, however, an over-simplification and utopian view. Majority in a pluralistic society, like India, is never clearly defined in terms of economic class or even socio-economic group. Moreover, even in a one-person-one-vote system, political influence of the poorer (but numerically larger) classes are found to be less than that of the richer (but numerically smaller) classes. Political compulsion, particularly election, does however influence economic policy in favour of the poorer classes. It is now well known that there are cycles in economic policy decisions in Western democracies: election year budget is softest in terms of taxation of middle and poorer households and immediate post-election budget is hardest. In India also ruling parties in the Centre and states have often adopted pro-poor economic policies on the eve of election, and discarded them either overtly or covertly, in the post-election period.

---

[3] Whiteley (1980) presents several studies on influence of economic factors on political decision-making in Western democracies. By and large, these studies show a significant influence of economic factors. However, there have been no stable relationships between economic factors and elections. Decision-making in a constitutional democracy is also analysed in Brennan and Buchanan (1985).

## Rationing and Public Distribution System

Rationing of food became an integral part of economic policy in India since the Second World War. The importance of rationing and public distribution of foodgrains was realized after the great Bengal famine of 1943 which, according to a reliable estimate, caused at least 3 million deaths (Sen 1981). What was important was that death occurred less due to shortage of food than due to mal-distribution. Rationing continued to be a necessity in the post-Independence period because of relatively faster growth of food demand over food supply. Rationing and public distribution of food was also important to keep the inflation rate in control in periods of excess demand. Finally, it was necessary to protect the real wages of politically volatile industrial workers and bureaucrats.

The rationing system covers mainly the urban population. Only in Kerala and partially in West Bengal and Jammu and Kashmir rural population is covered by rationing and public distribution of food. Even in urban areas many poor households belonging to informal sector are also not covered by the rationing system because of lack of any fixed residential dwellings. Construction labourers who typically change their place of work every few months are deprived of rationed food supply. Thus the vast majority of poor households belonging to agricultural labourers, non-agricultural rural households and urban informal sector households, who together constitute a sizable proportion of population, do not get the benefit of the public distribution system in India. These classes also do not have price indexation of wage or income. Being poor, and mostly below the poverty line, their consumption consists mainly of foodgrains. Thus when food prices rise the real consumption of these classes falls.

The manner in which the rationing and public distribution system work makes the condition of these vulnerable classes far worse than what it would have been without rationing. The rationed food is supplied out of government procurement and imports. The gap between the procurement and import price plus operational cost of public distribution, on the one hand, and issue price of foodgrains in urban ration shops, on the other, is borne out of the government budget as subsidy. Presently the food subsidy is more than Rs 2000 crores per annum or about 4 per cent of the total central government expenditure. Since subsidy is one of the causes of government deficit financing, which in turn affects inflation, the poorest economic classes—agricultural labourers, non-agricultural rural households and urban informal sector households—are in effect sharing the burden of supplying cheap ration food to the relatively better-off urban households.

More important is that if there was no urban rationing of food supply the free-market prices of food, which are paid by the households who are not entitled to ration, could have been lower.[4] This is so because if government supplies less ration food to the urban consumers then the free-market supply of food would increase, and given the demand for food, this would put a downward pressure on the free-market food prices, particularly in rural areas. This is particularly true of the recent years when large-scale procurement (at a fairly attractive price) has led to an excess accumulation of stock with the government, thus reducing the free-market food supply for the rural poor. In fact if the government now reduces procurement price of food, it can derive two benefits for the poor: first, it will reduce budget subsidy on food; and second, by procuring less food (when it has an excess stock), it can bring down the free-market price of food in rural as well as in urban areas, thereby increase food consumption of the poorer class and decrease the incidence of poverty.

Ideally, rationing and public distribution should protect the interests of the poorest economic classes. In India it does the same for the middle income classes. Worst of all, the urban middle and even rich income classes are enjoying the benefits of rationing and the public distribution system not at the expense of capitalist farmers and industrialists but at the expense of the poorest economic classes. The capitalist farmers receive procurement price of foodgrains on the basis of cost of cultivation. Thanks to stock accumulation with the government the free-market price of food these days is also higher than what it would have been without government stock accumulation. In net terms the capitalist farmers are therefore no worse-off, if not gaining, due to public distribution system. Industrial capitalists

---

[4] For a formal proof of this, see Bhattacharya and Dasgupta (1984).

also do not suffer due to rationing and public distribution, except that they have to share the burden of government food subsidy. On the other hand, industrialists are gaining from public distribution: first, it enables them to restrict wage cost of industrial workers (rationed food supply restricts growth of cost of living of industrial workers), and second, lower expenditure on food in urban areas increases expenditure on non-food consumer goods supplied by industrialists. On balance, the industrialists may gain out of rationing and public distribution. Industrial workers, both private and public bureaucrats as well as urban self-employed professionals gain from food rationing system, although many of them can afford to spend a higher proportion of their income on food. So the real losers from food rationing in India are the poorest economic classes.

It may be noted that the anomaly in the distribution of gains from food rationing and public distribution system arises not so much from the principle of rationing as such, but from a partial or imperfect rationing system. If the rationing system could cover not only the urban poor but also the rural poor, agricultural labourers and other poor rural households, there would be no adverse effect of rationing. In that sense partial rationing is more dangerous than no rationing as far as economic welfare of poorer economic classes are concerned. It is high time the government either restricted ration food supply only to the real urban poor or extended the same to the rural poor.

### Agricultural Pricing Policy

In recent years the pricing of agricultural inputs (fertilizer, electricity, irrigation, etc.), output-procurement and support prices have become a subject-matter of controversy. The conflict arises partly on account of growing subsidy for food production and distribution, partly on account of inter-sectoral growth and equity and partly on account of inter-sectoral resource transfer. Each of them has some implications for inter-class income distribution.[5] The most controversial in this

---

[5] For a general discussion on this, see Mellor (1978), Chichilinsky and Taylor (1980) have developed a simple general equilibrium model for this.

regard is the fertilizer price and fertilizer subsidy. Fertilizer subsidy is paid by government to fertilizer plants—public as well as private—for selling fertilizer to farmers below cost (plus normal profit) price. The question that arises in this context is who is the gainer and who is the loser, or who is ultimately bearing the burden of fertilizer subsidy. First of all, it may be noted that to the extent fertilizer subsidy results in deficit financing and which in turn results in inflation, it affects all consumers, poorer consumers more than the rich. Secondly, if underpricing of fertilizer results in greater fertilizer consumption and consequently larger food production, then fertilizer subsidy would benefit the poorer economic classes. Fertilizer subsidy also benefits industrial capitalists through the retention price system.

Until recently fertilizer consumption was confined to irrigated land. Capitalist farmers also accounted for the bulk of fertilizer consumption. Even now, with greater application of fertilizer in dry farming and also by small peasants, the bulk of fertilizer consumption is accounted for by the capitalist farmers in Punjab, Haryana, western Uttar Pradesh and Andhra Pradesh. Given this uneven consumption of fertilizer across regions and farms, it is doubtful whether peasants and poorer agricultural classes derive any benefit from fertilizer subsidy. Perhaps on balance it benefits the rich more than the poor. Similarly, underpricing of other agricultural inputs (water, electricity, pesticides, etc.) benefit rich farmers more than the poor. They also benefit rich farmers at the expense of other economic classes.

### Administered Pricing Policy

Administered pricing policy is often used as a covert or even overt means of benefitting one or more classes at the expense of others. Administered prices are generally based on cost plus normative profit. Costs are often artificially manipulated. Through administered pricing these high costs are transmitted to the rest of the economy. Sugar industry is an example of this artificial cost escalation. Most sugar mills in India, particularly those located in Uttar Pradesh and Bihar, have worn out machines, as a result of which they have one of the worst crushing capacity in the world. This results in the high cost of domestic sugar. In a competitive system these high-cost mills would have been closed years ago and in their place new mills would have come up. But under the present administered pricing formula, mills with worn-out machines dominate and consequently they determine the average cost, which then becomes a basis for administered pricing. This is a clear case of capitalists benefitting at the expense of not only other urban classes but also farmers.

Administered prices also benefit the public sector employees at the expense of others. In recent years prices of petroleum products have increased all over the world as a result of the policies of the OPEC. In India also prices of petroleum products have been increased in relation to international prices rather than in relation to domestic costs and demands. Public-sector oil companies have earned handsome profit as a result of this policy. (In fact they now account for most of the profits earned by public enterprises.) Since bonuses of public-sector employees are linked to profits, real wages of employees in public-sector oil companies have gone up substantially without any increase in labour productivity. Real wages in public-sector banks and financial institutions have also gone up substantially in recent years. In many cases real wages have gone up without any increase in profit, and in many cases even with increasing loss (Coal India). Since a fall in profit results in lowering resources for public investment, a higher wage (faster growth in relation to productivity) in the public sector is a covert means of transferring resources in favour of volatile public sector employees.

Underpricing is also used as a means of benefitting one or more classes at the expense of others. Most public enterprises are now suffering losses due to various reasons, notably, managerial inefficiency, inappropriate location, labour-intensive but high-cost technology and low labour productivity. Underpricing is also one of the basic reasons for losses of many public enterprises, particularly urban road transport and rural electricity. A perfect example of this is the Delhi Transport Corporation, which until recently charged only 40 paise for a bus journey up to 16 kilometre. At this rate it was perhaps the cheapest road transport in the country. For the same journey of 16 km, Bombay, Madras and Calcutta transport used to charge about Rs 2, Rs 1.80 and Rs 1.60 respectively. As a result of this underpricing and also managerial inefficiency DTC now has an accumulated loss of more than Rs 1000 crores (in recent years more than Rs 150 crores per annum). Since the loss is adjusted through budgetary support, this means that the rest of India has either paid extra taxation worth Rs 1000 crores or borne the cost through inflationary deficit financing to provide cheaper transport to Delhi/New Delhi commuters. According to official statistics, Delhi has the highest per capita income among all states and union territories, except Chandigarh. This means that poorer people all over India are contributing to the higher standard of living of the rich Delhi government servants and other economic classes.

Another case in this regard is the deliberate underpricing of electricity supplied to capitalist farmers. In states like Uttar Pradesh, Haryana and Punjab, electricity rates for rural consumers who are mainly rich farmers are even below the marginal wage cost of supplying rural electricity. No wonder these electricity boards suffer huge losses, which are then covered through overt or covert budgetary support.

## Taxation vs Deficit Financing

The share of direct tax revenue in national income has fallen over the years, partly due to lowering of tax rates, but mainly due to evasion and avoidance. While the share of direct tax revenue has declined that of total public expenditure, both plan and non-plan, has increased. This means that the financing of public expenditure has become more regressive over the years. Within direct tax, the share of agriculturists has declined even further. Indirect tax revenue, though more buoyant than direct tax, has also become relatively stagnant in recent years. In contrast, the share of public debt in general and that of deficit financing in particular has risen significantly. The overall means of financing public expenditure has, therefore, become more regressive.

Deficit financing, which is the most regressive form of financing public expenditure, now accounts for nearly 10 per cent of public expenditure. Deficit financing affects consumers more than producers. It also affects salaried or fixed income groups more. The increasing dependence on deficit financing is, therefore, a covert means of transferring real resources not only from private to public but also from salaried income groups to producers, notably capitalist industrialists and farmers. The worst sufferers of deficit financing are perhaps agricultural labourers whose incomes, unlike the government employees' and industrial workers', are not indexed to the price level.

## Concluding Remarks

State economic policies in India have distinct class biases. There is a difference between avowed and 'revealed preference' of government economic policies. Although majority of households belong to poorer economic classes, state economic policies are often heavily biased against them. Parliamentary democracy based on majority rule has not been able to protect the interests of the poor in this regard. State economic policies, however, have not been static. Compulsions of democratic elections have resulted in a shift in interests of various economic classes from time to time. On balance government policies regarding rationing of food, prices of agricultural inputs and outputs, administered prices, financing of public expenditure, have become more regressive in recent years.

### REFERENCES

P. K. Bardhan (1984), *Political Economy of Development in India* (Delhi: Oxford University Press).

B. B. Bhattacharya (1984), *Public Expenditure, Inflation and Growth* (Delhi: Oxford University Press).

B. B. Bhattacharya and A. K. Dasgupta (1984), 'Pricing Policy and Inter-class Income Distribution in India: An Analytical Model', paper presented in Silver Jubilee National Seminar (Institute of Economic Growth, Delhi).

G. Brennan and J. M. Buchanan (1985), *The Reason of Rules: Constitutional Political Economy* (Cambridge: Cambridge University Press).

J. Burton (1980), 'The Demand for Inflation in Liberal Democratic Societies' in Whiteley (ed.) (1980).

G. Chichilinksy and L. Taylor (1980), 'Agriculture and the Rest of the Economy: Macro Connections and Policy Restraints', *American Journal of Agricultural Economics*.

W. Grant (1983), 'The Political Economy of Industrial Policy' in R. J. B. Jones (ed.) (1983).

P. M. Jackson (1983), *The Political Economy of Bureaucracy* (New Delhi: Heritage Publishers).

R. J. B. Jones (ed.) (1983), *Perspectives on Political Economy: Alternatives to Economics of Depression* (London: Frances Pinter).

G. Locksley (1980), 'The Political Business Cycle: Alternative Interpretations' in Whiteley (ed.) (1980).

John Mellor (1978), 'Food Price Policy and Income Distribution in Low Income Countries', *Economic Development and Cultural Change*.

A. Mitra (1977), *Terms of Trade and Class Relations: An Essay in Political Economy* (London: Frank Cass).

C. H. H. Rao (1975), *Technological Change and Distribution of Gains in Indian Agriculture* (Delhi: Macmillan).

J. Roemer (1982), *A General Theory of Exploitation and Class* (Cambridge: Harvard University Press).

D. J. D. Sandole (1980), 'Economic Conditions and Conflict Processes' in Whiteley (ed.) (1980).

Amārtya Sen (1981), *Poverty and Famines: An Essay on Entitlement and Deprivation* (Clarendon: Oxford University Press).

P. Whiteley (ed.) (1980), *Models of Political Economy* (London: Sage Publications).

# Implications of Agricultural Development Policies for Rural Poverty in India: A Note*

K. SUBBARAO

If one looks back, with the advantage of hindsight, at the Indian agricultural development policies since Independence, broadly three sets of policy packages seem to have been adopted. The first set of policies related to building up of infrastructure including irrigation, flood control, etc., which may be termed 'public investment policy package'. The second related to institutional reform including all land redistribution policies, tenancy reform policies, consolidation of holdings, etc., which may be termed 'institutional reform policy package'. The third set of policies related to provision of incentives including price support, input subsidies, subsidized institutional credit, etc., which may be termed 'incentive policy package'.

The relative importance of these three sets of policy packages varied from time to time. Thus, prior to the advent of new seed varieties (i.e. prior to the mid-sixties), the first two sets of policies were emphasized more than the third. The 'incentive policy package' received an impetus following the Green Revolution.

---

\* This presentation is based on the author's two recent papers: (*i*) 'State Policies and Regional Disparity in Indian Agriculture', *Development and Change*, vol. 16 (1985), pp. 523–46; and (*ii*) 'Incentive Policies and India's Agricultural Development: Some Aspects of Social and Regional Equity', *Indian Journal of Agricultural Economics* (forthcoming). Readers interested in detailed quantitative evidence and methodology adopted may refer to these two papers.

The effectiveness of these policy packages also varied inasmuch as some were implemented more successfully than others. Thus the 'institutional reform policy package' was implemented much less successfully than the other two policy packages.

I wish to argue in this Note that the relative shifts in emphasis in the above three policy packages, and the varying degrees of effectiveness of their implementation, have important implications for inter-regional equity and inter-farm equity. Before I develop this argument I would first like to provide the broad quantitative dimensions of the relative shifts in emphasis in these policy packages.

Public expenditure on subsidies going to agriculture and rural development has risen from Rs 10,000 million in 1974–5 to Rs 25,000 million by 1980–1 *at constant prices*. Subsidy on fertilizer alone rose from Rs 2,660 million in 1977–8 to Rs 18,060 million by 1985–6. This subsidy is entirely borne by the central government. More recent data on other subsidies which are borne by the state governments (such as subsidy on irrigation) are far more difficult to obtain but their growing magnitude has been a major source of concern to the state governments. It is interesting that the ratio of expenditures on direct assistance (input subsidies) to public investment on crop production programmes including irrigation fell during the Fifth Plan period from 0.45 in 1974–5, to 0.22 in 1976–7 but rose sharply to 0.48 by the beginning of the Sixth Plan (i.e. 1980–1). Though available data are not complete in all respects, even conservative estimates suggest that the ratio has risen to 0.65 by 1985–6 owing to sharp escalation of public subsidies.

The above broad quantification suggests that since the mid-1970s, the third policy package consisting of various incentives (direct assistance programmes) has grown in importance relegating the 'public investment' and 'institutional reform' policy packages to the background. What are the implications of this shift from a public investment-cum-institutional reform-oriented development strategy to a subsidy-oriented development strategy, for equity and social justice? I would like to illustrate these implications with reference to input subsidies and price support.

In terms of cost to the treasury, I have already indicated the massive magnitude of fertilizer subsidy. The distribution of this subsidy violates regional as well as size-class equity. For example, four states (Punjab, Uttar Pradesh, Andhra Pradesh and Tamil Nadu), which accounted for only 30 per cent of the nation's gross cropped area, claimed nearly 60 per cent of the nation's fertilizer subsidy. Five states (Madhya Pradesh, Rajasthan, Bihar, Orissa and West Bengal), which accounted for 40 per cent of the nation's gross cropped area, claimed only 16 per cent of the fertilizer subsidy.[1]

More interesting is the inter-state variation in the bias against the small farms. In seven states which include two Green Revolution states (Madhya Pradesh, Rajasthan, Uttar Pradesh, Bihar, Orissa, Haryana and Punjab) the share of small farms (less than 1 hectare size-group) in fertilizer consumption of each state in 1978-9 was lower than their share in gross cropped area in each state and, interestingly, *substantially* lower than their share in the gross irrigated area of the respective states. The exceptions are West Bengal and Kerala, where the share of small farmers in fertilizer consumption is substantially *higher* than their shares in gross cropped area and gross irrigated area. In other states (Karnataka, Gujarat and Maharashtra), small farmers' share in fertilizer consumption roughly corresponds with their share in gross irrigated area.[2]

Pre-empting of supplies by better-off states and by large farmers within each state led to low fertilizer use in the rainfed eastern India and the semi-arid tropics where the potential is least tapped. This is one of the important reasons for the prevailing wide gaps between actual consumption and potential demand in a number of backward states (such as Assam, Bihar, West Bengal, Madhya Pradesh, Uttar Pradesh, Rajasthan and Jammu and Kashmir).

We now turn to the implications of the extensive use of price supports. That rising prices stimulate agricultural employment both through supply response in production and through increased demand associated with rising producers' incomes is now well-recognized. At the same time, a rise in staple food price may have the effect of reducing its consumption levels,

---

[1] For details, see K. Subbarao (forthcoming).
[2] Ibid.

especially for the poor consumers. It would be interesting to explore the *net* effect of these direct and indirect effects of a rising food price on the welfare of various social classes. This will enable us to evaluate the payoffs to a particular price policy intervention more clearly.

Studies based on partial equilibrium methodologies are not very helpful in capturing the above-mentioned direct and indirect effects of food price movements. An empirical simulation model of the impact of food price policy in a computable general equilibrium framework (Janvry and Subbarao 1988) shows that, while all social classes gain from weather or irrigation (technology)–induced output growth, *under flexible prices* the rich farmers derive their largest benefits from a system of technological change under price support policy. Even when one makes allowance for output response to price incentives the poor classes lose while the rich farmers gain substantially.[3]

Clearly, an upward pressure on food prices—both free market and administered—would worsen the real income position of farm labour, marginal and small farms and urban workers and urban marginals when its general equilibrium consequences are evaluated. Excessive rise in support and free-market prices has been an important factor behind the impoverishment of the nation's rural poor who are concentrated in the eastern states, and in the arid zone. It needs to be stressed that the rural poor in the eastern states are virtually out of the purview of the publicly distributed subsidized food.

Now let us turn to regional equity considerations. The available cross-section data for the recent period reveal significant differences in both costs of production and market prices across the states. In general, in the high productivity regions, both unit costs and market prices are lower than in the backward regions.

While *theoretically* all farmers and regions can avail of the facility of selling their output to the government at support prices, given the cost and market situations in the high and low productivity regions outlined above, in actual practice only the farmers in the high productivity region could avail of the facility

---

[3] For details, see Alan de Janvry and K. Subbarao, *Agricultural Price Policy and Income Distribution in India* (Oxford University Press, 1988).

of support prices. It is interesting that at least since the mid-1970s, the surplus-growing farmers in *both* advanced and backward regions were protected: the former by government intervention, and the latter by the prevailing market situation. Clearly, those who are left out are the rural poor (deficit producers as well as poor consumers, who are net buyers of foodgrains) in the backward poverty zones, essentially because of the disadvantage of having had to face higher market prices for foodgrains, with virtually no government support in the form of an effective rural public distribution system.

*Conclusion*

To sum up, the shift in emphasis towards incentive policy package undoubtedly succeeded in increasing production, but not in feeding the teeming millions. We have only generated production capacity but not consumption capacity, as is evident from the growing volume of food stocks. We failed in generating consumption capacity essentially because the incentive policy package failed to touch the millions of small and marginal farmers, especially in the backward states whose contribution to *incremental output* growth has been negligible.

If agricultural development is to subserve the interests of the poor there is a need to restore primacy to public investment and institutional reform policy packages. Unless poor farmers and landless labour become participants in the increasing production basket, there is no chance of ensuring household level food security. And it is just not enough to ensure only macro-level balancing of aggregate effective demand and supply. This is of course important but not enough. Now that we have achieved macro-level food security, we should take steps to ensure micro-(household) level food security. The most cost-efficient way of achieving this is to ensure participation of the poor farmers in the incremental output via appropriate public investment and institutional reform policies.

# Poverty Eradication: A Review of Policies and Programmes

### S. D. TENDULKAR

I will confine myself to the area of poverty. Here the major factor basically shaping our policy perspective is the sheer magnitude of the poverty problem. It affected 40 per cent of the population even in an exceptionally good agricultural year, 1977–8, and using a fairly moderate poverty line. This meant that there were about 200 million rural and 60 million urban poor in 1977–8. I am quoting the latest available figure. Equally significant is the trend increase in the number of the poor, at an annual average rate of two and a half million in rural areas and a little over one and a half million in urban areas.

The policy towards poverty eradication basically had two facets. One is the minimum needs programme under which the state mainly provides the essential services like education, health, drinking water and so on. The other facet has been to generate purchasing power in the hands of the poor either through a specific target-oriented programme or through the general growth process.

The problem of poverty in India has two distinct segments: urban poverty and rural poverty. As far as urban poverty is concerned, one finds that the major chunk of the urban poor are basically self-employed in the unorganized manufacturing, trade and services sector. Here if one were to raise their levels of living, the only way out is basically to step up the general growth process so that the demand for the services and the commodity that the urban poor produce go up. I think it is quite clear that the redistributive components of the urban growth process should be strengthened and it must also partly provide for redistribution to the rural poor. All the same, how to devise a substantial programme in the urban areas for eradicating urban poverty is a difficult question on which very little can be said.

Let me turn to the question of rural poverty. The strategy of fighting rural poverty has two strands. The first is a set of special target-group-oriented programmes: Integrated Rural Development Programme (IRDP), the National Rural Employment Programme, and the Rural Labour Employment Guarantee Programme. The second strand consists of programmes in raising agricultural crop production. A considerable degree of centralization marks both types of programmes and the two sets of programmes run parallel which not only fails to exploit the possibilities of beneficial integration but also unnecessarily burdens an already over-burdened development administration. I wish to stress the urgent need for a decentralized approach to the design and implementation of the programmes both for redistribution and growth and highlight the possibility of integration between the two.

The Integrated Rural Development Programme has turned out to be the principal programme. It is basically a centrally initiated programme aimed at making the beneficiary household economically viable through self-employment by transfer of finance, partly loan and partly subsidy. The aim is to transfer not only finance but a blueprint for the development of the household involving the creation or improvement of productive assets or skills. There are now three sets of problems that afflict IRDP arising from the centralized character of the design and implementation of the programme.

In an attempt of apparent fairness the financial allocation to each development block is the same and each block is targeted to cover the same number of beneficiary houses. Since these centrally stipulated norms and targets are unrelated to the incidence of poverty in the block, there is considerable mismatch across states between the incidence of poverty and the coverage of beneficiaries under the programme. In Punjab which has 1½ per cent share in the set of poor households and 3 per cent share in financial allocation, the number of beneficiaries exceed the total number of estimated poor houses. West Bengal, on the other hand, has 9 per cent of the poor houses and 1.3 per cent of the finances and here the coverage is less than 5 per cent of the poor till 1982-3.

The second problem with IRDP is the centrally determined targets of coverage of beneficiary households. This imposes a near impossible burden on local level administration. One village level worker on an average has to identify, assist and monitor the progress of 120 new beneficiary households each year and monitor cumulatively increasing number of households in successive years.

Thirdly, the financial limits of investments in different schemes are fixed centrally without reference to the actual cost which in turn results in the amount actually being transferred to the beneficiary, bearing no relation to the investment flow required by the beneficiary household to become viable. There has been a mechanical transmission of a fixed set of programmes to all beneficiaries irrespective of their background and management capability and here the important assumption underlying IRDP is the finance bottleneck. Each beneficiary assumes that the real linkages in the system, from input supply to production to marketing, are basically taken care of. Now it is also important to understand that the well-off people work out linkages in the production process on their own, but the poor cannot. This is why it is quite important that these real linkages are worked out satisfactorily.

The other problem is the emergence of middlemen between the beneficiaries and the development administration who cut substantially into the resources flowing into the hands of the beneficiaries. There is also the problem of non-poor and not so poor gaining access to credit and subsidies under the programme at the expense of those who are actually poor.

The failure to forge the crucial linkages between the finance, production and marketing systems which is important precisely because the poor are unable to forge these links on their own and the emergence of middlemen and their cuts carry with it the danger that the recipient views the loan subsidy operation as a one shot income transfer. As this perception becomes widespread and the numerical target-oriented approach speeds up this process, the resulting bad debt can seriously choke the flow of credit in the aggregate and threaten the profitability of the banks. On the other hand, if repayment is insisted upon I think that would definitely lead to greater indebtedness. It must therefore be stressed that a mere raising of the financial transfer under IRDP without resolving the problems of linkages with the production system would do little to solve the problem of persistent poverty in rural India. Establishing adequate linkages alone would raise the income-earning capability of the household in a sustained manner. Merely raising the size of the development administration, while preserving the centralized character of the programme, design and implementation would do little more than eat into the resources, meant to be transferred to the beneficiaries.

It follows from the assessment of IRDP that if it is to raise the economic viability of the sister households, a more decentralized approach is absolutely essential. Programmes must have their origin in an understanding of local level constraints and possibilities with the technical expertise being provided by somewhat higher level authority, possibly at the district level. One is of course presuming that the local level institution, such as *gram panchayat,* could be revived and strengthened through a process of financial devolution and democratization.

Now the case for decentralization extends well beyond the needs of redistributive social justice. Even for achieving the objective of accelerated growth a decentralized approach is required, especially in the rural context. In most rural areas, agricultural growth can be taken to be a focal point around which non-agricultural employment and trade may be expected to emerge. With tremendous regional diversity in a country of India's continental dimension, the relative importance of technological, institutional and resource constraints operating on agricultural growth would certainly vary from region to region.

In this connection, the current approach dominated by the near total preoccupation with crop cultivation, has severe limitations. This should be changed to an approach making a rational choice amongst alternative uses of available land mass, which in turn is conditioned by the quality of soil and moisture available. For example, there are locations characterized by combination of soil and moisture condition where crop cultivation is an expensive and wasteful use of land. From a social point of view this land can be better utilized for increasing the vegetal or forest cover. Such conditions are known to exist in those rainfed areas which have been brought under cultivation due to demographic pressure, but which are intrinsically unsuitable for sustained cultivation either because of the steepness of their slope or shallowness of their soil, or both.

However, it is important not to overplay the either-or-character of the allocation of land between crop cultivation and forest and vegetal cover, for the vegetal and forest cover would not only increase moisture availability but also prevent soil erosion. In fact the case for mutually reinforcing conservation and development of land and water resources has been persuasively argued by B. B. Vohra in many of his recent writings. Interestingly, many elements of the integrated land and water development programmes suggested by Vohra, such as land levelling and contour bunding for soil and moisture conservation, construction of channels and afforestation are part of the schemes of compulsory consolidation and land development suggested by B. S. Minhas way back in 1970. These elements along with integrated rural energy systems have also been emphasized recently by K. N. Raj while arguing for decentralization. The point is that there seems to be a certain consensus about this and that is why I am raising this issue. It is important to emphasize that these programmes must take into account local level constraints and local possibilities and hence require a decentralized effort. However, it is equally important to emphasize that the land and water development programme suggested by Vohra and Minhas and Raj necessarily involve community action which in turn cannot emerge without active political mobilization and support.

In the context of rural unemployment and poverty, the programme of integrated land and water management has three implications. First, several elements of this programme are essentially labour-intensive which, if implemented through the National Rural Employment Programme, can be used to generate employment for assetless rural households who account for the substantial share of both poverty and unemployment in rural India. Second, in so far as these programmes relate to agricultural productivity, they would also generate additional permanent employment, particularly at least for the family labour and self-employed households and possibly also for the casual wage labour. Finally, asset and skill development programmes under the IRDP would have a better chance of success in a growing rural economy organized around land and water development. The present problem is that IRDP is operating in a vaccum so to say and in a stagnating rural economy. IRDP has absolutely no chance because for self-employment the market cannot develop in the absence of growth in the rural areas.

One final point. The implicit political judgement underlying not only IRDP but other centrally and state sponsored programmes—whether for general development or oriented towards redistribution—is that development administration that is distanced from the local level pulls and pressures is more likely to operate in the interest of the weaker sections than the local level structure. Further, that the benefits of this outweigh the costs associated with centralized design and implementation of programmes for solving the problems which are essentially dispersed and decentralized. In my view, this judgement is not universally valid. One should not underestimate the strength of the countervailing forces that a process of organization of the weaker sections—whether prompted by the benefits at stake or autonomously as part of the general process of politicalization—can and will generate. It is the forces of the weak and the poor which need to be supported at the political level rather than suppressed as in the past.

# Industrial Policy in India, 1947–85

KAMAL A. MITRA CHENOY

It is commonly believed that the policies and regulations in the sphere of industrialization, i.e. industrial policy, has acted as a brake on the industrial development in India. In particular it is believed that these policies have been unduly restrictive, because of ideological and other considerations, in so far as, 'the permit-quota Raj' has severely hampered the growth and development of the private sector, in particular the industrial houses or big business groups. It is argued, however, in this discussion note that industrial policy has been consistently 'liberalized' since its inception around 1948, and that the manner of implementation of industrial regulation has in fact facilitated the growth of the upper strata of industrial enterprenors, in particular the industrial houses or 'monopoly' groups.

*Congress Formulations on Industrial Policy, 1938–48*

The National Planning Committee (NPC), set up by the Congress in 1938 with Jawaharlal Nehru as its Chairman and K. T. Shah as its Secretary, broadly formulated an industrial policy, in its various sub-committees, in which the major role was to be played by the state sector. Basic, 'key' and defence industries, as well as public utilities were to be in the State sector. Immediately after Independence, the AICC Economic Programme Committee (EPC), also headed by Nehru, submitted its report in January 1948, where an even more major role was advocated for the state. The EPC recommended that all existing privately owned units in key and public utility industries be nationalized within five years, that all large scale units competing against small and cottage industries be State controlled, and further that all undertakings in the nature of monopolies, i.e. whose activities or market extended to more than one province, be nationalized. The nationalization of banks and insurance was also recommended, together with indigenous control over units where there was substantial foreign equity participation. Business lobbies reacted stridently to the EPC Report recommendations, and these were later played down, and scarcely incorporated in the 1948 Industrial Policy Statement.

## Industrial Policy, 1948–56

The April 1948 Industrial Policy Statement sharply reduced the area to be reserved for the State: with only three industries exclusively reserved for the State as compared to the above (1938) formulation and with new undertakings reserved for the public sector in six more industries. Moreover, the takeover period for privately owned units in reserved areas, which was five years in EPC Report, was extended to ten years, and further even after the expiry of the ten years period, the matter was to be reviewed.

In April 1949, Prime Minister Nehru made a 'Statement on Foreign Investment in India', in the Constituent Assembly Legislative, wherein he explicitly assured foreign investors that they would be treated at par with domestic capital. In yet another withdrawal from its earlier position, the Government accepted foreign control of Indian undertakings for a 'limited period'.

In April 1956, the Industrial Policy Resolution, which even now formally shapes industrial policy, was accepted by Parliament. The Resolution divided all industries into three categories:

  i. the first group considered to be of 'basic and strategic' importance, numbering 17, were put in Schedule 'A' in which future development was to be exclusively in the public sector;
 ii. the second group of 12 industries were listed in Schedule 'B', and in these industries new undertakings were increasingly to be in the public sector; and
iii. the largest group of industries which were not listed in

either Schedule were to be wholly open for the private sector.

However, the reservations for the public sector were in effect relaxed by 1957.

Consequent on a meeting between Nehru, Morarji Desai (Commerce and Industry Minister) and T. T. Krishnamachari (Finance Minister) sometime in mid-1957, it was decided to throw open both Schedule 'A' and 'B' industries to the private sector.

### Industrial Policy, 1956–66

The Report of the Industrial Licensing Policy Inquiry Committee (ILPIC) revealed that the bulk of the licenses issued in both Schedule 'A' and 'B' industries between 1956 and 1966 went to the large private sector. In the Schedule 'A' industries the private sector received: (a) 42 out of 46 in the iron and steel industry; (b) 306 out of 312 in heavy castings and forgings of iron and steel; (c) 103 out of 106 for heavy plant and machinery; (d) 58 out of 61 for heavy electrical plants; (e) 344 out of 390 for coal and lignite; (f) 12 out of 12 issued in shipbuilding; and so on. Similarly, in Schedule 'B' industries the private sector received: (a) 226 out of 235 licenses issued for machine tools; (b) 9 out of 11 for ferroalloys and tool steels; (c) 233 out of 250 in the basic and intermediate products required by chemical industries; (d) 334 out of 335 in plastics, antibiotics and essential drugs; (e) 42 out of 54 in fertilizers, (f) all 46 in alluminium; (g) all 87 in other non-ferrous metals; and so on.

Therefore, even during the Second and Third Plan periods, when industrial regulation was at its height, the licensing system operated in favour of the private sector in general, and the large industrial houses in particular. As the ILPIC report put it, 'the licensing system... provides considerable scope for favours to be granted and... these favours mostly... are secured by firms belonging to the Large Industrial Sector.'

By the mid-sixties, a substantial delicensing of industry took place. In May 1966, 11 industries (many of which were in Schedules 'A' and 'B') were delicensed; in July 1966, two more industries were delicensed, and in November 1966, licensing was withdrawn for 23 more items.

### Later Trends, 1970 onwards

In February 1970, the new industrial licensing policy threw open 17 'core sector' industries for investment by larger industrial houses and foreign private capital. These industries were generally Schedule 'A' and 'B' industries, and this policy change marked the culmination of the jettisoning of the 1956 Industrial Policy Resolution. The February 1973 licensing policy decisions further expanded this list to 19 industries, listed in Annexure I. Thus with these policy changes the large private sector was officially encouraged to invest in areas formally reserved for the public sector (in the 1956 Industrial Policy Resolution).

The MRTP Act has been considered to be a regulatory mechanism restricting the growth of the large industrial houses. This is why the recent Budget increased the asset limit of an MRTP group from Rs 20 crores to Rs 100 crores. However, as the Sachar Committee has shown, the vast majority of applications made under the MRTP Commission were approved. Moreover, the bulk of the applications, both with government and the MRTP Commission, are cleared. In fact, the latest available data shows that the larger MRTP groups have grown remarkably despite, or perhaps because of, the MRTP Act and industrial regulation. From 31 December 1980 to 31 December 1983, the combined assets of the 25 largest MRTP listed groups increased from Rs 8,225.82 crores to Rs 14,651.64 crores, an increase of 78.1 per cent. In the same period, the sales turnover increased from Rs 11,298.76 crores to Rs 17,401.35 crores, i.e. by over 54 per cent. Some of the smaller groups increased faster, e.g. Reliance Textiles increased its assets from Rs 166.33 crores in 1980 to Rs 562.98 crores in 1983, i.e. by 238. 5 per cent.

### Conclusions

It is evident from the foregoing discussion that industrial policy has developed in a manner in which it favours the growth of big business and monopolies. Indeed, as Marx showed in the last century, the centralization and concentration of capital are two fundamental features of the general law of capitalist accumulation. As a consequence of the operation of this law, the top twenty MRTP groups, which controlled 25.1 per cent of the assets of the private sector in 1969, controlled as much as 34.7 per cent in 1975 (Sachar Committee Report).

# New Economic Policy: From Disenchantment to Discontent*

BALRAJ MEHTA

The dull and drab statistics about the performance of the Indian economy in 1986 have been widely publicized in the last few weeks. What they portend for the political economy of the country is, however, attempted to be obfuscated in a calculated manner by the political-power establishment which has been making claims of success for its policies and management.

The overall growth rate of the economy during the year is estimated to be 4.5 per cent, the same as in the last year as against the annual rate of growth of 5 per cent claimed to have been achieved during the Sixth Plan period and projected for the Seventh Plan. This too has been possible only because the tertiary sector, or the services sector, which already accounts for 40 per cent of the GDP, is estimated to have grown at the rate of 7 to 8 per cent in 1986. In contrast the primary, or the agricultural sector, is estimated to have grown by only 2 per cent and the secondary, or the industrial sector, by less than 6 per cent.

For the growth rate of the primary and secondary sectors to lag behind the growth rate of the tertiary sector at the present stage of the development of the Indian economy is ominous, and this, unlike in the case of the developed economies, is bound to weaken its growth potential. This is so all the more when, within the tertiary sector itself, the weight of wholly unproduc-

* Reprinted with the author's permission from *Saturday Times, Times of India*, Delhi, 10 January 1987.

tive and consuming services increases at a rate faster than that of the services which help to accelerate the growth of the primary and secondary sectors.

The growing expenditure on what is euphemistically called security, internal and external, with reliance placed on a large standing army, expansion and proliferation of such organs as law and order and civil bureaucracy testifies to this position. The problem is only compounded by the emergence, with the accumulation of public debt, of a large rentier class in the economy and consumerist tendencies among the upper classes which the official policy is encouraging. The productive base of the economy is simply not able to meet the growing consumerist cravings of upper classes and the military-strategic ambitions of the ruling establishment.

The result is that the high saving–investment base which had been achieved within the framework of development planning for economic growth is beginning to erode and the ground gained in the past is being cavalierly lost by the so-called economic liberalization policy under the present political dispensation. This is what the resource crunch for development and the danger of being caught in an internal and external debt trap is really all about.

The inflationary pressures which had been somewhat dormant or within tolerable and manageable limits in recent years have also become active in these conditions. The wholesale price index has risen by 6.5 per cent and measured in terms of the consumer price index, inflation in 1986 has already touched the dreaded double digit rate.

Agricultural production, having touched a plateau in 1983–4, has since tended to sag and a marked upswing in the agricultural sector is nowhere in sight. Production of foodgrains in the current year, though above 2 per cent from last year's, will be nearly three million tonnes below the 1983–4 peak. If the supply of foodgrains is still seen to be comfortable, this is to be attributed to the fact that effective demand (for want of purchasing power) for foodgrains, as indeed of all wage goods, has remained stagnant. This also falsifies the loud claims of poverty alleviation.

The demand factor has, in fact and admittedly so, emerged as a major constraint not only in investment in industrial growth but also fuller utilization of established industrial capacity. Industrial growth rate has sagged during the current year compared to last year's 6 per cent, as against the target of 8 per cent per annum set in the Seventh Plan. Growth in the manufacturing sector has decelerated more markedly from 5.8 per cent of last year to 5.1 per cent this year. With inflationary pressures becoming active, demand constraint on industrial investment and production can only become more severe.

The balance of payments position has deteriorated and with a decline in concessional aid flows and payments obligations arising out of servicing past debts and large trade deficits, it is becoming more and more difficult to persist with fanciful schemes of modernization with the help of credit financed liberal imports of capital goods and sophisticated technology. It is also becoming difficult to import mass consumption goods such as edible oils in order to augment their supplies for maintaining price stability.

The hope that there will be a dramatic spurt in private investment, Indian and foreign, which will make good the drastic cut made in the Seventh Plan in the provision for investment in the public sector industry for policy and ideological reasons, is turning out to be misplaced. Much is made of the approval of capital issues which added up to Rs 2000 crores in 1984-5 and are expected to be of the order of nearly Rs 4000 crores in the current year. Past experience shows that nearly half of the proposals for investment in the private corporate sector as well as under foreign collaboration arrangements do not materialize.

The stock market boom has already given way to despondency. The initial unguarded reaction of the investing public to the promise of a spurt in economic growth with the launching of the new market-oriented economic policy has given way to caution by the actual performance of the economy. The expected mobilization of public savings for an investment of the order of Rs 66,000 crores in the private corporate sector during the Seventh Plan period is nowhere in sight. The spokesmen of the private corporate sector are bewailing resource stringency for implementing their investment intentions as much as the government about resource crunch for investment in the public sector. A fierce competition has started between public and private sector enterprises seeking public savings for shares, debentures and bonds floated by them.

The problem really is that faith of the public in trading in shares and stocks tends to be easily shaken considering the narrow and weak social base of private corporate enterprise in India. It is not surprising, therefore, that while public enterprise has been emasculated, private enterprise remains stagnant. The result is that investment and growth are not picking up and the development process is arrested.

It is misleading in this context to be concerned with resource crunch holding up the development process as primarily a financial problem which is reflected most sharply in the increasing budgetary imbalance. It is a problem which is multidimensional and the growing budgetary deficit is one of its facets. There is, in addition, the misutilization of budgetary resources as well as underutilization and misdirection of material and human resources.

There are two features of the resources crunch at present which are most glaring. One is the growing deficit in the revenue budget, especially of the Central Government, and the second is the underutilization of the material and human resources available in the economy which may be seen in the form, above all, of slump in capital goods and machine-making industries and growing unemployment, especially of skilled and semi-skilled manpower. These features manifest themselves in a variety of ways and forms, among them shrinking of budgetary support for investment, especially in the public sector, and credit-financed imports of goods and services which are competitive to domestic production capacities and capabilities.

The Union Finance Minister has admitted that in order to contain budgetary deficit within manageable limits it may become necessary to make cuts in budgetary allocations for meeting expenditure of the government on plan as well as non-plan schemes and programmes. He is, at the same time, drum-beating about buoyancy in revenue collection because of the government's much-applauded 'reasonable' tax policy, flexible enforcement of tax laws and efficient tax collection. But he misses the point that vigorous revenue collection is not the same thing as resource mobilization for development. It should have by now dawned on him that in spite of his expectation of an increase of Rs 12,500 crore in the collection of tax revenues than earlier estimated during the Seventh Five-Year Plan period, he will still not be able to provide funds and direct human and material resources for the implementation of the public sector part of the plan. The projections of the Finance Ministry show that there will be a step-up in the plan outlay next year.

The Finance Minister is said to be keen to keep deficit financing which, beyond a point, can only stoke the fires of inflation, within manageable limits by controlling and cutting down expenditure of the government. But hilarious in this context is his claim that he has wiped out the overdrafts by the state governments by advancing interest bearing loans out of funds created by deficit financing at the central level, and is ironic. The fact indeed is that the annual plans and the budgets, let alone the five-year plan, are being treated with utmost disdain by the Union government. The obligations towards and discipline of planning and a budget approved by Parliament are conspicuous by their absence in the government's decision-making process. The manner in which the Prime Minister goes about announcing financial grants and allocations as his personal gifts has been widely noted. But the Finance Minister too has tended to destroy the sanctity of the budget and its discipline by frequent and impromptu adjustments in fiscal and budgetary measures on the side of both revenue collection and expenditure, especially consumption expenditure of the government.

The so-called resource crunch in the form of growing budgetary deficit has assumed its present rigour and dimensions over a period of time and to get out of it is not going to be painless, economically or politically. The fact indeed is that the Union budgets have ceased to play a positive role in a planned development process. There are no revenue surpluses available for financing development. On the contrary, the revenue budgets of the Union government have tended to run in an increasing measure into large deficits, larger than the overall deficits. The overall deficit estimated in the budget presented by V. P. Singh for this year was Rs 3650 crores. But the revenue deficit was estimated to be Rs 6870 crores and this deficit is likely to swell very much by the close of the year. The position is going to worsen in the coming year and it is likely that revenue deficit will grow to Rs 900 crores. This means that the revenue raised by the government by measures strictly within the frame of the budget have been falling increasingly short of the government's non-development, maintenance expenditure, including expenditure on security, external and internal. The government has to draw upon resources mobilized, including loans from internal and external sources, ostensibly for development, for non-development purposes. This has led to the emasculation of the planned development effort and dilution of the role of government in the development process.

It is economically and socially impermissible and untenable to let the budgetary deficit emerge and grow to its present dimensions. Taxation is a prerogative of the state which it must exercise to close this gap. The official planners have rightly warned that the declining trend in the ratio of tax revenue to gross domestic product must be reversed. The tax ratio must rise by at least two percentage points from the present level of about 16 per cent to 18 per cent and the overall savings rate must thereby be stepped up by as much as 1.2 per cent of GDP. This is considered by the planners crucial for achieving the modest growth targets set in the Seventh Five-Year Plan. The idea that taxes, especially on incomes and wealth, can be substituted by market borrowings and raising of deposits is misplaced and counter-productive. It piles up public debt and encourages the growth of parasitic rentier classes with all its adverse implications for the economy and society.

In broader socio-economic terms, the official policy can be seen to be designed to swell disposable incomes of the upper classes which they have the opportunity to use partly for current consumption and partly to step up investment to satisfy in future their elitist consumption demand, that is, demand backed by adequate purchasing power in the market. Side by side, price adjustments are being made and more will be made which will curb current consumption of the mass of the people without, of course, impairing the profitability of investment. Priority in this dispensation is being given to ensure return on capital and measures are underway to regulate reward to labour. What is being attempted is austerity, ruthlessly imposed from above, for the mass of the people and liberalization for commercial enterprise and investment, above all, in the private sector, Indian and foreign, which is presumed to be more efficient than investment in the public sector.

It is not surprising, therefore, that disenchantment with official economic policy and management which became palpable early in 1986 when wide-ranging hikes in administered prices were made has turned into mass discontent towards the close of the year. The middle classes, especially the technocrats and professionals, which were looking forward to a bonanza under a political dispensation which promised fast rate of economic growth and modernization, high reward for skilled labour and low taxes, are also getting disillusioned. The ardour of even private industry which looked upon the economic liberalization policies as opening up new opportunities for gainful business enterprise has become subdued as the economy remains stuck in the mire of stagflation. The problem for private enterprise has been further compounded as reliance on foreign capital and credit-financed imports have exposed indigenous enterprise to unequal and unfair competition.

In the countryside, with progress of the so-called Green Revolution stalled, the middle and upper peasantry is beginning to grouse and the landless and poor farmers are becoming desperate. Caste and class violence in the rural areas is spreading and assuming fierce features in many landlord-dominated areas where feudal social relations and practices are entrenched and brook no protest.

In the midst of growing social unrest, economic growth on competitive market principle by unleashing private enterprise and inviting foreign capital is turning out to be shibboleths which mock at reality in the context of the given socio-economic and political conditions. Some among even the starry-eyed admirers and ardent advocates of what has come fashionably to be titled as a new economic policy of the government have, therefore, begun to show uneasiness about its adverse consequences and implications as they have unfolded in a short period of less than two years.

The new economic policy of liberalization and free play of market forces, it should have become clear by now, cannot break the barrier of mass poverty and a highly skewed income distribution to self-sustaining economic growth on a sound and strong socio-economic basis. While growth is bound to remain sluggish, the free play of market forces can only boost labour-saving technologies and concentration of economic assets and power, shrink employment opportunities and intensify the exploitation of labour. While relaxation of bureaucratic regulation may be necessary as well as desirable for unshackling industrial activity, meaningful planning and management with public investment setting the pace for development is an essential pre-condition in Indian conditions for orderly and self-sustaining economic growth.

The dilemmas which have surfaced in 1986 for policy-makers and planners are of a wider relevance and implication than short-run adjustments and *ad hoc* measures can solve. When the government launched the drive for liberalization, import-liberalization included, and took a series of fiscal and administrative steps to boost private enterprise and open up the Indian market for foreign capital, many liked to argue that equity and self-reliance might be traded off in the short-run for accelerating growth to the longer-term advantage of the Indian economy and society. It transpires that, while equity and self-reliance have been wantonly sacrificed, growth has remained elusive and social tensions are growing.

# On Economic Stagnation, Past Development Strategy and New Economic Policy—A Summing-Up

ARUN BOSE

### INTRODUCTION

I don't think it is either possible or useful to try to summarize *everything* that was said at the wide-ranging, fairly exhaustive and rather exhausting discussions we have had of 20-odd papers or presentations over the past two days. When invited by the organizers of the seminar I agreed to sum up rather than summarize the main classes of issues that came up, adding some comments of my own.

When I attended my first seminar as a final year undergraduate 45 years ago, I found the participants—I remember Lionel Robbins and Friedrich Hayek with Piero Sraffa, who had invited me, along with the others, holding the ring—every one of them, determined to present seminal or original ideas. Nowadays, so many seminars are organized so often that we say a good seminar is one at which *new* questions are asked; an even better one is that in which at least one *new* answer is found. Our seminar worked very hard in discussing almost threadbare the key themes of (1) economic stagnation in India (hereafter the 'stagnation thesis'), (2) India's past development strategy and (3) the new economic policy (or strategy) that is being talked about over the past one year. In what follows, I shall try to assess the main points made on these three themes, referring also to some points which were not made but appear to be highly relevant if one is to sum up the discussion. (I leave it to readers to judge whether it was a 'good' seminar or among the 'better' ones).

### Economic Stagnation in India

I do not think any one either present at this seminar or anywhere else any longer believes what Paul Baran in his *Political Economy of Growth* (1957, ch. 5, specially pp. 143–50) set the fashion in believing, viz. that India suffered, both before and after Independence, from absolute as well as extreme economic stagnation because in India 'there has been capitalism *without* the accumulation of capital'.

What most participants at our seminar seemed to stress (with the possible and partial exception of Professor A. M. Khusro who seemed to think there has been no economic stagnation in India at all since Independence) is that India has been cursed with a stable or steady long-term rate of growth, which, though positive, placed India at the bottom of the table of third world growth rates. (All of us nowadays admire the Marxian and Schumpeterian unsteady or unbalanced growth rather than the Nurksean or Von Neumannian unsteady or unbalanced growth.) An exasperated Professor Raj Krishna used to hammer away derisively at India's never-changing Hindu rate of growth which placed India at the bottom of the score-card of third world countries. At our seminar Professor Siddharthan presented figures to show that even in the South Asian region (i.e. the Indian sub-continent plus Burma), Burma had the highest agricultural growth rate (under a military socialist regime) of 4.7 per cent p.a. in the decade 1970–81, a significant rise from 4.1 per cent p.a. in the decade 1960–70. But in spite of this step-up in agricultural growth, and a significant step-up *also* in growth rate of manufactures in the second decade compared to the first—her 20-year annual average growth rate of GNP per capita was as low as India's at 1.4 per cent p.a. So even if we accept without question Burma's official statistics (about which we do not know a fraction of what we do know about India's statistics), Burma too seems to suffer from economic stagnation overall, like India. Siddharthan's figures also reveal that Malaysia—*not* so far as I know famed for its success story—was *on top* as regards agricultural growth in the decade 1970–81, taking both South and East Asia together, with 5.2 per cent p.a. But doubts arise when we note that the 1960–71 figure for Malaysia is missing and that her overall growth of GNP per capita over

1960–81 was *below* Thailand's (whose agricultural growth rate as well as manufacturing growth rate was *below* Malaysia's). On the other hand, it seems from Siddharthan's table that the rather aggressively Buddhist Sri Lanka too had a Hindu 'unchanging' growth rate, albeit higher than India's being at 3 per cent against India's 1.9 per cent in agriculture in both decades (1960–70 and 1970–81). Finally, we find from Siddharthan's table that China's agricultural growth in the first decade (1960–70) at 1.6 per cent p.a. was below India's (1.9 per cent p.a.). But in the second decade (1970–81), China's agricultural growth was far above India's (2.8 per cent p.a. against India's 1.9 per cent p.a.). But is it not a fact that collection of economic statistics and/or their use to compile national aggregates was abolished for a long period in China after the failure of the Great Leap Forward, when there were cyclical ups and downs in the growth of statistics rather than in the growth of agricultural output? (Let me stress that there is nothing particularly Chinese about the politicization of statistics.) When both Professor P. C. Joshi and I were working at the Indian Statistical Institute, Calcutta, in the 1950s there was the strange and shattering 'Kidwai-Mahalanobis effect' on India's official food statistics. Every year India's food deficit was growing by leaps and bounds, state after state was becoming deficit, queueing up for food aid from the USA via the Centre. Kidwai declared he did not believe in the statistics of the food department, when he took over as Food Minister; Mahalanobis checked official statistics, derived from impressionistic village patwaris' reports, with the results of sample crop-cutting surveys. Within a year began the long climb upwards of India's statistics of food production, which has never stopped since! Evidently, with all its defects, Mahalanobis' crop-cutting surveys sent state-level (and central) food ministers—in pursuit of the political power which mounting food-deficits bring—out of business!

Let me insist that I am *not* being cynical about statistics, I am merely asking awkward questions which, as I said at the outset, *should* be asked at every good seminar. Let me ask two or three more awkward questions about the statistics of India's economic stagnation (or is it the stagnation of India's statistics?) *First*, even if we take the recently published NCAER figures (which are *lower* than the official figures) India's aggregate saving-investment rate has risen impressively from around 16 per cent (1960) to 23 per cent (1981). Why then is India's growth rate of GNP so impressively steady? I conjecture that it is just *possible* that it is not so unimpressive in reality, that the savings-investment rate is based on better reported financial statistics (better reported because higher savings and investment earn tax rebates) than output growth figures in the 'formal' sectors or the 'formal economy' (which have been systematically underreported to evade excise duties). This leads on immediately to my second awkward question, about the dark no man's land of what the Americans refer to as the 'informal economy' and in India we refer more often to it as the 'black economy'. From the time many years ago when the 'black economy' was sighted on the Indian economic horizon by Nicholas Kaldor and I. S. Gulati, it has cast a larger and larger shadow over our economic discussions. Even at the inauguration of this seminar Professor Khusro referred to it. Of course, he referred to it only to reassure us that it is still a 'qualitative' idea rather than a 'quantified' or 'quantifiable' economic fact, and, in any case, since it exists in the form of *hoarded* assets, it is *sterile* and makes no difference to the actual performance of the Indian economy. Now, since the matter has hardly been properly investigated, except by some investigative journalists at least some of whom go after what is sensational rather than what is authentic, unfairly damn some and protect others, it is tempting to agree with Professor Khusro's view. But suppose the proportions of idle, sterile, hoarded assets, to total assets are roughly the same in the 'formal' and the 'informal' economies—can it not explain in part India's low rate of growth of GNP as an *under-reported* growth rate, limited in coverage to the relatively stagnant 'formal sector'? Also, suppose the 'black economy' is *not* strictly what an Indian judge has named as a 'parallel economy', but intersects the 'white economy' at multiple points, and is served by the 'white economy' more than it serves the white economy. What if the savings and investments of the formal economy enterprises (state-owned and managed as well as private) are being *increasingly* used to generate unreported growth of output and income in the 'black economy'? Can this not also explain in part why India's income-output growth is so low compared to other third world countries where the black economy operators are less dynamic, efficient and ingenious?

I find that I have spent many more minutes on the statistics of India's economic stagnation than I intended to. I would like to conclude this section of my summing-up by asserting that if I am arguing in favour of reconsidering the 'stagnation thesis' vis-à-vis India, I am not alone in doing so.[1] Also, a priori, adopting a 'qualitative' approach to economic phenomena, I am certain that if the difficult study of the political economy of the 'black economy' in quantitative terms were seriously undertaken, we would have a higher long-term average growth rate of the Indian economy than we have at present, both absolutely and in comparative terms (i.e. vis-à-vis other third world economies). But the main reason why I have struck my neck out and touched on this topic is that I am convinced that the main cause for concern about India's long-term economic performance is her unequal, uneven and in this sense 'unreal' growth for a stable or a growing majority rather than no growth[2] or Baran's 'capitalism without capital accumulation'. Obsessed with 'economic stagnation' we tend to be fatalistic about unevenness and inequality (region-wise, sector-wise and white economy/black economy wise), telling ourselves that the slices of the cake can be made larger only *after* we have increased the size of the cake, as Nehru insisted.[3]

## Past Development Strategy

On the development strategy adopted or implemented in India over the past 35 years or so, I have less to say, partly because I

---

[1] Cf. Paul Mattick Jr. entry on Baran, Paul A. (pp. 41–2) and entry on Sweezy, Paul M. (pp. 317–18) in Robert Gorman (ed.), *Biographical Dictionary of Marxism*, Greenwood Press, Westport, Connecticut, USA (1986).

[2] Cf. Ngo Manh-Lan, Introduction, in Ngo Manh-Lan (ed.), *Unreal Growth*, vol. I, pp. xxi–ix, Hindustan Publishing Corporation (India), (1984).

[3] Cf. The Prime Minister, *Strategy of the Third Plan*, Publications Division, Government of India (n.d.), Problems in the Third Plan, p. 39: '... production comes first, before any kind of equalisation or division. There is no point in having an equal measure of poverty for all.'

agree more than I disagree with the ideas that emerged on this theme.

For years, discussion of India's development strategy has been very narrowly constricted to focus *only* on 'institutionally-neutral' quantitative aspects of strategy, such as whether industry can or should grow faster than agriculture (whether it can or should grow faster than the 'tertiary sector' being largely ignored), whether heavy industry capacity/output (the two being conflated at some risk) or light industry capacity/output can or should grow faster, whether there can or should be increasing economic dependence followed by increasing self-reliance (if so, to what extent and in what degree and *how*), whether there should be import-substitution or export-led growth or growth-led exports, etc. In so far as attention was at all paid to institutional aspects of strategy, there were vague assumptions, more implicit than explicit, about greater growth of the state-owned and state-managed or state-controlled 'public sector' than the private sector being an indicator of a march towards a 'socialistic pattern' (if not socialism), whether there should be state-directed choice of technique in agriculture, small-scale industry (*without* paying much attention to the question as to *how* this was to be done), etc. To be sure, some writers, mainly Baran and Bettelheim,[4] spoke confidently (but not too convincingly) of India's 'capitalist path of development', while Kalecki with his thesis of 'intermediate regimes' visualized India following some kind of ambiguously conceived 'non-capitalist path of development'. But *no one*, to the best of my knowledge, spoke of India's 'state-monopoly capitalist path of development' (though I have come across Professor Pranab Bardhan writing about India's 'state-feudalist path of development'[5]).

In refreshing contrast to all this, I was happy to note that in not less than three papers presented at our seminar, it is *explicitly* stated that in India we have had a 'state-monopoly capitalist strategy' in operation. Furthermore, in one paper it is correctly stated that within this 'regulatory frame', 'new' monopolies

---

[4] Cf. Charles Bettelheim, *India Independent*, MR Press, New York, 1968.
[5] In private correspondence with me.

have been promoted to join the 'old' monopolies in the high-status club of Indian and multinational monopoly houses. In another paper it is recognized that large capitalist farmers have also emerged on the basis of heavy subsidies to agriculture provided by this 'regulatory frame' of state-monopoly capitalism and utilized by them.

All this is music to my ears (although the quality of the music is rock or pop rather than classical) because for at least twenty years I have been arguing that the hypothesis that India has undergone state capitalist development is worth considering as an empirically verifiable hypothesis. (It is only in the past two years or so that I have realized that—taking into account the role of statutory state monopolies or 'public sector' enterprises *no less* than that of the privately-owned Indian and multinational monopoly houses—the hypothesis should be reworded to refer to state-monopoly capitalist development.) In other words, to adopt a metaphor used by a participant in our seminar in his remarks on India's 'new economic policy', I am of the view that in India all along (in fact since the 1930s at least, and certainly since the feverish 'primary accumulation of capital' in the 1940s during the war) capitalist enterprise has been the 'prime engine of growth'.

Having said this, let me hasten to add that all we have done as yet is to float a promising hypothesis, the first step in a 1,000 kilometre march; we have a long way to go before we can hope to verify it empirically and, hopefully, gain some acceptance from rather conservative Indian economists of the left and the right.

First, it is *not* easy to establish or to prove as true the hypothesis of state capitalist or state monopoly capitalist development in India without going beyond the narrow compartmentalized limits of neoclassical economics or even going beyond classical English (or French) political economy to Marxian political economy (with some leaves taken out of one of the oldest texts of political economy in the world, viz. Kautilya's *Arthashastra*).[6] It is simply not enough to rely on

---

[6] Cf. R. Shama Sastry, trans., *Kautilya's Arthasastra*, Mysore Printing and Publishing House, Mysore, 1967.

making a mystique of the mysterious 'political element' in economic analysis (as Myrdal has set the fashion in doing). Once we allow for the close inter-dependence between economics and politics, it is not so difficult to frame logically a proper hypothesis about India's state-monopoly capitalist development or to verify it empirically. There is nothing mysterious about the hypothesis.

Second, if we adopt this approach, the landmarks—the Bombay Plan of the 1940s, the long-term projections appended to the First Five Year Plan (whose authorship is credited to Professor K. N. Raj), Mahalanobis' Draft Plan-Frame drawn up on the eve of the Second Five Year Plan (but severely whittled down in the final drafts of the Second and later Plans), the 'Nehru doctrine' expounded during the 'crisis of planning' during the Third Five Year Plan where he recommended a permanent commitment to the co-existence of both the public and private sectors, and the growth of both, in the interests of promoting the *efficiency* of both[7]—all these landmarks stand out. They stand out as landmarks in the evolution of a highly original Indian strategy of state-monopoly capitalist development (if only because, though Nehru wanted 'concentration of economic power' to be checked, as we all know, he allowed the industrial licensing procedures, and even the curbs on private monopoly houses, Indian and foreign, to be used to *promote* them, and, secondly, like the English Fabians he ignored the restrictive monopolistic tendencies in the rapidly growing state monopolies). True, the Bombay Plan was quite explicitly for withdrawal of all state controls as in the Japanese model of development, once continuous development at a high rate, relying mainly on Indian capital, had been achieved. In contrast, Mahalanobis accepted the state monopoly capitalist strategy with some regrets, simply because there was no 'instant socialist alternative' available (especially when the Indian political left agreed with the right that India must *inevitably* and *desirably* go through a period of 'independent *capitalist* development' on the basis of a rapidly growing state-monopoly capitalist sector). But these contrasts between the Bombay Planners (Tata and Birla and the other top Indian monopoly houses) and Mahalanobis'

[7] Cf. **The Prime** Minister, ibid. (n.d.), p. 39.

Draft Plan Frame, or the contrast between both and Nehru's thinking just noticed, are *secondary*. For different reasons, from different angles, all were agreed on the necessity of state-monopoly capitalist development in India. (In this context, let us note that Dr Aurobindo Ghose's point that India's planning models represented the strategy *intended* by their authors, which were not implemented in practice because the authors of the economic models were not the actors on the economic stage, is valid. But both the intended strategy summed up in the models as well as the strategy implicit in actual practice were state-monopoly capitalist. It is not as if the models (at least Raj's and Mahalanobis') were 'socialist' while reality turned out to be state-monopoly capitalist.)

Third, state monopolies, whether they are indirectly controlled by private owners, or are directly controlled by technocrats imbued with a bourgeois ethos, or—this can no longer be ignored—partly controlled by monopolistically *united* trade unions with left or right political affiliations—have to be controlled in the public interest as much as private monopolies. I regret that in one paper read at this seminar, the author seems to rely on the panacea of state monopolies being promoted to check private monopolistic malpractices. But the malpractices of the first breed and under-write the malpractices of the second, more often than not!

Fourthly and finally, to flesh out our understanding of India's state-monopoly capitalist strategy, we have to investigate India's highly developed 'black economy' realities as significant vehicles of state-monopoly capitalist development. This has to be stressed because the role of the black economy as an *antidote* to, rather than an aid to, state-monopoly capitalist development is sometimes exaggerated (in the literature emanting from the ILO for example).

### New Economic Policy

On the theme of the New Economic Policy on the anvil in India, the strong Schumpeterian overtones of two papers presented at our seminar made me wonder: have we all become Schumpeterians now? On this important, and even exhilarating, new trend, I have already said this morning what I wanted to say: while making good use of his innovation-oriented paradigm, we should beware of misunderstanding Schumpeter, and being misled by him (see annexure: On Schumpeterian Recipes for India).

Let me make, in addition, as briefly as I can, three points. First, as Professor K. N. Raj put it in a recent talk at the Delhi School of Economics, in discussing India's development strategy, the Delhi School of Economics is all for promoting 'productive forces', while the Economics Department of Jawaharlal Nehru University is all for changing 'production relations' as panaceas. May I point out that contraposing the two sounds absurd nowadays, when western Reaganomics and Thatcherism stress the importance of 'market miracles' (a matter of 'production relations') and all communist societies (from China to the Soviet Union) stress the importance of 'perfecting social production relations'? Production relations are not established once and for all either under capitalism or under socialism, they change, and *have* to be changed periodically (even if it is doubtful whether in any social system, capitalist or socialist, they can ever reach 'perfection'). One has to change production relations if one wants to promote changing productive forces.[8]

Secondly, productive forces also are interdependent. There is no such thing as *one* productive force to be promoted, what is changing and ought to be changing are the 'material balances' involved in producing the national product, as the Soviet Marxist economists pioneered in pointing out long ago.

Thirdly, it follows from all this that India needs a truly New Economic Policy or strategy in which the dice is loaded against conservatism *both* as regards the complex of inter-dependent productive forces, as well as the complex of production relations (which is a Marxian euphemism for the sum total of property relations, production, distribution and management

---

[8] The terminology is Marxian. As annotated by Oskar Lange, *Political Economy*, vol. 1, Pergamon Press, ch. 1, 2, 'productive forces' are manual and mental labour-power, machines, raw materials; 'production relations' are 'social relations into which men enter' governing ownership and management of productive forces, and distribution of what is produced.

relations). If workers, peasants and professionals will not innovate *in their own interests*, innovations will be imposed by employers, managers, planners *against* their interests. Conservative resistance to all innovations will not protect them for long. On that note, let us conclude our seminar.

ANNEXURE

*On Schumpeterian Recipes for India*

The incidental Schumpeterian admonition to euphoric Indian entrepreneurs, viz. 'the trees (i.e. gains) of the budget are counted but the wood is missed—which is behaviour very uncharacteristic of the Schumpeterian innovator' by Professor Minocha, and the more elaborate Schumpeterian argument put forward by Professor Siddharthan are welcome. It is high time we became impatient with tinkering with development problems *without* innovations. It is time we were inspired by Schumpeter's stress on innovations (not only technological, but also, let us not forget, *institutional*) which, as he himself acknowledged, he first found in Marx.

Let us, by all means, learn from Schumpeter's restless innovation-oriented vision. But, let me also add, let us not misunderstand him, nor be misled by some of his fetishes and foibles. For, if Marx must be updated, taken with a few grains of salt, and, above all, 'Indianized' for use in India, so must Schumpeter be. Let me remind you that while Siddharthan seems to be right in portraying Schumpeterian innovations in terms of non-price variables (like skills, market structures, etc.), let us not forget that his *successful* innovations are always identified as successful in terms of price variables. So let us not misunderstand Schumpeter on this point and think price variables have no role to play in his analysis.

Nor should we be *misled* by Schumpeter. The early Schumpeter insisted, realistically that 'many (innovators) try, few succeed . . . the successful profits of the successful ones are earned out of the bankruptcies and losses of the failures'. The late Schumpeter, in his *Capitalism, Socialism and Democracy*, got carried away to expound a highly unrealistic doctrine of 'the institutionalization of innovations' in modern private and state monopolies, such that *all* innovations are guaranteed to be successful! On any interpretation of the facts, the early Schumpeter was nearer the truth.

# Index

accumulation process, 155–6
agricultural
  capitalist farming, 261, 268
  capital-labour ratio, 230
  coarse grains output, 230
  Drought Prone Area Programme, 224
  dry land crops, 217–18
  dry land projects, 221
  fertiliser consumption, 58, 214, 266
  frontier lands, 127–9
  growth, 196, 208; foodgrains output, 207; inter regional variation in, 203, 205; region wise; dry land region, 199–202; eastern region, 199–202; northern region, 199–202, 211; southern states, 199–202
  incentive policy package, 271–2, 275
  Intensive Agricultural Development Programme, 91, 96, 195
  inter-state indicators, 47
  inter-state variations, 216–18, 273
  irrigated area, 213
  marginal farmers, 205, 210
  National Commission on Agriculture, 208
  policy, 207, 271; pricing, 265
  procurement, 207
  reforms, 157, 271; Land Reforms, 174, 178, 181, 194–5, 249, 290; Ceilings Laws, 195; Consolidation of Holdings, 195; Legislations, 194; Security of Tenure, 195; Zamindari Abolition, 161
  Relations, 166
  Restructuring, 157
  Small Farmers' Development Agency, 73, 80–1, 83, 224
  Spatial Diversification, 208
  Technology, 195–6; Dry Farming, 199, 218–20; Fertiliser, 208; Green Revolution, 4, 33, 92, 166, 205–10, 212, 214, 224, 259, 261, 271, 293; High Yielding Varieties, 210, 214, 218, 219; Seed-Fertiliser, 199
Ahluwalia, M. S., 46, 85
Ahuja, Kanta, 228
AICC Economic Programme Committee, 282–3
Aird, John S., 19, 21
Alagh, Y. K., 57, 85
All India Manufacturing Organisation, 257
allocative efficiency, 148
Americans, 298
Avadi budget, 170

Bagchi, A. K., 193
Banerjee, N., 193
Baran, P., 296, 300
Bardhan, P. K., 259–60, 300
Baru, Sanjaya, 179
Basu, Kaushik, 106
Bettelheim, Charles, 175, 300
Bengal-Bihar coal belt, 137
Bengal Famine, 263

Bhagwati, J. N., 245, 252
Bhalla, G. S., 57, 85, 194, 210
Bhatia, B. M'., 206
Bhatia, M. S., 229
Bhattacharya, B. B., 259, 269
Birla, G. D., 171, 175, 303
black economy (*also see* informal economy), 298, 303
black marketing, 165
black money, 95
block level planning, 40
Bombay Plan, 170, 302
Bose, Arun, 4, 295
Brenan, G., 262, 269
Britain (*also see* England, United Kingdom), 117, 122
British Rule, 7, 155
Buchanan, J. M., 261, 262
budget, union, 1985–6, 256
Burton, J., 269
Butterfield, Fox, 18, 21

Calcutta, 297
capital
  accumulation of, 156, 296
  primitive, 155, 180, 182
  capital deepening, 156
  capital formation, 174
  capital goods sector, 38
  capital intensive enterprises, 62, 162
  capital intensive techniques, 162
capitalism, 5
  competitive, 153
  indigenous, 180
  industrial, 157
  state, 179–80, 187, 300, 302–3
  capitalist framework, 178
  capital market, 189–90
  capital-output ratio, 33, 35–6, 162, 300
  capital theory, neo-Austrian, 120–1, 129
  foreign capital, 170, 192

Central Ganga Authority, 126
Centre for Monitoring Indian Economy (CMIE), 47, 49, 52, 55, 59, 82, 85
centre-periphery problem, 42, 63
centre-state relations, 134
Chakravarty Committee, 63
Chakravarty, S., 1, 23, 63
Chandrapur, 70
Chenoy, Kamal A. Mitra, 282
Chichilinsky, G., 265, 270
Chile, 247
Choudhury, R. A., 1
Christians, 15
civil liberties, 178
Coale, Ansley J., 19, 21
coalition of interests, 104
Command Area Development Programme, 80, 226
compensation controversy, 118
Costa Rica, 108
credit: creation, 182; expansion, 182
Cuba, 108
Culturable Command Area, 67
Cultural Revolution, 18

Dalal, Ardeshir, 171
Dalal street, 170
Dandekar view, 5
Dasgupta, A. K., 269
Dasgupta, P., 128, 135
D.C.M., 101
Delhi School of Economics, 304
Delhi Transport Corporation, 267
demand recession, 170
democratic framework, 155
Desai, Meghnad, 8, 21
Desai, Morarji, 284
devaluation, 185
development block, 277
disparity indicators, 43
dualism, socio-economic, 39

## Index

East Asian countries, 5, 35, 239–41, 244
  China, 10, 11, 15, 18–20, 221–3, 240–1, 297, 304
  Japan, 42–7, 68, 107, 115, 239–41, 248, 250
  Malaysia, 240–5, 295–6
  Philippines, 240–5, 296
  South Korea, 13–14, 64, 239, 241–8
  Taiwan, 64, 115
  Thailand, 96, 240–5, 296–7
  Vietnam, 207
Economic Programme Committee, 282–3
economic stagnation, 177, 295, 296, 299
economic surplus, 183
Economic Survey 1981–2, 234–8
elite consumption demand, 188–9
Emergency, 177
employment
  Effect 139, 163
  Employment Guarantee Scheme (EGS), 83
  Food for Work Programme, 224
  wage employment, 111
  National Rural Employment Programme (NREP), 29, 110–11, 224, 226–7, 229, 232, 277, 280
  Rural Labour Employment Guarantee Programme (RLEGP), 277
  self-employment, 111
  unemployment, 43–5, 44–5, 62, 63, 134
energy transition, 139
England (*also see* Britain, United Kingdom), 107
Ethiopia, 207
Europe, 152
European coffers, 180

Far East, 249
Fascism, 177
Federation of Indian Chambers of Commerce and Industries (FICCI), 171
Feder, E., 127, 135
Fields, G. S., 35
Fifth Modernisation, 20
Finance Commission, 74, 76, 78, 134
Food Corporation of India, 209
food imperialism, 207
food scarcity, 4, 6
food security, 207
  macro, 4, 6, 275
  micro, 275
foreign trade
  balance of payments, 164
  export demand, 235
  export promotion, 115, 148
  foreign exchange, 169; reserves, 108, 169
  imports, aid financed, 185
  liberalisation, 104, 121, 140, 141, 169
fossil fuel, 139

Gamkhar, Shama, 1
Gandhi, Indira, 18, 19
Gandhi, Rajiv, 4, 190, 191
George, K. K., 74, 78, 86
Germany, 122
Ghose, Aurobindo, 1, 169, 303
Gini-coefficient, 100, 107
Gorman, R., 299
government
  central, 290
  Uttar Pradesh, 59, 76, 85
gram panchayat, 279
Grant, W., 270
Great Bengal, Famine, 8, 12, 19

growth
 balanced, 30–1
 classical model of, 31
 consumption-led, 191
 export-led, 169, 245, 247
 Hindu rate of, 296
 impulses, 139
 is beautiful, 121
 self-sustained, 153, 172
 trickle-down effect of, 3, 5, 110, 154, 174, 189
 unbalanced, 145
Guha, Ranajit, 14, 21
Gulati, I. S., 74, 78, 86, 298

Habib, Irfan, 8, 10, 21, 126, 135
Haldia Fertiliser Plant, 254
Haque, T. H., 229
Hayek, Friedrich, 295
Heavy Engineering Corporation, 137
Hecksher-Ohlin, 114
Heston, Alan, 7
Hicks, J. R., 118–20, 135
Hindustan Aluminium Corporation, 176
Hindustan Motors, 94
Hirschman, 145
Humber, 7
Hungary, 250–1
hydro-geological surveys, 70

income distribution, 186, 189, 203
 food-poor states, 6
 food-rich states, 6
 high-income states, 74
 inter-state disparities, 56
 low-income states, 74–5
 middle-income states, 74
Indian Council of Social Science Research, 55, 86

industrial
 automobile industry, 188
 foreign collaborations, 175
 indicators, 50, 59
Industrialization
 de-industrialization, 181
 district-wise, 3, 114, 134, 169
 heavy, 3, 170, 175–6
 import-intensive, 185
 spatial, 137
 —policy
 Enquiry Committee Report, 170, 175
 import-substitution, 115–16, 144, 163–4, 167, 239, 245–6
 Industrial Licensing Enquiry Committee Report, 284
 negative-protection, 140
 resolution of 1956, 100, 175, 283, 285
 statement of 1948, 283
 —recession, 175
 —stagnation, 186
 technology
 forward-biased technological progress, 119
 forward-biased labour intensity, 117–18, 120
 high cost of, 267
 import of, 188
 transfer, 248
 unstable, 39
 workers, 260
Industrial Revolution, 39, 117, 152, 154
infant mortality, 107
informal economy (*also see* black economy), 298
informal sector, 161
infrastructure
 bottlenecks, 108
 drinking water supply, 60
 electrification, 60

indicators, 51-2, 60, 62
policy, 64
road-lengths, 60
socio-economic, 152
Institutional Reforms Policy, 271-2
Integrated Rural Development Programme (IRDP), 96, 226-31, 277-81
intermediate regimes, 180, 300
international demonstration effect, 191
international division of labour, 24
Ishikawa, S., 252

Jackson, P. M., 260, 271
Janvry, Alain de, 274
Japanese model of development, 302
Japan External Trading Organisation, 247
Jha, Prem Shankar, 137
Jodha, N. S., 126, 135
Johnson, Chalmers, 246
Johnson, Lyndon B., 206
joint-sector, 171
Jones, R. J. B., 270
Junker-style landlord capitalism, 181

Kabra, Kamal Nayan, 151
Kaisar Aluminium, 175
Kaldor, N., 27, 28, 159, 298
Kalecki, M., 28-30, 179-83, 193, 300
Kautilya, 301
Keiretsuization, 246
Kennedy, Charles, 118
Kerala, 15-16, 108
Keynesion theory, 26
Keynes, J. M., 30, 35, 92, 115, 135
Kidwai-Mahalanobis Effect, 297
Kindleberger, Charles P., 27
Khusro, A. M., 87, 107, 296, 298
Kornai, J., 25, 26, 29

Krishnamachari, T. T., 209, 284
Krueger, Anne O., 245

labour productivity, 203
labour surplus economy, 173
Lal Bhai Kastur Bhai, 171
land distribution, skewness in, 195, 203-4
landless labour, 10, 205
landlord capitalism, 181
land-man ratio, 161
Lange, O., 304
Latin American countries, 39, 89-90, 247, 251
Laxminarayan, H., 210, 211
Lewis, Arthur, 31-2, 145
Liberalisation, 147, 167, 168, 170, 189, 247, 251, 288, 293
life expectancy, 108, 241
Little, I.M.D., 252
Locksley, G., 270
Luxemburg, R., 27

Mahajan, O. P., 53, 86
Mahalanobis, P. C., 302-3
  model, 23, 87, 167, 209, 302
Majumdar, Madhavi, 53, 86
managerial reforms, 250
Manh-Lan, Ngo, 299
manufacturing, proportion of workers, 59, 60
marginal lands, 127
market deepening, 162
market miracles, 304
Marx, Karl, 2, 17, 26, 118, 123, 248, 257, 285, 305
Marxian, 296
  political economy, 301
  euphemism, 304
Mathai, John, 171
Mathur, Ashok, 53, 86
Mattick, Paul Jr., 299
Mehta, Balraj, 254, 287

Mehta, G. L., 42
Mehta, Ved, 9, 21
Mellor, John, 265, 270
Middle East, 11
MIG Project, 137–8
military dictatorship, 262
Mill, James Stuart, 118
mimetic nationalism, 154
Minhas, B. S., 280
Mining and Allied Machinery Corporation, 138
Minocha, V. S., 143, 305
Mitra, A., 259, 270
Monopolies, 175, 188
  Birla, 303
  Modi, 101
  Nandas, 101
  Tata, 303
Monopolies and Restrictive Trade Practices Act, 249, 285–6
Multinational Corporations, 160, 164, 169–70, 173–6, 188, 301
Morishima, Michio, 252
multilateral institutions, 184
  I.B.R.D. (also see World Bank), 184–5
  I.D.A., 184
  I.F.C., 184
  I.M.F., 13, 184
  World Bank (also see I.B.R.D.), 10, 22, 245
Myrdal, G., 302

Nabar, Veena, 224
NABARD, 229
National Institute of Public Finance, 75, 86
National Sample Survey, 46, 63, 228
natural resource indicators, 48, 49
Nayyar, Deepak, 24, 193
Nehru, Jawaharlal, 92, 175, 282–4, 299, 302; doctrine, 302; era, -170; University, 304

neo-Classical ideal, 2, 239, 247, 251
neo-colonialism, 185
neo-Marxist critique, 172
neo-populist critique, 172
new computer policy, 190
New Economic Policy, 2, 3, 170, 295, 303–4
non-banking financial intermediaries, 182, 189
North America, 152
North Eastern Council, 79
Nurkse, R., 115, 296

Organisation of Petroleum Exporting Countries, 267
Othello, 11
over-subscription, 190

Palestinian War, 206
Patnaik, Prabhat, 24, 193
Patnaik, Utsa, 181, 192
permit-quota raj, 282
PL 480, 206
Planning
  Commission, 78
  crisis of, 302
  democratic, 160
  draft Sixth Plan, 78
  Kerala Board, 228
  manpower, 160
  material balances, 304
  multi-level, 65, 66
  National Planning Committee, 282
  Seventh Plan, 287–9
plateau of prosperity, 123
pluralistic society, 262
political democracy, 153
political economy, 2, 259
poverty
  anti-poverty programmes, 261
  health, 96
  housing, 96
  inter-state dispersion of, 59

literacy, 96
Minimum Needs Programme, 64, 224, 276
  rural, 276
  rural poverty ratios, 46, 56
  urban, 276–7
  vicious circle of, 115
power famine, 113
Prebisch, R., 23, 163
prices
  administered, 266–7, 274
  inflationary spiral, 29
  retention pricing, 266
  supports, 273
  support prices, 273, 275
primitive stagnation, 28
private corporate investment, 188
private sector, 255
privatization, 170, 247, 254–5, 258
property relations, 304
protectionist policies, 246
public distribution system, 263–4, 275
  fair price shops, 232–3
  rationing system, 263–5
  rural, 275
public enterprises, 267
public financial institutions, 187, 191
public investment, 5
  in agriculture, 181
  decelaration in, 188
  policy, 271
public sector, 93, 175, 187, 254–5, 299–300
  excess capacity in, 174
  inefficiency of, 187
*Puranas*, 126
Pursell, G., 247, 253

Quality of Life Index, 61, 96

Raj Committee Report, 236–7
Raj, K. N., 24, 27, 280, 302–4

Raj Krishna, 1, 42, 296
Rakshit, M., 27
Ranade, M. G., 145
Ranis, Gustav, 86
Rao, C. H. H., 260, 270
Rao, D. C., 86
Rao, S. K., 182–3, 193
Rath, Nilkantha, 226, 227
Raychaudhury, Tapan, 7, 10
Reaganomics, 304
recession, 170
redistributive social justice, 279
regional development, 114
regulatory frame, 147, 300–1
rental income, 102
Report of the Presidential Commission on World Hunger 1980, 207
Report on Currency and Finance, 235, 237
Reserve Bank of India, 121
resources
  boom, 179, 290
  crunch, 179, 290
  deficit financing, 165, 182, 268–9
  fiscal crisis of the state, 103, 179, 185
  foreign aid, 184–5
  mobilization, 180
Rhee, Yung W., 247, 253
Ricardo, D., 117–18, 259
Ricardo Machinery Effect, 118–20, 134
Robbins, L., 295
Robinson, Joan, 28, 118
Roemer, J., 270
Romania, 250
royalty repatriation, 188
Roy, R. K., 234
rural oligarchy, 182
rural population, 221
rural-urban hiatus, 115
Russia (*also see* Soviet Union), 122, 173, 304

Sachar Committee Report, 286
Saith, Ashwani, 221
Samuelson, Paul, 27, 118, 128–9, 135
Sandole, D. J. D., 270
Saraiya, R. G., 171
Sau, Ranjit, 113, 135, 137
Scheme Flood II, 84
Schumpeter, 2, 37, 146, 249, 251–2, 304, 306
Schumpeterian paradigm, 247–8
  principles, 3, 5, 248, 305
  variables, 239, 248–9, 251, 305
Scitovsky, T., 115, 136
Second World War, 143, 146, 263
Sen, Amartya, 1, 2, 7, 22, 263, 270
Sen, S. R., 126, 136
Shah, K. T., 282
Sharma, V. K., 229
Shastri, Lal Bahadur, 209
Shetty, S. L., 193
Shroff, A. D., 171
Siddharthan, N. S., 239, 249, 252–3, 296–7, 305
Singh, V. P., 291
Sivaraman, 206
socialism, 5, 147
  transition to, 190
socialist
  democracy, 178
  Fabian, 159
  ownership, 178
  pattern of society, 158, 170, 179, 300
social service indicators, 54–5, 61
social welfare programmes, 154
socio-economic classes, 186, 259–61, 264
  administrators, 100
  bureaucracy, 261
  rentier, 3, 102, 104
  industrial bourgeoisie, 100–1, 104

monopoly capitalists, 186
political brokers, 101–4
property-owning, 186
proprietary, 102
rural landlords, 100
untouchables, 16
South-Asia, 14, 239, 296
  Bangladesh, 10, 240–5
  Burma, 15, 296
  India, 239–45, 249, 296
  Pakistan, 13, 240–5
  Sri Lanka, 13–15, 108, 241–5
South East Asia, 35
  Malaysia, 95
Soviet Union (also see Russia), 122, 173, 304
Sraffa, Piero, 120, 136, 295
Sri Ram, 171
stagnation thesis, 299
state feudalist path, 300
state policy, 169
state terror, 177
Statistical Abstracts, GOI, 125
statistical empirical method, 2
stock market boom, 289
structural bottlenecks, 5
structural change, 3, 5, 26
Subba Rao, K., 271, 274
Subramanium, C., 206, 209
subsidy
  fertiliser, 266, 272–3
  food, 263
  —oriented development strategy, 272
sugar mills, 266
Sun Yefang, 19, 22
supply-side bottlenecks, 27, 113
supply-side policies, 237
Swaminathan, M. S., 206
Swamy, Dalip S., 99, 106
Swarup, Govind, 83, 86
Sweezy, Paul, 299
Swiss Accounts, 169

tariff walls, 170
Tata, J. R. D., 171
Tata Memorandum, 171
Tata, Naval, 171
taxation, 183, 268
  direct, 184
  evasion of, 165
  income tax on agriculture, 175
  indirect, 184
Taylor, L., 265, 270
technological choices, 151, 172
Tendulkar, S. D., 276
Thakurdas, Purushottamdas, 171
Thatcherism, 304
time profile of costs, 119
totalitarianism, 153

under pricing, 67–8, 266
United Kingdom (*also see* England, Britain), 188
United States of America, 88, 97, 185
*Upanishads*, 126

Vaish, R. R., 223
value added by manufacturing, per capita, 59

Vanishing Frontier Lands, 123
*Vedas*, 126
Velayudhan, T. K., 193
vertically integrated industries, 120, 139
Vohra, V. V., 280
Von-Neumann, 296
Von-Thunen, 129

Walicki, A., 27
wasteland development, 126, 128, 134, 169
Weber, 261
Wei Jingsheng, 20
Welfare State, 154
West Bengal, 17
Western democracies, 262
Westphal, Larry E., 247, 253
Whitley, P., 262
Williamson, 53

Yugoslavia, 250–1

Zaibatsu, 248, 250
Zero-Sum Game, 156
Zhu Zhengzhi, 19, 22